16.95.

Risk Issues
and Crisis
Management

Praise for *Risk Issues and Crisis Management*

"It used to be said that 'reward is commensurate with risk'; now I fear more apt is 'risk is likely to end in crisis'. Who better to guide us through the risk/crisis minefield than Mike Regester and Judy Larkin, who have guided so many so well for so many years. Read it before you need to would be my advice."

Robert Worcester, Chairman, MORI

"As one involved in MBA teaching and executive development, I find this book invaluable – not only for students, but also for managers seeking insights into these crucial areas of modern management. It's a clear and highly readable overview of the requirements of risk, issues and crisis management, informed by the expertise and experience of two leading practitioners and consultants, as well as by skillfully chosen and 'classic' case studies. The book is recommended early reading for any manager involved in risk assessment, in trying to understand and manage issues, and concerned to prepare him or herself for the demands of crisis management."

Jon White, Associate, The John Madejski Centre for Reputation,
Henley Management College

"In a world where the hardest won corporate reputation can disappear overnight, this is required reading. Industry has learned little from the mistakes of the past, say the authors, who go on to give a compelling account of just how much there is to learn. Their first-hand experience in dealing with reputational issues and managing crisis shines through."

Paul Marriage, Head of Corporate Communications, Standard Chartered Bank

"Regester Larkin is a key business partner helping us to shape our thinking on proactively managing our reputation. This book is a leading work on reputation management."

Isobel Hoseason, Director of Communications, National Grid Transco

"This book is full of wisdom, insights and practical advice from two of the real gurus in the PR industry. It's also one of the few books on public relations which is a pleasure to read. We keep it as a standard reference in our offices and I recommend it to anyone, at any level, who wants to know more about corporate communications under extreme pressure."

Adrian Wheeler, Chairman, GCI UK and Europe; Chairman, PRCA,
1999–2000

PR IN PRACTICE SERIES

Risk Issues and Crisis Management

A Casebook of Best Practice

Third Edition

Michael Regester
& Judy Larkin

CIPR

CHARTERED INSTITUTE OF PUBLIC RELATIONS

KOGAN
PAGE

London and Sterling, VA

for

Paul

Lucinda, Alice, Kimberley and Daniel

Publisher's note

Every possible effort has been made to ensure that the information contained in this book is accurate at the time of going to press, and the publisher and authors cannot accept responsibility for any errors or omissions, however caused. No responsibility for loss or damage occasioned to any person acting, or refraining from action, as a result of the material in this publication can be accepted by the editor, the publisher or any of the authors.

First published in 1997
Second edition published 2002
Third edition published 2005

Kogan Page Limited
120 Pentonville Road
London N1 9JN
UK

Kogan Page US
22883 Quicksilver Drive
Sterling VA 20166–2012
USA

British Library Cataloguing in Publication Data

A CIP record for this book is available from the British Library.

ISBN 0 7494 4382 0

Library of Congress Cataloging-in-Publication Data

Regester, Michael.
    Risk issues and crisis management: a casebook of best practice/Michael Regester and Judy Larkin – 3rd ed.
        p. cm.
    Includes bibliographical references and index.
    ISBN 0–7494–4382–0
    1. Issues management. 2. Social responsibility of business. 3. Crisis management. I. Larkin, Judy. II. Title.
HD59.5.R44 2005
658.4′056–dc22
                                                    2005000815

Typeset by Jean Cussons Typesetting, Diss, Norfolk
Printed and bound in Great Britain by Clays Ltd, St Ives plc

Contents

PART 2 CRISIS MANAGEMENT

PR in Practice Series

**Published in association with the Chartered Institute of Public Relations
Series Editors: Anne Gregory and Gro Elin Hansen**

Kogan Page has joined forces with the Chartered Institute of Public Relations to publish this unique series, which is designed specifically to meet the needs of the increasing numbers of people seeking to enter the public relations profession and the large band of existing PR professionals. Taking a practical, action-oriented approach, the books in the series concentrate on the day-to-day issues of public relations practice and management rather than academic history. They provide ideal primers for all those on CIPR, CAM and CIM courses or those taking NVQs in PR. For PR practitioners, they provide useful refreshers and ensure that their knowledge and skills are kept up to date.

Anne Gregory is one of the UK's leading public relations academics. She is Director of the Centre for Public Relations Studies at Leeds Business School, a faculty of Leeds Metropolitan University. Before becoming an academic, Anne spent 12 years in public relations practice and has experience at a senior level both in-house and in consultancy. She remains involved in consultancy work and is a non-executive director of South West Yorkshire Mental Health NHS Trust with special responsibility for financial and communication issues. Anne is Consultant Editor of the PR in Practice series and edited the book of the same name and wrote *Planning and Managing Public Relations Campaigns*, also in this series. She was President of the CIPR in 2004.

Gro Elin Hansen is the in-house Editor of the PR in Practice series, as well as being Editor of *Profile*, the Chartered Institute of Public Relations' member magazine.

Other titles in the series:

Creativity in Public Relations by Andy Green
Effective Media Relations by Michael Bland, Alison Theaker and David Wragg
Managing Activism by Denise Deegan
Online Public Relations by David Phillips
Planning and Managing Public Relations Campaigns by Anne Gregory
Public Relations: A practical guide to the basics by Philip Henslowe
Public Relations in Practice edited by Anne Gregory
Public Relations Strategy by Sandra Oliver
Risk Issues and Crisis Management in Public Relations by Michael Regester
  and Judy Larkin
Running a Public Relations Department by Mike Beard

Forthcoming titles:

Effective Internal Communications by Lyn Smith and Pamela Mounter
Introduction to Public Affairs by Stuart Thompson and Dr Steve John

The above titles are available from all good bookshops. To obtain further information, please go to the CIPR website (www.ipr.org.uk/books) or contact the publishers at the address below:

Kogan Page Ltd
120 Pentonville Road
London N1 9JN
Tel: 020 7278 0433   Fax: 020 7837 6348
www.kogan-page.co.uk

About the authors

Michael Regester is an international authority, author and lecturer on crisis management and is regarded as having pioneered many of the systems, procedures and training programmes which companies can put into place to handle the communication aspects of crisis situations.

His involvement in crisis management started in 1979 when, as public affairs manager for Gulf Oil Corporation, Europe, West Africa and the Middle East, he had to handle the communication aspects of one of the oil industry's worst disasters – at Bantry Bay in Ireland.

In addition to many papers on public relations and crisis communications, he is author of *Crisis Management*, published by Century Hutchinson in 1987. His second book, *Investor Relations*, co-authored with Neil Ryder, was published by Century Hutchinson in 1990. Both are the first books on their respective subjects to be published outside the USA and have sold internationally.

He is a former board member of the International Public Relations Association, a Fellow of the UK Chartered Institute of Public Relations, and a regular visiting lecturer on crisis management at British universities.

He is a founding partner of crisis and issues management consultancy, Regester Larkin.

Judy Larkin is a founding partner of Regester Larkin and has 20 years' experience in international corporate communications and marketing.

She has worked both in-house and as a consultant, primarily in research and development-driven industries such as information technology, pharmaceuticals and petrochemicals.

A former head of corporate relations for Logica plc, she has held board-level positions with a number of major UK and US consultancies.

She has collaborated with Michael Regester on many crisis management consultancy programmes and, more recently, has been responsible for devising and introducing issues management systems into a number of international corporations.

She is a fellow of the Chartered Institute of Public Relations and of the Royal Institution, a member of the Issues Management Council in the United States, and an advisory board member of the Centre for Risk Management at King's College London. She is a regular writer, speaker and visiting lecturer on issues management and risk communication.

Foreword

We live in a world where corporate reputations are fragile and where crises seem to be occurring more and more. The role of the communicator in this environment is critical. Furthermore, the communication planner who might foresee and prepare for such eventualities is a significant player in our interconnected and changing world.

In this book, Michael Regester and Judy Larkin outline a comprehensive approach to managing situations that may turn into crises and handling crises once they occur. Their proposition is that it is impossible to live without risk and, therefore, it is important that organizations are in constant dialogue with all the stakeholders with whom they operate. This means that lines of communication must be open, regularly evaluated and that a basis for understanding needs to be established.

The authors go on to define issues and how they can be managed and, critically, who should be responsible for issues management. They discuss in detail the issues life cycle, from the point at which an issue is just a potential, right through to its development into a crisis, when it is either resolved or left to lie dormant and pop up at some later stage.

Despite the best endeavours of the most insightful and professional managers and communicators, crises do happen. So what happens then? Well it depends on the type of crisis! Regester and Larkin carefully outline a number of scenarios illustrating different crises and take the reader through the practicalities of the legal issues involved, the crisis-management planning process and the nitty-gritty of handling crises as they unfold. This includes setting up a press centre, managing the media, handling relatives, keeping employees informed and dealing with the emergency services.

Of course, it doesn't end there. Work is still to be done after the immediate crisis is over. Again, the authors suggest the necessary steps that have to be taken to manage the aftermath of a crisis and to learn from it.

Sprinkled with detailed and informative examples and case studies, *Risk Issues and Crisis Management* is a must for the modern-day public relations practitioner. The authors have gained a great deal of knowledge and experience of issues and crises management over many years, having been involved in developing issues and crises management practices and handling a number of large-scale crises. The public relations practitioner who is able to manage risk issues and crises for his or her organization is an invaluable asset, so a good knowledge and understanding of the issues covered in this book is a must for anyone involved in public relations today.

Anne Gregory
Series Editor

Preface

If your responsibility involves managing or advising on any facet of communication which has a bearing on corporate reputation or operational performance, this book is intended for you.

No matter how well organized and in control you may feel about your day-to-day tasks, extraneous events may suddenly place you and your colleagues in a vulnerable position.

Something as seemingly trivial as an opinion advocated in a trade publication, a minor but continuing increase in product complaints, an unsubstantiated claim about your company's performance or an apparently unconnected trend in social behaviour could have the potential to emerge as an issue, the maturing and long-term consequences of which could be devastating for your business.

Equally, the totally unexpected could happen – in the next hour or week – in an alarmingly fast and dramatic way, creating a true crisis situation. In either case, if you are unsure of your organization's ability to anticipate the probability of such a risk actually happening, let alone have the expertise, resources and infrastructure to cope, these 12 chapters are designed to provide a practical operational framework for pre-emptive action planning.

Risk Issues and Crisis Management is a best practice casebook, completely updated in 2005, drawing on the authors' considerable experience in working alongside senior management teams from many different industry sectors and on a cross-border basis. In addition, they refer to many well-documented case study examples and assess the lessons – both positive and negative – to be learnt from each.

Research conducted on behalf of Regester Larkin among major international corporations operating in the UK highlights the lack of a systematic approach to identify, prioritize, analyse, strategize and action issues programmes among the majority of respondents.

This book attempts to define and apply the emerging discipline of issues management with particular reference to assessing and dealing with risk in a communication context. A principal focus is on techniques for anticipating, planning and proactively managing issues to minimize negative commercial impact and create competitive opportunities.

Furthermore, while there is a greater acceptance on the part of business of the need to plan and organize for potential crisis situations, the continuing failure of senior executives to seize the initiative in explaining what has happened, what is being done to sort out the mess and, crucially, how the organization feels about what has happened, is amply demonstrated in the continuing succession of damning cases that fuel the appetite of a global media and sophisticated advocacy industry.

Guidelines for anticipating, planning, preparing and training are provided together with suggestions on how they can be applied inside your organization. These are summarized from the personal advice and experience of the authors who have made a detailed study of, and been directly involved in, handling major risk issues and corporate crises.

Acknowledgements

We would like to thank our colleague Jeremy Clarke for research for this book.

Introduction

WHAT PRICE REPUTATION?

There is no doubt in our minds that business is a formidably positive force in society today. Good business – performing and behaving with a sense of responsibility – underpins successful communities. It influences who we buy from, work for, supply to and invest in, and plays to both the rational and emotional attachments that we have with an organization. Strategic business development and revenue growth are reflections of a company's performance, but so is perceived leadership through greater visibility. Reputation is, therefore, a vital commercial asset and one which companies squander at their peril.

The influence and resources of big business today are huge, and that is not necessarily a bad thing. At the turn of the millennium fifty-one out of the world's top 100 economies were corporations, representing annual revenues of $4 trillion (Anderson and Cavanagh, 2000) The annual revenues of Royal Dutch/Shell are greater than the GDP of Morocco; those of Wal-Mart greater than the GDP of Poland, and those of General Motors greater than the GDP of Denmark. Against a backdrop of economic globalization, political transition and technological transformation, business has emerged as the principal engine of growth and development in the new world order, and so it has everything to play for.

Companies can, on occasion, lose sight of the right course to navigate by focusing on short-term requirements at the expense of longer-term impacts – no surprise when share-price is king and the average life expectancy of a CEO is three years. Ignoring the wider consequences of what companies are doing can, however, create unwanted market volatility, negative scrutiny and opportunities for the growing influence of anti-business activism. Companies travelling along this route are charting a course towards a field of operational and reputational icebergs that can quickly sink the most water-tight business strategies.

Threats to reputation – whether real or perceived – can destroy, literally in hours or days, an image or brand developed and invested in over decades. These threats need to be anticipated, understood and planned for. Public perception of risk has become a constant and recurring threat to reputation. Understanding and communicating effectively around risk perception can help to reduce conflict and gain support and trust – critical attributes in securing and maintaining customer, investor and employee loyalty. This is even more important at a time when the forces of globalization and the internet are pushing us from a so-called 'old world' or 'industrial' economy, dependent on the value of physical assets such as property and equipment, to a 'new world' or 'knowledge' economy characterized by the intangible assets of reputation, knowledge, competencies, innovation, leadership, culture and loyalty.

These intangible assets are valued in the balance sheet as goodwill or 'intellectual capital', of which reputation and brand attributes play important parts. Some 53 per cent of the value of Fortune 500 corporations is accounted for through intangible assets – an estimated $24.27 trillion. Research conducted by Interbrand with Citibank in 1998 found that the total value of the FTSE 100 companies was £842 billion, with goodwill accounting for 71 per cent of total market capitalization. In contrast, 10 years ago goodwill accounted for less than 44 per cent of the total, although this figure had been steadily rising over preceding decades. Another recent study by Interbrand concluded that one-quarter of the world's total financial wealth is tied up in intangible assets (Clifton and Maughan, 1999).

Why is it then that corporations are surprised when they are faced with controversy? Exxon, Shell, British Airways, BP Amoco, Coca-Cola, Railtrack, McDonald's, British Nuclear Fuels, Nike, Marks & Spencer, TotalFinaElf, Singapore Airlines, Renault – some of these companies are potent symbols of globalization, others are or were powerful local or regional brands, some successfully reinvented themselves from nationalized backgrounds – most have spent fortunes developing or redesigning and promoting their corporate or brand image. And yet all have failed at some point to acknowledge the commercial impact of adverse public perception on reputation in a risk setting, with chilling results.

Since we have worked in the field of crisis and issue management for many years, it seems extraordinary to us that business has learnt so little from its past mistakes. Coca-Cola learnt nothing from Perrier when it faced product contamination scares in Belgium and France in 1999. TotalFinaElf learnt nothing from the *Exxon Valdez* disaster a decade before when it had to deal with a major oil spill off the coast of Brittany at the end of 1999. By the end of 2000 Monsanto had wrecked an entire industry, as well as its own brand. Wrangling over who was to blame for a major vehicle safety failure has left the asset base of Bridgestone/Firestone in tatters and has created a serious dent in the balance sheet and reputation of Ford Motor Company, ejecting top management in the process. The British rail infrastructure company, Railtrack, self-destructed with help from incompetent policy makers in late 2001, and confidence in corporate America has slipped in the aftermath of scandals associated with Californian energy trading, Enron and Arthur Andersen, Sotheby's and Tyco.

Government performance has fared no better. Surely some lessons could have been learnt and applied about 'joined-up government' in the UK from the BSE outbreak in 1996, the fuel crisis and the floods of 2000 and the foot and mouth epidemic of 2001? The US administration continues to be accused of an unhealthily close relationship with business; and European politicians are being dragged, kicking and screaming, into a new world order which calls for transparency at the expense of personal and party political corruption.

In many Western societies today, we are living in an environment of unprecedented risk aversion and perceived lack of trust. This is strange, because for much of human history we have relied on gut instinct in the face of uncertainty and fared pretty well.

Reputation is built on trust and belief. Our own reputations matter to us a great deal – whether we are good at what we do or fun to be around. But in the commercial world reputation appears to have become a Cinderella asset – easily overlooked but with terrific potential. After all, it should be the biggest asset in most corporations and a high priority in the boardroom. Yet reputation isn't properly valued, is rarely fully understood and is seldom managed in a cohesive way by the people at the top.

As the examples cited above demonstrate, traditional models simply don't work any more because they ignore the essential building blocks of trust and belief. Senior managers need to think and behave differently: first, by demonstrating a clear acknowledgement of the importance of reputation in the boardroom, and second, by adopting an integrated approach to reputation management across the organization in exactly the same way that conventional operational risks are assessed, audited and managed. The maxims explored in this book for avoiding the pitfalls and delivering successful reputation risk management are as follows:

- Acknowledge that reputation is a valuable asset and needs to be actively managed at board level.
- Develop a finely tuned radar and become a listening company.
- Design clear and robust management systems that integrate with routine risk management processes.
- Create your own code of good behaviour and assure your licence to operate.
- Treat your stakeholders intelligently.
- Work as if everything you say and do is public.

Part 1

Risk Issues Management

1

Outside-in thinking

WHO CAN WE TRUST?

Minds are like parachutes; they work best when open.

Lord Thomas Dewer

Business today suffers from the perception that its leaders are complacent, greedy and unconcerned about the long-term welfare of their
companies and the employees that have not been shown the door
through downsizing. Government regulators are considered to be in the
pockets of industry, examples of bureaucratic sloth. The media is widely
believed to sensationalize the news as a means to establish its own
agenda. Consumer activists, often considered to be agents for constructive change, are being criticized for exaggerating the dangers facing
society. To understand why, it is worth examining some interesting trends
affecting the changing relationship between business and society.

First, there are many dynamic forces – political and regulatory,
economic, social and technological – that are shaping the way organizations work, perform and behave. They are expanding:

- the quantity, quality and speed of information globally;
- the impact of new broadcast and multimedia technologies on public
  opinion;
- the competition for reaching and influencing consumers;

- the knowledge, values and behaviour of constituents;
- the association between product and corporate brand reputation.

Second, the role of government and corporations in society is being challenged to a much greater degree than before. Here are some examples.

Public policy formulation is still an evolutionary process. We are quite naturally confused over government roles at local, regional, national and federal levels. This is characterized by uncertainties at a national level of the benefits of a unified Europe and the perceived responsibilities of newly democratized systems of government in central Europe.

Corporate and institutional behaviour is under much greater scrutiny. Critical media reports highlight concerns over excessive profits and senior executive pay, a lack of adequate corporate governance and corruption scandals in the financial and public services sectors. Monopolistic practices are questioned as industries consolidate and integrate for global competitiveness. 'Dirty tricks' campaigning, aggressive lobbying tactics that compromise the credibility of executives and public officials, and too much interference by business in government typify the populist braying of newspaper and broadcast editors alike.

We are less trusting of those in authority. In most developed countries, government promises on taxation and healthcare reform continue to be broken, and we are challenging industrial performance, for example, over the environmental reputation of oil and chemical companies. Even the ethical stance of companies focusing on socially responsible business practices, such as Body Shop, Ben & Jerry's and Levi Strauss, is being called to account.

Corporate loyalty is no longer a given. Redundancies, relocations, the erosion of workers' rights and job security have taken their toll. Demographic changes mean fewer young people are entering the market, the demand for skilled workers is gradually increasing while unskilled jobs are in decline. Employment is likely to become a sellers' market.

The social landscape is changing. Populations are getting older, resulting in several European countries raising the retirement age at a time when people generally want to stop work earlier. Our traditional family structures are under intense pressure. Nearly one in two marriages are ending in divorce in the UK. Coupled with declining job security, domestic property prices, pension and elderly welfare provision, a staggering change in family cash flow through an average lifecycle is illustrated in Figure 1.1.

Opinion polling in the United States and Europe indicates that some of the principal shifts occurring in society that give rise to concern relate to:

- safety and security, including economic security;
- environment, including workplace;

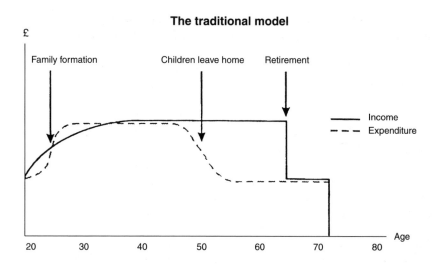

The traditional model

£

Family formation   Children leave home   Retirement

——— Income
- - - Expenditure

Age

20   30   40   50   60   70   80

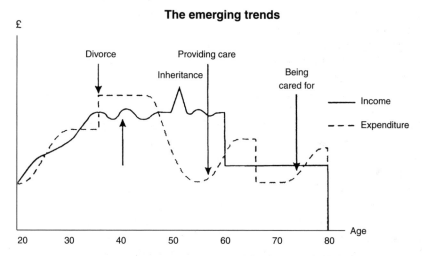

The emerging trends

£

Divorce   Providing care

Inheritance   Being cared for

——— Income
- - - Expenditure

Age

20   30   40   50   60   70   80

Source: Henley Centre Future of Work Forum, 1996, London

Figure 1.1   *Family lifecycle cash flows changing*

- gender/equality;
- service quality/value for money;
- institutional accountability;
- empowerment.

Changes in these and other areas are bringing about a big increase in activism. We are now much more likely to vote with our feet on issues of major concern, by picketing, boycotting and litigating. In the past 10 years, the proliferation of single-issue groups has outstripped anything in the past. Powerful and well organized, there is rarely a sandal-wearing extremist in sight. They have money and are well connected, often with sophisticated cross-border links.

CONSUMER POWER AND THE RISE OF A NON-GOVERNMENTAL ORDER

More often than not we now trust ourselves. We have much greater access to information through the internet, greater confidence in the validity of our own opinions and our 'consumer rights', and we increasingly back our ability to make a difference.

As business is becoming the main target for evidence of 'responsible behaviour', consumers are becoming the most vocal task-masters. Now, the active consumer:

- demands and exercises personal choice;
- responds to single-issue politics;
- is more likely to question the value of new developments;
- regards environmental issues as fundamental.

The active consumer is uneasy about corporate power. In a *Business Week* survey (14 September 2000), nearly three-quarters of Americans felt business has gained too much power in recent years. The active consumer not

Who Do The Public Trust To Do The Right Thing?

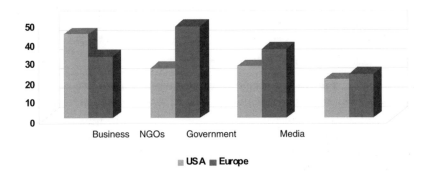

Source: Edelman PR

Figure 1.2 *Who do the public trust to do the right thing?*

only has greater affluence, access to mountains of information and with increased longevity, thinks longer-term, but also – certainly in Europe – looks to NGOs to drive the CSR agenda and places more trust in the legitimacy of what they say than in business, government or the media.

NGOs in Europe are masterminding increasingly sophisticated campaigns. Their own research reinforces the view that social as well as environmental responsibility is a key issue for the public. According to Peter Melchett, former Executive Director of Greenpeace UK, 'The vast majority of people are not anti-science, nor are they Luddite. But people are increasingly aware, and mistrustful, of the combination of big science and big business.' He continued, 'people scorn patronizing assumptions based on the premise that they don't know what is good for them. On the contrary, people insist that it is their society and their world, and they will decide what is acceptable, and what is not.'

This vocal and energetic movement is growing in line with corporate unpopularity, tackling issues as diverse as food and health safety, pollution, animal welfare, trading standards, smoking, ageism, racism, nuclear disarmament, sexism in the workplace, litter, noise, pornography, pesticides and disclosure of information. There are now more than 1,000 single-issue campaign groups in the UK, ranging from big organizations

Table 1.1 *Some of the issues that concern active consumers*

Marketplace	Workplace
• Impact on society of core products and services • Issues around buying and selling • Supply chain management • Vulnerable customers • Cause-related marketing	• Workforce diversity • Work–life balance • Health and safety • Human rights • Training and lifelong learning
Environment	**Community**
• Emissions to air, land and water • Use of natural resources • Environmental risk • Transport impacts • Impact on environment of core products and services	• Impact of local operations on the community • Business investment in the community

Source: Business in the Community, 2000

like the multinational Greenpeace with 4 million members to specialist outfits such as Surfers Against Sewage. One way or another, they have the power to inflict long-term damage on companies, and like shareholders and politicians, they need to be factored into corporate planning and decision making.

Effective consumer campaigns have contributed to a rise in popular sensitivity to a range of environmental and social issues and a plea for restraint in corporate activities. Global companies are the main targets of these demands because of their visibility and their perceived ability to shape economies and politics for their own ends. In our newly transparent, internet-driven world, businesses have no place to hide, no time to think and no second chances.

Charities, consumer groups and other NGOs are building enormous influence. Direct action campaigns clearly pose threats to reputation risk. Protestors at the World Trade Organization (WTO) meetings in Seattle, Washington DC, Prague and Genoa from 1999 to 2001 expressed concern about growth of big corporations, environmental degradation and the widening global gap between the 'haves' and 'have-nots'. They also criticized the IMF, the World Bank and WTO as three undemocratic institutions whose policies deprive people of food and water, and thus start wars.

NGOs have become increasingly sophisticated and powerful in targeting government and business at local, national and international levels. Under greater scrutiny and with expectations of more open governance and accountability, businesses are being pressured from many different quarters to respond to a culture of growing individuality and assertiveness, where every opinion is perceived to matter.

Campaign tactics are varied, often well managed and increasingly coordinated through internet and mobile communication technologies. The boycott is one of the oldest and most effective – a threat that can haunt any company today that fails to consider the ethical as well as environmental consequences of its commercial activities. This has ranged from student boycotts of Barclays Bank in the apartheid South Africa of the 1980s, through boycotting Exxon products over the Valdez spill in Alaska in 1989 and Shell gas stations over Brent Spar and its interests in Ogoniland in 1995, to PepsiCo in Myanmar through the mid-1990s, and clothing manufacturers such as Levi Strauss, Nike, Gap and Marks & Spencer over employment practices in developing countries.

One of the longest running boycotts has been against Nestlé. Baby Milk Action has been waging a record 25-year-long war against the company over the way it has marketed infant formula products, which it claims contravene the World Health Organization (WHO) code. In the 1970s, when the company was accused of selling infant formula in developing countries at prices that could not be afforded and where clean water was virtually non-existent, the company decided to ignore allegations of irresponsible behaviour and greed. Baby Milk Action became a powerful, critical force against Nestlé, generating negative media coverage and succeeding in targeting the company where it hurt – for example, through campaigning for boycotts of its market-leading Nescafé coffee brand. Nestlé suffered significant reputational and commercial damage by refusing to debate the issues in public. By the time the company woke up to the need to build bridges with campaigners and other stakeholders, the iceberg had well and truly struck. No amount of resource or attempts to align with the WHO through the development of a health code for infant feeding and nutrition made a difference. Furthermore, the student leaders and activists of the 1970s have become the media and social commentators and business people of today, consolidating the polarization of opinion.

Source: Regester Larkin

Figure 1.3 *NGO tactics*

The effect of these developments has been to shift the power of 'voice' in the formation of corporate reputations away from companies themselves and towards their stakeholders. As new opinion leaders emerge via the internet, reducing the share of voice of corporations, reputation risk management is becoming defined increasingly by external stakeholder perceptions rather than by what a company says and does.

Activists deal with problems; companies tend to deal with issues, and there is a difference. A problem has a wide context: pollution; bad employment practices; poverty; human rights abuse; hunger; racial discrimination. An issue tends to be more specific, and involves considering potential solutions – regulation to curb emissions; codes of practice to improve workers' rights or reduce bad behaviour; financial or regulatory penalties for failing to meet required standards. Activist groups today are focusing more on winning issues and seeking solutions, rather than merely creating awareness of problems. A key maxim for avoiding a collision course with activists is for companies to switch on and monitor the radar. The objective is to scan stakeholder attitudes in relation to emerging, current or linkage issues that may have the potential to impact on commercial or reputational objectives, and become familiar with the profile, personalities and working practices of activist groups.

The activist's checklist for developing a campaign strategy around an issue is likely to consider whether it will:

- result in a real improvement for people;
- give people a sense of their own power;
- be worthwhile and winnable;
- be felt in an emotional way;
- be easy to understand;
- have a clear target and timeframe;
- build leadership;
- have a financially beneficial angle;
- enhance profile to support subsequent campaigns;
- raise money and membership;
- fit with objectives and values.

(Source: Adapted from *Organizing for Social Change*, Midwest Academy, 2000)

In the same way that an NGO will develop its campaign agenda, a company facing potential direct action from an NGO must *analyse the problem and decide what kind of solution to work towards*. It requires answers to these questions:

- Can a credible argument be made against the company's position on the issue?
- Does the issue evoke emotion?
- Is the issue media and internet-friendly?
- Are there linkages to other issues, and are there legacy problems?
- How strong are the key activists?

- How far have the dynamics of the issue lifecycle developed?
- What impact will dealing with this issue have on the organization?
- What are the risks (and opportunities) if we ignore the issue?
- How are the company's key stakeholders likely to react, and how strong is our support base on the issue?
- How confident are we that we can influence the issue in the way we want?
- What potential resources will be required?
- What is the simplest solution and what is the most far-reaching?
- What are the potential benefits from actively seeking a solution?

(Source: Adapted from Winter and Steger, 1998)

Once again, accountability and transparency are the watchwords for corporate response to NGO attack. The view of one senior reputation risk practitioner is that 'public opinion demands accountability and transparency from business today and it will expect performance delivery on social and environmental issues pretty soon after'.

Post September 11, the global economic justice agenda championed by these groups is once again gaining momentum. However, the vast majority of NGOs are seeking solutions and change, not all-out war. Activists are far more willing to enter into partnerships with business to achieve their objectives. A greater self-confidence has emerged from the more militant tendencies of the 1970s and 1980s – a shift in mindset from 'anti-business' towards a more goal-oriented approach that accepts that partnerships that deliver results is not a compromise of principles.

Companies are seeking NGO advice on strategies for environmental, social and supply chain management. The WWF, (formerly the World Wide Fund for Nature) for example, has worked extensively with industry to establish the Forest Stewardship Council and Marine Stewardship Council.

Even Greenpeace, amongst the most aggressive of campaigners, is collaborating more with business. It cultivates industry outsiders that could be potential allies, encourages them to adopt environmentally friendly technology, and then targets its members to place orders. This approach led to the launch of chlorine-free paper and Greenfreeze, a CFC-free refrigerant. The group also developed smILE, a fuel-efficient prototype car based on a Renault Twingo and designed to demonstrate that a 50 per cent reduction in carbon dioxide emissions from cars is feasible. Greenpeace has established a unit to find technical solutions to environmental problems, and believes that it can bring technology to the market which would not otherwise happen. Marketing pressure is a key driver for the organization's campaigns, together with a streamlining of tactics based on research, the use of the media and the law, and targeted lobbying.

However, the strength of NGOs should not be misinterpreted as an issue fait accompli. No company should feel bullied into automatic capitulation over NGO demands if the tactics employed involve unfounded allegations or misinformation. These should be rebutted in a clear, credible and consistent manner. Many companies by their nature are involved in complex manufacturing and supply chain issues where accidents can happen or trade-offs need to be made. And many NGOs get their facts wrong or don't consider secondary issues or consequences of their demands. There is no doubting, however, that NGOs are among the most sophisticated and effective communicators, backed up by greater latent trust from the public. Business needs to be attuned to the issues communications 'playing field' defined by NGOs, and to be well equipped to succeed on those terms.

CASE STUDY: SHAC ATTACK

Even if they are not believed, special interest groups can still play havoc with an organization's ability to conduct its daily business. The vicious attacks on Huntingdon Life Sciences by Stop Huntingdon Animal Cruelty (SHAC) brought the company to the brink of collapse early in 2001. As well as targeting staff with hate mail, abusive phone calls and firebombing cars, Huntingdon's chief executive, Brian Cass, was attacked with baseball bats outside his home.

The company became a target after workers were filmed allegedly mistreating dogs three years previously. Then, in a sinister new move, SHAC began targeting investors and bankers to the company using the same aggressive tactics. Eventually, Huntingdon Life Sciences was plunged into financial crisis when the Royal Bank of Scotland called in a £22 million loan. Barclays Stockbrokers, a subsidiary of Barclays Bank, cut its stake in HLS, also blaming the campaign against it by the extremists.

Finally, in an unprecedented move, the Bank of England – which usually only offers facilities to commercial banking operations and government departments – stepped in and said it would provide banking services to the company.

Science Minister Lord Sainsbury played a key role in brokering the deal after warnings that if HLS was forced to close, research into vital treatments for cancer, Alzheimer's and other diseases would suffer serious setbacks.

In today's complex environment, organizations have to understand and respond to our rapidly shifting values, rising expectations, demands for public consultation and an increasingly intrusive news media. It is no longer enough to focus on internal objectives alone: *outside-in thinking*, illustrated in Figure 1.4, is an essential prerequisite for achieving the tacit acceptance of society to continue to operate.

There is a growing expectation, on the part of a broad range of stakeholder groups, that organizations should perform and behave in a more open, socially caring and responsible way. These principles are even more important in times of intense pressure, for example where there is a *real* or *perceived* risk to public health, safety or the environment.

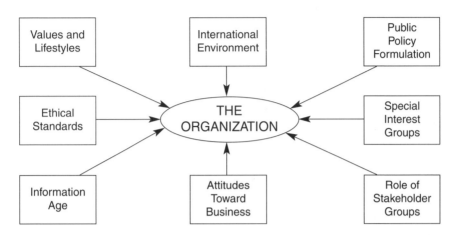

Source: Ashley and Morrison, 1995

Figure 1.4 *Outside-in thinking*

DEALING WITH RISK

The so-called 'risk society thesis' identifies new patterns of political and public anxiety. This conflict is being brought about by a combination of:

- continuous societal change and uncertainty;
- the remorseless pace of industrial and technological innovation;
- time and cost pressures that do not allow for adequate scientific evaluation of the risks versus the benefits of new innovation;
- a trend towards greater individuality and assertive public opinion.

In combination, these factors are intensifying a host of risk issues.

Traditional reliance on the judgement of experts to interpret levels of risk in using new products and processes is now paralleled by a growing ability on our part – reinforced by a modern media – to challenge political and corporate reassurance couched as scientific or technical fact. The perceived risk of contracting CJD through BSE-infected cattle is an example of the potential and real business impact of exaggerated public fear.

Risk is a measure of the adverse effect of an issue. It is about assessing and communicating the possible *hazards* associated with a particular process relative to the *safeguards* and *benefits* which it offers. This helps us, as consumers, to make choices about our health and safety, and the protection of the environment in which we live.

Risk assessment is essential when:

- a *new risk emerges* – such as the threat of contracting CJD or the safety of the Channel Tunnel following the fire in 1996;
- the *degree of existing risk changes* – such as the dangers of hand guns following the Dunblane massacre in 1996 or the perceived risk of thrombosis from sitting still during long-haul flights; or
- a *new perception of risk occurs* as in the potential impact of so-called gender-bending chemicals (phthalates) on animal and human health, and the environment.

All too often during public health and safety scares, the basis for sensible decision making has remained buried beneath an avalanche of scientific or technical data. According to US crisis management specialist Peter McCue, each crisis follows a similar pattern:

1. a special interest group sounds the alarm;
2. the media creates widespread awareness of the claim;
3. industry responds with reams of data and proclaims its products safe;
4. in the face of increasing shrillness, the public becomes anxious and avoids the products in question until more reliable information is available;
5. sales decline as regulators equivocate and issue confusing guidelines;
6. relying on exaggerated public fear, the activists step up the campaign;
7. the media faithfully covers everything they do and say;
8. industry reacts strenuously, occasionally resorting to exaggerations of its own in an attempt to restore calm and boost sales;
9. for a period of time everyone loses perspective on the issue;
10. eventually, a more accurate and balanced assessment emerges;
11. industry braces itself for another day;
12. those who make their living from consumerism find somewhere else to spread doom and gloom;
13. the media moves on to the next crisis, giving little attention to clarifications of the original inflated charge;
14. government returns to studying the issue so that it can write new and confusing legislation.

So, there are a number of dilemmas facing organizations endeavouring to understand and manage the dynamics of a risk issue:

- *Risk means different things to different people* – we overestimate sensational risks, like flying or contracting CJD, while we underestimate common risks such as driving a car or taking a short cut through an alley at night.
- *Basic attitudes are hard to change* – they are forged by a range of social and cultural factors and reinforced by our own contact with and opinions advocated by friends, colleagues, family members and others. These attitudes shape the way we interpret, understand and act upon new risks.
- *The public is not looking for zero risk* – we each constantly make risk/benefit choices, consciously or unconsciously, but there is a basic unease about two things: where is the benefit and can the people responsible for managing the risk be trusted? This is particularly true in areas of food and health safety, for example in food processing, biotechnology and synthetic chemical usage.
- *The source of information about risk is critical* – research in the UK indicates that consumers are totally confused about who to trust on food safety. A MORI public opinion survey after the Brent Spar incident in 1995 asking 'Who did they trust?' gave an 82 per cent score to Greenpeace, 48 per cent to Shell and 28 per cent to the UK government. A similar question in the same environmental issues poll to assess public confidence in scientists gave a 97 per cent rating to scientists working for environmental groups, compared with 77 per cent for government scientists and 64 per cent for industry scientists (see Figure 1.5). In other words, third-party expert allies play a crucial role in risk issue management.
- *Emotion* is the most powerful influencer of all. Emotional symbols – water cannon jets aimed at Greenpeace activists attempting to occupy the Brent Spar, aerial shots of the oil spill in Alaska, the cloud hanging over Chernobyl, debris floating in the water off Long Island following the crash of TWA flight 800 and the Snowdrop campaigners at Parliament – can overwhelm and *totally negate scientific fact*.

CASE STUDY: MMR

The government's failure to listen to people's worries and answer their fears led to a reduction in the uptake of the measles, mumps and rubella (MMR) vaccine and confusion about who to trust on the issue. Although the MMR vaccine has been given to children in the UK since 1988, in 1998 research led by Dr Andrew Wakefield of the Royal Free Hospital appeared in *The Lancet*, claiming a possible link between the vaccine and bowel disorders and autism in children. Organizations such as the Medical Research Council (MRC) reacted by dismissing these claims. The government set out to persuade parents that

Public confidence in scientists working for…

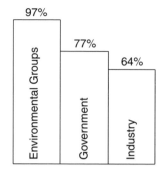

Media confidence in scientists working for…

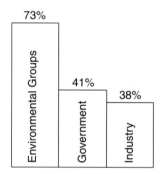

Who would you trust more to make the right decisions about the environment?

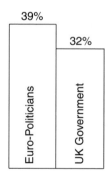

Source: MORI, 1995

Figure 1.5 *Sources of information and trust*

giving the MMR vaccine to their children would be the most sensible option, considering that the alternative would be to deal with a measles epidemic.

Dr Simon Murch, one of the doctors involved in the original research, changed his opinion and announced that he did not believe a connection exists between MMR and autism. Tony Blair would not comment on whether his son Leo had received the MMR vaccine or not. Parents very quickly became deeply confused. The prime minister's silence led to understandable assumptions that Leo had not received the MMR jab, and this contrived to create a feeling of deep mistrust in the government's advice. This, combined with conflicting medical opinion and a clear lack of authoritative scientific facts to alleviate the perceived risk, caused parents to refuse the combined jab.

Although many reports were published rebuking Dr Wakefield's original claim, this did little to ease parents' minds. The number of parents willing to allow their children to receive the jab fell significantly from 92 per cent in 1996 to 82 per cent in 2003 and even 60 per cent in some areas. Public calls for the introduction of single vaccinations grew louder. The government responded by claiming that the rejection of the combined jab in favour of single vaccinations could potentially lead to a measles epidemic.

It is important in emotive cases to understand and be sensitive to the emotional triggers of those affected. Not many things are as emotive as the health and welfare of children. The government failed to do this, and instead of listening to and answering health concerns in the call for single vaccines, it concentrated on pushing the MMR jab. Added to this was its attempt to fight fear with fear, telling parents that if their children weren't given the vaccine they could die from a measles outbreak. This was a clear case of pouring oil on the fire. Rather than seeking to address the emotional concerns, sensitively and dispassionately presenting the risks and benefits and taking the emotion out of the debate, it heightened the scare factor.

The government's immediate reaction to the original 1998 research was handled through a rapid and effective report form the MRC. Unfortunately, over the next five years there was no commitment to monitoring the issues and maintaining an open flow of information. Public mistrust evolved rapidly on the back of dismissive behaviour and a lack of openness, capped by doubts surrounding Leo Blair's inoculation.

As Liam Donaldson, Chief Medical Officer for the Department of Health, said, 'People are entitled to make claims, and when those claims cause anxiety to parents then we have a responsibility to respond to parents' concerns and look at the evidence again and continue looking at it every time that a claim is made.'

HANDLING THE ORGANIZATIONAL RESPONSE

For organizations facing emerging risk issues, some of the principal guideposts for effective risk communication are:

● To understand the dynamics of public emotion and the working practices of special interest groups and the media who may strive to

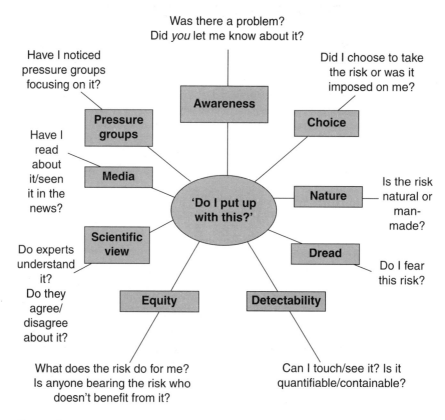

Was there a problem?
Did *you* let me know about it?

Have I noticed
pressure groups
focusing on it?

Did I choose to take
the risk or was it
imposed on me?

Awareness

Pressure groups

Choice

Have I
read
about
it/seen
it in the
news?

Media

Nature

Is the risk
natural or
man-
made?

'Do I put up
with this?'

Scientific view

Do experts
understand
it?

Dread

Do I fear
this risk?

Do they
agree/
disagree
about it?

Equity

Detectability

What does the risk do for me?
Is anyone bearing the risk who
doesn't benefit from it?

Can I touch/see it? Is it
quantifiable/containable?

Source: Regester Larkin

Figure 1.6   *Risk perception wheel*

raise and legitimize a stance on an issue for public debate and, ultimately, public policy formulation.
- To familiarize the organization with the cyclical development of an
  issue; to focus appropriate resource on early identification and monitoring of information relevant to the emerging issue and organized
  activity for response. This should include a clearly defined policy and
  associated communication strategy.
- To appreciate that it is not realistic to change public opinion about the
  size of the risk (even if the true risk of an unfamiliar hazard is small),
  and so for the organization or industry:
  - to communicate in language that relates to and alleviates public
    anxiety;
  - to establish and build *trust* about the commitment to *control,
    reduce and contain it.*

THE ADVOCACY APPROACH

According to Howard Chase (1984), more often than not activist groups are setting the public policy agenda by combining propaganda techniques with computer-age technology.

First, they create a perceived need for their reform idea (eg, that phthalate levels in synthetic chemical manufacture are destroying our reproductive systems and the environment) in both special interest and establishment press and before groups of opinion leaders.

Second, they create the appearance of legitimacy for the idea through studies, third-party validation and, ultimately, through public opinion polling and public policy lobbying.

Finally, they use other information dissemination techniques such as widespread editorial, direct mail and grass roots mobilization to extend their viewpoint on a cross-border basis.

From a corporate perspective, our own research on issues management carried out at the end of 1995 indicates that corporations were most concerned about/involved in dealing with the types of issues shown in Figure 1.7.

At its simplest, a campaign may consist of gathering information and passing it on to the media and government. Often, by using research, a pressure group can win public support for its cause and the courts can be brought into the equation to challenge corporate performance. Members

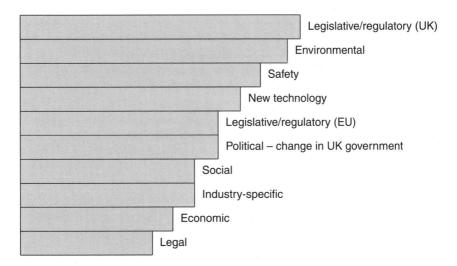

Source: Opinion Leader Research for Regester and Larkin, 1995

Figure 1.7 *Costs and choices*

and supporters can be mobilized to write to companies complaining about actions and policies. More pressure can be exerted by a boycott. Lufthansa agreed to stop transporting animals for laboratory testing 10 days after European anti-vivisection groups launched a campaign urging travellers to use another airline. The student boycott of Barclays Bank due to their operating in South Africa lasted 15 years, and was one factor that contributed to its eventual withdrawal in 1986.

Shareholders can also be tapped for support. Pensions and Investment Research Consultants claim there has been a rapid rise in ethical unit trusts over the last five years. Demonstrations at company annual meetings are now regular events, targeting companies such as British Gas with its 'Cedric the pig' campaign in 1995, attacking executive pay levels. Furthermore, financial institutions have experienced the damage inflicted by legal claims resulting from environmental pollution. Claims relating to toxic waste, asbestos and radioactive waste contributed about 20 per cent of the recent serious losses at the Lloyd's of London insurance market.

The new litigious culture of the late 20th century is costing corporate America $43 billion a year in product liability insurance. Even a small high street solicitor in the UK who paid an annual premium of £1,000 for professional indemnity 20 years ago is faced with a bill of £60,000 today. The burgeoning lottery of compensation claims for personal injury – physical and emotional – is achieving Alice in Wonderland status. UK health authorities are one of many public bodies in the firing line, anticipating an annual increase of between 15 per cent and 20 per cent in compensation claims. A recent landmark judgment centred on a 20-year-old who accepted an out-of-court settlement of £30,000 over claims that he had been bullied at a school in south-west London.

In the United States, the top 12 environmental pressure groups have operating budgets totalling around $400,000,000 a year, from a donor base of around 13,000,000 contributors. That works out at over 10,000,000 more people and an extra $250,000,000 than the entire combined Democratic and Republican parties have available to them.

The volume of work created by these advocacy groups, particularly in the area of environmental protection, is forcing organizations to focus on the introduction of issues management systems and new functions to manage them. In recent years, big businesses have shifted their thinking, believing there are commercial as well as social advantages to communicating about the steps they are taking to reduce their impact on precious resources without redressing the imbalance in some way. Many companies now publish environmental policy statements and employ specialists to devise strategies for cleaning up manufacturing processes and developing environmental initiatives in the community. Similarly, some organizations are implementing marketing and sponsorship programmes designed to promote brand awareness but in an ethically sustainable manner. 'Advocacy advertising' and 'cause-related marketing' campaigns are run by companies such as Levi Strauss, Benetton, J&B, Body Shop and many retail banks.

In his book, *The Critical Issues Audit* (1984), Eli Sopow refers to news content analysis research which shows a consistent pattern by advocacy groups or individuals who are attempting to gain public support for their action. The steps are listed below and shown in Figure 1.8:

Step 1: A key point of conflict is established, generally presented in simple terms. Action words are used by advocates to create a sense of urgency. Those words include *unique, new, first, only, last.*

Step 2: Once the issue has been identified as important/urgent it requires legitimacy. This is provided through apparent scientific and technical confirmation, with action words like *research, evidence, studies, tests.*

Step 3: The issue now has a sharp focus, and is backed up with scientific research. This step incorporates the necessary ingredient of broad-based public support. Action words are *people say, public demand, strong support.*

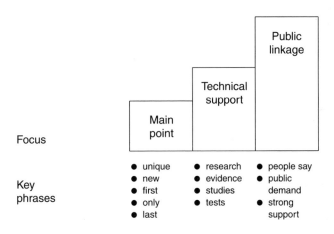

Source: Sopow, E, 1994

Figure 1.8 *Advocacy approach*

In formulating a potential strategy relating to an emerging issue, it is possible to anticipate some of the types of tactics that advocacy groups are likely to adopt. These tactics help to mobilize public opinion in such a way that pressure for public policy change – ie greater industry regulation – can be brought to bear.

Using our phthalates example, these tactics will include:

- Advocating, through the media and independent scientific experts, the need for a (long-term) comprehensive and independently commissioned research programme (to be funded by government and industry) to established 'benchmark criteria'; the aim is to pressurize government to take action to eliminate synthetic chemicals that disrupt hormones and a key objective here is to shift the burden of proof to chemical manufacturers.
- Proposing the development of a model similar to the 1987 Montreal Protocol, an international treaty that mandates the phase-out of CFCs and other ozone-depleting chemicals on an international basis (see Chapter 5).

In addition, advocacy groups could encourage activists at grass roots level via calls to:

- prevent exposure to hormone-disrupting chemicals through their total elimination;
- regulate every new compound so that before it is allowed to enter commercialization it is subjected to tests by manufacturers to ascertain what risks the chemicals pose;
- protect against the vulnerability of children and the unborn, taking into account that the effects of exposure on developmental processes are usually irreversible;
- change specific regulations and laws to take into account the additive and interactive effects of chemicals, not simply the effects of each individual chemical;
- assess contaminant levels from any single source within the context of total cumulative exposure rather than on an individual basis;
- manufacturers to provide comprehensive labels for their products so consumers have the information they need to protect themselves and their families from hormonally active compounds;
- force manufacturers/distributors to accept responsibility for monitoring their products for contamination;
- companies to detail the quantity of hormone-disrupting compounds incorporated into their products;
- collate comprehensive records of birth defects and symptoms of impaired function to determine whether significant changes are occurring;
- force governments to collaborate cross-border to act in the face of a genuine threat to human welfare.

So, the industry or organizational 'issue action plan' needs to factor in the methods of working and approaches of special interest groups in order to effectively respond to this type of agenda setting. In addition, companies now need to be taking steps to actively consult with the communities of which they are a part.

PUBLIC CONSULTATION – BUILDING DIALOGUE INTO THE COMMUNICATIONS PROCESS

In today's disaffected political environment, leaders in government and business are being called upon to embrace genuine public input. Public consultation is an increasingly important facet of *outside-in thinking*. It is about building dialogue into the communications process to minimize conflict and to achieve as much consensus as possible in balancing the scales of protectionism and developmentalism.

Simply assuming that being aware of upcoming issues, distributing some literature, placing some ads and holding a few 'town hall' meetings would create the result the company wanted in the first place is completely outdated. Public concern over what constitutes 'sustainable development' will continue to increase. As we learn more about the real pressures on the environment, it is argued that many of us will feel a desire to push for a slow-down in the remorseless progress of industrialization. The result is that a company's well-researched and very reasonable proposal relating to seeking planning permission for a new development on the edge of a green belt area may not seem so reasonable to people who already feel threatened by environmental degradation.

We were involved in such a case in 1996, when a company waiting for confirmation of planning permission to operate a low-level radioactive waste facility was confronted – much to its surprise – by a well-organized, articulate and highly vocal local community campaign. In spite of stressing that the type of waste that would be stored at the facility posed virtually no risk to human health, local teachers, parents, children and government officials, already living in a catchment area of research establishments working with nuclear materials, felt that enough was enough. One more facility, however safe it might be, was one too many in the risk/benefit equation. Anxiety over the perceived additional risk to their health and that of the environment, and a failure on the part of the organization involved to develop a more proactive public consultation process during the application for planning permission, created mistrust and a militant response. Parents and children marched on the premises of the company, under the watchful eye of local television, radio and newspaper reporters. Although we don't expect zero risk, we do want to get as close to it as possible.

THE RISE OF THE PRECAUTIONARY PRINCIPLE

A lack of *outside-in thinking* by organizations is giving rise to the 'precautionary principle', with potentially disastrous consequences for both business and society.

In this era of the triple bottom line – the achievement of a balance between commercial success, environmental responsibility and social justice – the stakes are becoming much higher for companies in their dealings with the outside world.

The cumulative effect of a succession of highly publicized health and food safety issues in recent years has contributed to a culture of blame and uncertainty. While consumers have become better informed and sophisticated – with rapidly rising expectations in relation to product and service choice, quality, value and access – they have also become more anxious about the complexity and pace of change that both drives and serves these demands.

Businesses should by now understand that successful companies are those which are outward-facing and which understand not only who their audiences are, but also what they think and what they want. So why are companies so often surprised by controversy? Probably because they are used to rational decision making based on technical and scientific data. They fail to understand that an issue can be viewed in many different ways and that emotion is a powerful changemaker.

There are many recent examples of companies that have failed to put this into practice: Monsanto, Marks & Spencer, Nike, McDonald's and Coca-Cola are just a few.

Added to which, some parts of the media have been directly responsible for manipulating sensible and justified calls for greater accountability to create a situation in which the public has become totally risk-averse. The genetically modified food furore during 2000 was punctuated by media coverage that *campaigned* rather than *reported* – to the extent that the media was driving the issue to fit its own agenda. Sensational headlines of the 'Frankenstein Food' variety quickly influenced a British public which has, for the most part, only a basic scientific education.

This, in turn, has been amplified by the workings of sophisticated pressure groups. Such situations can all too readily be channelled through pressure on government agencies to introduce tougher and costlier legislation and, ultimately, litigation.

In the wider context of corporate responsibility, the precautionary principle is a gift to those campaigning for greater restraints on business. It was first mooted in 2000 as justification for the delay in approving GM crops across Europe and there are now demands for a no-testing policy.

More recently, a government-sponsored report on mobile phones advocated a precautionary stance, while acknowledging the absence of evidence that mobile phones are damaging to health. The result has been a very confused British public.

If this trend continues, there is likely to be a stalemate with all new technologies. The discovery of the genetic blueprint for life was triumphantly welcomed in headlines around the world – but in today's climate of hostility to change, the ability to apply this new knowledge for the benefit of mankind may well be hampered.

It is clearly time for the balance to be redressed. This can only be done through early and open communication. Policy-makers need to work alongside industry to communicate in ways to which the public can relate; they need to reclaim the 'middle ground' and demonstrate both competence and honesty. Unless they do, the gap between their own efforts and the machinations of the media and other self-interested groups will grow ever larger, and 'caution' will undermine progress.

CASE STUDY: PHTHALATES IN TOYS

Phthalates have been used in a wide range of products for almost 50 years, because of their ability to turn rigid polyvinyl chloride (PVC) into a flexible product. In the mid-1990s the safety of phthalates, particularly in children's toys, was called into question amid claims that they could cause cancers, liver damage and hormonal disruption. Environmental NGOs in Europe and the United States launched a concerted campaign to ban phthalates in children's toys, and despite a lack of clear scientific evidence that phthalates could pose a health risk, the EU eventually banned phthalates at the end of 1999 in teething rings and toys that could be sucked by children under the age of three. Similar measures were subsequently introduced in the United States.

Greenpeace was the most influential campaigner against phthalates in toys, and for many years had highlighted environmental health risks from chlorine and associated plastics manufacture. In 1996 it began contacting leading toy manufacturers requesting meetings to discuss concerns about PVC toys, and began targeting the European Commission.

By April 1997, the Danish Environmental Protection Agency (EPA) stated that the level of phthalates in teething rings was 'unacceptable', and Danish importers voluntarily withdrew teethers from the market pending further research. The European Commission referred the concerns regarding phthalates to the newly appointed Scientific Committee on Toxicity, Ecotoxicity and Environment (CSTEE) for investigation.

In September 1997 Greenpeace launched its 'Play Safe' campaign in New York and London, 100 days before Christmas. The campaign increased direct action against manufacturers and retailers – a list of PVC and non-PVC infant toys was made available to parents in an attempt to target manufacturers such as Mattel and retailers such as Toys'R'Us. Greenpeace's claims continued to be widely and sensationally reported by the media. The following month saw requests from the Austrian consumer affairs minister and Belgium's public health minister for the voluntary withdrawal of PVC toys on the basis of precautionary consumer protection. A domino effect followed across Europe, with similar restrictions being introduced in Italy, Germany and Spain. Retailers in these countries began to withdraw branded PVC products from sale. In December 1997, a German toy retailer association responded by calling for a total withdrawal of PVC toys.

Although scientific evidence indicated no adverse human health effects, under growing media and NGO pressure, the European Commission requested that the CSTEE set up a working group to investigate the impact of phthalates on children's health, and to suggest appropriate limits and test methods. The Commission removed all PVC toys from its childcare facilities as 'a precautionary measure' in February 1998.

Throughout 1998 there was considerable scientific debate on phthalates, but not much in the way of a concerted response from industry. The World Health Organization (WHO) denied phthalates had carcinogenic properties, but under concerted NGO and media pressure the European Commission still agreed a non-binding recommendation to withdraw teething rings from use. Member states were invited to adopt appropriate safety measures while Community legislation for permanent protection was prepared. Between 1998 and 1999, eight EU countries introduced their own restrictions on the production and sale of phthalates. The government bans gave Greenpeace considerable ammunition to advance its crusade against the plastics industry.

In July 1999 the European CSTEE reported that scientific research showed there was no immediate health risk. However, in December 1999 the EC went ahead with a three-month renewable ban on PVC toys and teething products intended to be put in the mouths of children under three, pending future legislation. The ban has been continuously renewed since then. On 6 July 2000 the European Parliament voted on a draft Council Directive on phthalates in toys, requiring the banning of all phthalates in plastic toys for children under three years of age. This was followed by a demand by the European Parliament for a policy to replace soft PVC.

In the United States, industry capitulation was also swift. Government agencies, toy manufacturers and toy retailers came under pressure to remove phthalates from their products following the regulatory action in EU countries. Greenpeace accelerated its campaign in the United States during this period; at the opening of the International Toy Fair in New York in autumn 1998, activists abseiled down the side of a building to unfurl a banner that said 'Play Safe, Buy PVC Free'. Relentless pressure from Greenpeace and the US environmental NGO Environmental Defense (ED) led some larger US manufacturers to remove phthalates from their products, and Mattel announced voluntary action to remove phthalates from soft toys in 1998.

In December 1998 the US Consumer Product Safety Commission (CPSC) asked industry, as a precautionary measure, to remove one particular phthalate (DINP) from soft rattles and teethers in spite of a CPSC study demonstrating that 'the amount ingested does not even come close to a harmful level'. The plastics industry was requested to remove phthalates from soft toys and teethers to 'alleviate the mood of fear and as a precaution while more scientific work is being done'.

Environmental Defense maintained the pressure. In October 2000, it wrote to 100 US toy manufacturers requesting voluntarily disclosure of the chemical constituents of their products 'either targeted for young children or that in use involves mouthing or extensive skin contact by children including older children'. Unwisely, the Juvenile Product Manufacturers Association (JPMA) and the Toy Manufacturers Association (TMA) responded by saying that they did not think this was necessary, enabling Environmental Defense to claim that 'they would say that, wouldn't they?' through ongoing media articles and advertising campaigns.

European and American regulatory reaction towards the phthalates campaign ultimately forced the plastics industry to withdraw its products. Companies producing, selling and using phthalates took a wholly unnecessary hit to their reputation and to their financial performance. Why? Because of a total failure to understand the dynamics of the issue lifecycle curve, the triggers that can escalate a risk issue out of control, and a complete inability to communicate early on and in any concerted way to offset public perception of a wildly exaggerated health risk. If you see national regulatory agencies calling for voluntary restrictions on products, recognize that you are already forfeiting any chance of navigating your way round the risk perception icebergs! (Source: Larkin, 2003.)

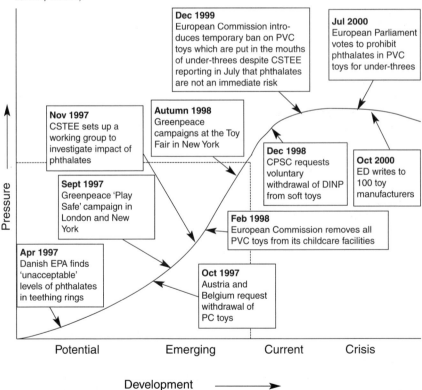

Dec 1999
European Commission introduces temporary ban on PVC toys which are put in the mouths of under-threes despite CSTEE reporting in July that phthalates are not an immediate risk

Jul 2000
European Parliament votes to prohibit phthalates in PVC toys for under-threes

Nov 1997
CSTEE sets up a working group to investigate impact of phthalates

Autumn 1998
Greenpeace campaigns at the Toy Fair in New York

Dec 1998
CPSC requests voluntary withdrawal of DINP from soft toys

Oct 2000
ED writes to 100 toy manufacturers

Sept 1997
Greenpeace 'Play Safe' campaign in London and New York

Feb 1998
European Commission removes all PVC toys from its childcare facilities

Apr 1997
Danish EPA finds 'unacceptable' levels of phthalates in teething rings

Oct 1997
Austria and Belgium request withdrawal of PC toys

Pressure

Potential   Emerging   Current   Crisis

Development

Figure 1.9 *Phthalates in toys issue lifecycle*

CASE STUDY: MOBILE PHONES AND RADIATION

In April 1996, *The Sunday Times* newspaper in the UK printed a story with the headline 'Danger – mobile phones cook your brains', which set off a long-running media and NGO campaign regarding alleged health effects from mobile phone electromagnetic frequency (EMF) emissions. The health effects from EMFs have been studied since the Second World War, and have been the subject of international media, NGO and scientific scrutiny in relation to links between leukaemia and emissions from electricity transmission pylons. Concerns over risk of brain tumours and other health effects from mobile phones began in the United States and then Australia in the early 1990s, following litigation alleging that a woman's fatal cancer was the result of prolonged exposure to a mobile phone.

Electromagnetic fields are emitted by all sorts of electrical equipment, from television masts and radio networks to hairdryers and ovens, and they also occur naturally. The science relating to EMF health effects is complex; it has been reviewed by expert panels and government-appointed inquiries and has formed the basis for national and international exposure guidelines. None has definitively concluded that EMF exposure within international guidelines causes adverse health effects. However some recent data examining both thermal and non-thermal effects have proved controversial, suggesting a range of unpleasant health conditions. So far, none of this science has been replicated for peer review, but further studies are under way. In line with public inquiries in different countries and international scientific reviews, the majority of experts have called for further research and the adoption of precautionary policy approaches, for example, recommending avoidance of prolonged use of mobiles by children. Scientific complexity coupled with uncertainty and risk aversion has provided the impetus for continued media coverage, mobilization of public opinion against mobile base station sitings, and ongoing attempts to demonstrate causation between EMFs and brain cancers through the courts. Some of the key triggers that have projected the issue through a roller-coaster ride in recent years are highlighted in Figure 1.10. Using a risk perception wheel model, it is not difficult to see how concern levels can rise.

These levels indicate active triggers for raising public concern. In the case of choice and equity, while we can choose whether or not we want to use a mobile phone, it is difficult to object to the siting of base stations close to our backyards. Residents who don't use mobiles but do live close to base stations are in a less equitable position regarding the risk–benefit equation. Moving house may not be a realistic option.

In 1997 Cable & Wireless was the first mobile company in the UK to recognize this issue's potential for public concern and impact on the reputation and commercial health of the mobile phone industry – and not just in the UK. Mobile telecommunications is by definition an international business, and companies like C&W, Vodafone, Deutsche Telecom, BT, France Telecom and Hutchison have invested enormous sums in creating global capabilities and global brands. Although there wasn't a shred of evidence that worry over health effects was affecting consumer purchasing or usage patterns, C&W

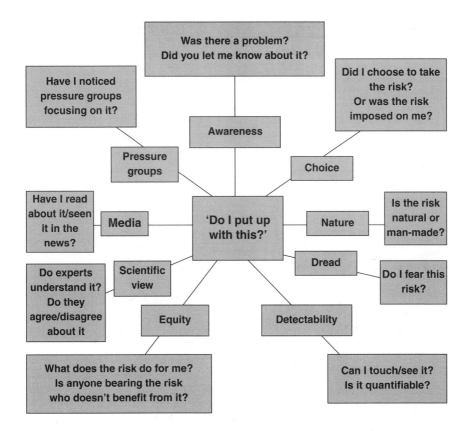

Figure 1.10 *Mobile phones and radiation risk perception wheel*

called on other mobile operators to work together to establish a consistent and responsible industry voice on health issues.

Quite naturally, some operators were sceptical of the need to do anything. After all, 40,000 mobile phones were being sold a month, the companies were making huge sums of money in a demand-led market, and it was crystal clear that consumers were becoming increasingly dependent on mobile phones for business and leisure use. C&W's senior director responsible for the issue, Ann Sullivan, commissioned Regester Larkin to undertake a risk assessment, present the findings to senior management and work to establish a risk issue management function within the corporate centre. The aim was to support local operating companies around the world to handle consumer, media, NGO and regulatory inquiries and requests for information on health issues. In particular, operating companies in Australia and Hong Kong were some years ahead of the emerging issue in Europe, so sharing experience and good practice in consumer communication and liaison with regulators and public officials

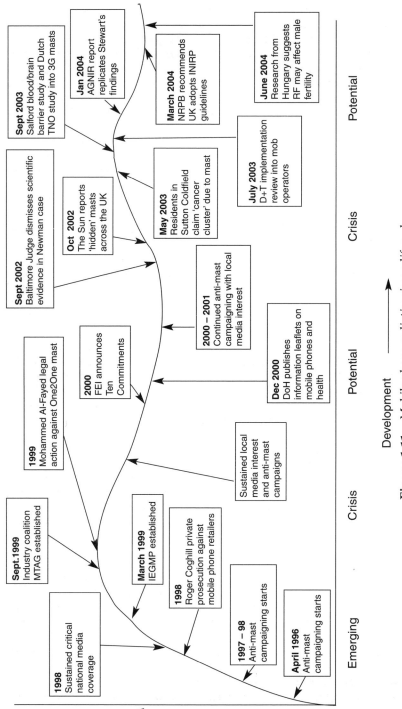

Figure 1.11 *Mobile phone radiation issue lifecycle*

Development ⟶

1998
Sustained critical national media coverage

Sept.1999
Industry coalition MTAG established

1999
Mohammed Al-Fayed legal action against One2One mast

Sept 2002
Baltimore Judge dismisses scientific evidence in Newman case

Sept 2003
Salford blood/brain barrier study and Dutch TNO study into 3G masts

Jan 2004
AGNIR report replicates Stewart's findings

March 2004
NRPB recommends UK adopts INIRP guidelines

June 2004
Research from Hungary suggests RF may affect male fertility

Oct 2002
The Sun reports 'hidden' masts across the UK

2000
FEI announces Ten Commitments

May 2003
Residents in Sutton Coldfield claim 'cancer cluster' due to mast

July 2003
D+T implementation review into mob operators

2000 – 2001
Continued anti-mast campaigning with local media interest

Dec 2000
DoH publishes information leaflets on mobile phones and health

Sustained local media interest and anti-mast campaigns

March 1999
IEGMP established

1998
Roger Coghill private prosecution against mobile phone retailers

1997 – 98
Anti-mast campaigning starts

April 1996
Anti-mast campaigning starts

Emerging   Crisis   Potential   Crisis   Potential

proved to be highly beneficial in briefing management teams around the world and developing clear and consistent communication tools. Figure 1.11 describes the responsibilities of the issue working group within C&W.

The health issue began to escalate in the UK in 1998 through 1999, with an increase in tabloid media reports highlighting the results of poorly designed studies connecting mobile phone usage with memory loss, headaches, increased blood pressure and fatigue. At the same time, an application for judicial review was made by Mohammed Al Fayed, the high profile owner of London's Harrods store, against the siting of a base station near his son Dodi's mausoleum on the multi-millionaire's Surrey estate. Calls for tougher regulation against operators were emerging in Australia, further litigation was being attempted in the United States, and the World Health Organization established a working group to review international science on the subject with a five-year timeframe for reporting. It was time for mobile phone operators in the UK to consider their position.

We helped to facilitate an informal group of senior managers from C&W, Vodafone, BT, One2One and Orange to consider options for establishing a coordinated strategy in response to public interest in mobile phone health effects. Participants trawled company experience in international markets, participated in international scientific and risk communication seminars, and tapped into equivalent global operational, regulatory, litigation and public consultation experience within the electricity industry over EMF issues. It didn't take long for the group to determine that organizing a single issue industry forum was the only realistic and credible route to go. What was needed was an executive director with appropriate experience, a decision as to whether the forum should be established as an entirely new entity or affiliated to an existing industry group, and a decent budget.

Group contacts, international networking and executive search identified an experienced corporate lawyer and risk communicator with direct experience over many years of the electricity industry situation. A forum was set up to coordinate policies around the issue through the Federation of Electronic Industries in London – a well-established group with expertise and links to equivalent groups around the world. Following a series of 'get to know' meetings and assessments of resourcing and policy requirements, the UK Mobile Telecommunications Advisory Group (MTAG) was established towards the end of 1999. Over the next two years the group developed a risk issue management framework along similar lines to the C&W model, designed to:

- acknowledge and respond to public concern;
- develop and disseminate information to anticipate and respond to public interest in the issue, directly and through the media and NGOs;
- prepare industry spokespeople for media management, inquiry handling and participate in international industry, scientific and risk communication events;
- create tools for liaison with local government officials in relation to base station planning applications;
- develop expertise in participating in public meetings;
- establish and support independent scientific assessment of, and research into, EMF health effects;

- liaise with public policy officials to achieve a balance between commercial, regulatory and public interests;
- implement regular consumer and other stakeholder opinion polling as a means to gauge opinion and potential attitudes towards industry responses;
- provide for contingency planning requirements.

Practical experience and learning also encouraged operators to establish their own EMF units, designed to communicate around company-specific network management requirements. Our work in this area was based on creating a risk management case to justify additional resourcing for an EMF unit against a background of:

- reducing increased cost of capital and loss of revenue through delays in network commissioning as a result of direct action by swifter and improved information quality;
- managing the 'opportunity costs' associated with significant additional handling of public and customer inquiries about health-related issues; a key measurement criteria was based on an inquiry response procedure with inbuilt escalation to process responses appropriately and within defined time periods;
- offsetting the potential for costly litigation or additional insurance liability through structured dialogue with public officials, local planning officers, regulators, technical and scientific experts and the media.

At the time of writing, attempts in US jurisdictions to win judicial approval for litigation on mobile phone health effects have not succeeded; however, high-profile plaintiff-friendly lawyers are determined to pursue legal action in this field, and it is possible that in the next few years, scientific data and expert opinion may make this strategy stick, with major liability consequences for industry. In addition, international scientific review programmes have yet to report their findings. While essential use of mobile phones continues to dominate and transcend global economies and cultures, public concern over mobile phone safety is not denting customer usage patterns. Public opinion polling in Europe is, however, suggesting more precautionary attitudes to the use of or exposure to mobile phone emissions in the case of children. It is also indicating that people are confused about the science and quality of information in making decisions; one clear indicator is that they are not inclined to trust the mobile phone companies in helping them to make decisions.

Who knows how this issue will roll on and roll out? Industry has done some excellent work in the area of acknowledging and responding to the emotions and vagaries of public risk perception associated with mobile phone health effects. A great deal of good practice has been pursued and implemented. What is worrying is that against this positive reputation risk management background but declining financial performance, there is a real risk that the companies will quickly lose sight of the benefits achieved so far and strip out the associated costs on short-term performance grounds. Applying the reputation risk radar now is more important than ever before. (Source: Larkin, 2003.)

SUMMARY

The difficulty for companies setting off down a more assertive public consultation route is that they should be prepared not to get their own way on every occasion. Unsuccessful consultation can actually polarize or further divide public opinion. Nevertheless, taking an active role in communicating about issues through adopting a more 'inclusive' approach in the influencing and consultation process will, we believe, prove to be an essential requirement if the current fault-line between financial and sustainable success is to be removed.

Outside-in thinking depends on an organization's ability to move away from one-way information flow towards active *dialogue* with a wide range of stakeholder groups. Institutions and companies, upon which we depend to provide and protect, must run much faster both to resolve potential conflict *and* achieve consensus about their role and relationship in society. Those who fail to address the need for this type of change, as we shall illustrate in the following chapters, may simply forfeit their licence to operate.

2

Issues management defined

One moment of patience may ward off disaster; one moment of impatience may ruin a whole life.

Anon

As we described in the previous chapter, organizations are running just to stay in place in their chosen markets as rapidly shifting public values, rising expectations, demands for public consultation and an increasingly intrusive news media present greater challenges.

A recent US public opinion survey of 1,000 consumers showed that half had actively boycotted a company at some time, with a further 26 per cent saying they had joined a boycott within the past year. Their outrage was caused by bad customer service, poor quality products and environmentally unsound actions. They objected to corporations whose values were out of sync with their own. The mismatch between political and public priorities, as we shall see in the following chapters, is even more pronounced. The actions of politicians and political institutions today are inconsistent with changing public attitudes leading to greater frustration, anxiety and lack of trust in the integrity and effectiveness of elected officials (Sopow, 1994).

How issues are handled can mean the difference between a crisis out of control and a proactive solution – between profit and loss. From our own experience, many issues can be anticipated and successfully managed. On the negative side, however, many organizations still fail to see there is a problem.

WHAT IS ISSUES MANAGEMENT?

Issues management has been around for almost 20 years, but while it has been adopted by some major corporations as a powerful strategic planning tool, it has not attracted the widespread attention we believe it deserves.

In the mid-1970s, an atmosphere of increased hostility towards corporations led business communicators to rethink the role of corporate communication. The groundswell of public suspicion about private sector management was reflected through two trends. While some 40 years ago public opinion surveys reflected a clear majority in favour of the practices of business management (an 85 per cent score was typical), 35 years on that figure had slumped to around 10–15 per cent. During the same period companies, increasingly subject to criticism, hired public relations firms in droves to defend them in the face of growing public opposition. Budgets grew tenfold, running into billions of dollars annually, but this did nothing to stop the decline of public support for corporate enterprise.

Issues management was an attempt to define the strategies that companies needed to use to counter the efforts of activist groups which were putting pressure on legislators for stricter controls of business activity. 'Despite the billions of dollars companies and their associations have spent on *external relations* business in general has been ineffective in defining and then validating its position on public policy issues' (Jones and Chase, 1979). So, a new area of corporate communication emerged – issues management was first implemented as a way in which companies could deal with their critics.

In 1978, the US Public Affairs Council defined it as 'a program which a company uses to increase its knowledge of the public policy process and enhance the sophistication and effectiveness of its involvement in that process'. Heath and Cousino offer their own explanation of issues management as 'a product of activism and the increasing inter- and intra-industry pressures by corporations to define and implement corporate social responsibility (CSR) – as well as the debate in public about what the standard of CSR should be' (1990).

Many saw the early role of issues management in the United States as an effective means to avoid large sums of clean-up money and a way to forestall incoming government legislation on employment and other social issues.

Tradition has it that in 1977 W Howard Chase coined the term 'issue management'. Chase drew upon his experience at American Can Company and the lead of another specialist who introduced the term 'advocacy advertising' to recommend a new kind of corporate communication response to the critics of business activities. Companies were advised to move from an information base to an advocacy position because 'companies should not be the silent children of society' (Chase, 1984). Since then, the relationship between business and society has become an important strategic factor in reputational and financial performance terms.

Chase and his colleague Barry Jones defined issues management as a tool which companies could use to identify, analyse and manage emerging issues (in a populist society experiencing discontinuous change) and respond to them *before* they became public knowledge. They felt that most companies reacted after the fact and were forced to accept what new regulations and guidelines were given to them.

> When challenged by today's activism, business tends to react to overt symptoms, rather than by identifying and analyzing fundamental causes of the trend which has led to a critical issue. It is not surprising, then, that when a critical issue reaches the public policy decision-making point, business finds itself the defendant in the court of public opinion.
>
> (Jones and Chase, 1979)

Public policy also needs defining and one expert says:

> Public policy is a specific course of action taken collectively by society or by a legitimate representative of society, addressing a specific problem of public concern, that reflects the interests of society or particular segments of society.
>
> (Buchholz, 1988)

Some experts describe the formation of public policy in terms of the interplay of government, the media and the public. As an issue gains momentum, a climate of opinion is created that puts pressure on government to do something about it. If, however, interest flags in any one of the three components then the issue will lose momentum (Ito, 1993).

Any section of society can and will exert some sort of pressure on government and its influence over corporations. Jones and Chase describe the formation of public policy as the result of interaction between public and private points of view. They state that a corporation has every moral and legal right to help formulate public policy instead of waiting for governments to pass legislation. As a result, more organizations, particularly in the United States, see issues management as an integral part of strategic planning and a basic ingredient for corporate survival.

Hainsworth, in a 1990 article, describes the importance of issues management:

Where legislation and regulation are concerned, issues are always resolved to someone's advantage and to someone's disadvantage. If it is the object of corporate management to maximize the organization's profits and minimize its losses in a socially responsible manner, then issues management should be seen as a critical element in overall corporate planning and management.

WHAT ABOUT THE SCEPTICS?

Critics of the term 'issues management' feel that it implies manipulation – 'of conditions or events which are the natural and freely occurring output of a pluralistic society' (Brown, 1979). Others argue that no organizational management can allow its environment to stand still, nor can it decide the direction in which the environment will change.

Scepticism about adopting issues management as a clearly defined function exists in the following areas according to Tucker and Broom:

Financial risk – the link between issues management and the bottom line is a tenuous one, normally only realizing benefit over the long term, if at all.

Boundaries – issues-based communication is just one tool used in conjunction with, for example, research, corporate planning, change management and other media and communication activities. It is both difficult to define and evaluate in isolation.

Diversity – the people actively conducting and taking part in the issues management function are not only from public relations backgrounds; they may include lawyers, corporate planners and analysts, researchers, etc. It may be inappropriate to assume that the public relations practitioner is the single driving force behind issues management.

Furthermore, some specialists question the degree to which a disciplined acceptance of and approach to issues management is actually applied inside the organization.

Recent research conducted across a sample of major public corporations in the UK on behalf of our own consultancy (Regester Larkin) indicated that while there was acknowledgement by corporate communication and public affairs functions of the importance of managing issues, only 10 per cent of the sample considered that their senior management proactively dealt with issues as part of the strategic planning process. Less than 5 per cent considered their organization applied an integrated approach – linking planning, communication, regulatory and other appropriate functions – to assess, prioritize and plan for the potential impact of near- and long-term issues on corporate objectives. Ninety-five per cent of the sample felt that issues were handled in a reactive and ad hoc manner, often to the detriment of reputational and financial performance goals.

However, academic research and practical case study examples do demonstrate that effective use of issues management techniques can:

- increase market share;
- enhance corporate reputation;
- save money; and
- build important relationships.

Failure to do so can lead to market share erosion, impact reputation, incur significant expense, put management in a negative spotlight and reduce corporate independence through increased regulation.

Newspaper articles quoting 'exploding toilets and a public relations disaster of epic proportions' surrounding the refit of the *QE2* ocean liner at the end of 1994 demonstrated how an issue can develop to a point where financial performance and corporate reputation are negatively affected.

Having worked across both areas for many years, our experience tells us that issues management is not crisis management and the two terms should not be used interchangeably. Part of the difficulty in defining and understanding the principles of issues management is that it is less action-oriented and more anticipatory in nature than crisis management. Issues management is proactive in that it tries to identify the potential for change and influence decisions relating to that change before it has a negative effect on a corporation. Crisis management tends to be a more reactive discipline dealing with a situation *after* it becomes public knowledge and affects the company. It is needed after there is public outrage.

Dealing with crisis situations is much more immediate and we have learnt to have an overnight bag at the ready wherever we are. There is normally a clear focus, and a finite set of actions and audiences and information that needs to be communicated within a short timescale. With issues management, organizations should be aiming to eliminate any possibility of outrage, often by trying to anticipate trends, changes and events that may have a bearing on the ability of the corporation to continue to operate or, indeed, achieve competitive benefit.

Issues management involves looking into the future to identify potential trends and events that *may* influence the way an organization is able to operate but which currently *may* have little real focus, probably no sense of urgency and an unclear reference in time.

According to US issues management specialists, Tucker and Broom (1993):

Issues management is the management process whose goal is to help preserve markets, reduce risk, create opportunities and manage image (corporate reputation) as an organisational asset for the benefit of both an organisation and its primary shareholders.

WHAT IS AN ISSUE?

It will come as no surprise to discover that there are many definitions of an issue offered by business communicators and academics on both sides of the Atlantic.

An issue arises, according to US specialists Hainsworth and Meng (1988):

> as a consequence of some action taken, or proposed to be taken, by one or more parties which may result in private negotiation and adjustment, civil or criminal litigation, or it can become a matter of public policy through legislative or regulatory action.

Chase and Jones describe an issue as 'an unsettled matter which is ready for decision'. Others suggest that, in its basic form, an issue can be defined as a point of conflict between an organization and one or more of its audiences. A simple definition that we like to use is that an issue represents 'a gap between corporate practice and stakeholder expectations'. In other words, an emerging issue is a condition or event, either internal or external to the organization, that if it continues will have a significant effect on the functioning or performance of the organization or on its future interests.

Example triggers for issues management include the potential for new legislation, an opinion or claim advocated through the media or other channels, a competitive development, published research, a change in the performance or behaviour of the organization itself or individuals or groups to whom it is linked.

Managing issues frequently involves dealing with change. An overall aim is to bring some control to the impact caused by discontinuity in the environment (Heath and Nelson, 1986). The ultimate goal, according to Hainsworth and Meng, is to shape public policy to the benefit of the organization through:

- early identification of the potential impact of the change; and
- organized activity, based on sound management principles and techniques, and allowing time for analysis and creative thinking to influence the evolution and, ultimately, the outcome of that change.

It is important to remember, however, that managing issues should not be considered a defensive activity. Although most of the time we are asked to advise companies on how to minimize the commercial risks associated with change, positive opportunities for repositioning a product or process, or communicating new benefits do exist *if they are looked for.* The creation of new issues or the gathering and management of information and opinion relating to an issue can be harnessed by an organization for significant competitive or social advantage.

WHO SHOULD PRACTISE ISSUES MANAGEMENT?

A major question relating to issues management is who is best placed to practise it? Chase feels that issues management derives strength from public relations, and from its various disciplines – public affairs, communications and government relations. He goes on to say that issues management is the highway along which public relations practitioners can move into full participation in management decision making (Chase, 1984).

> Public relations practitioners understand that they are expected to play increasingly complex and involved roles in promoting the bottom line, building harmonious relations with stockholders, and protecting corporate interests in ways that must be sensitive to the needs of a variety of external interests.
>
> (Heath and Cousino, 1990)

We believe public relations practitioners are well placed to help manage issues effectively but often lack the necessary access to strategic planning functions or an appropriate networking environment which encourages informal as well as formal contact and reporting.

WHAT ARE THE FUNCTIONS OF ISSUES MANAGEMENT?

The US Public Affairs Council (1978) states that the functions required of issues management are identifying issues and trends, evaluating their impact and setting priorities, establishing a company position, designing company action and response to help achieve the position and implementing the plans.

These functions must occur constantly and be integrated and focused on the central task of helping the organization – through its management. The key tasks of this activity are *planning, monitoring, analysing* and *communicating.*

Heath and Cousino (1990) identify four broad functional requirements for a company to maximize its position and positively sustain its public policy environment, with a principal focus on nurturing relationships with stakeholders.

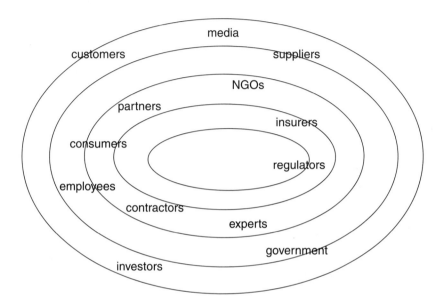

Figure 2.1 *Stakeholder risk radar screen – charting the importance to organization and influence on issue*

Smart planning and operations

If issues managers are doing a good job of capturing the critical changes in the public policy environment then that information should be integrated into the strategic business plan and corporate management strategies. The rationale is that this kind of information can offer business opportunities, justify the curtailment or change of business activities, and guide the standards by which the company operates. 'Issues management can positively affect corporate performance by enhancing the firm's responsiveness to environmental change' (Wartick and Rude, 1986).

Tough defence and smart offence

Issues management offers the rationale, tools and incentives for becoming involved in the discussion of public policy issues as early as possible. If companies get involved before issues have solidified, they can increase the likelihood of their communication campaigns succeeding. In other words, what needs to be said to whom and with what intended effect to exert influence in the public policy arena?

Getting the house in order

According to the authors this is about examining requirements to achieve appropriate commitments to matters of corporate social responsibility. Research in the United States found that market forces alone do not shape the fate of corporations – public policy change plays its role. In addition, public affairs must be sensitive to public policy forces and assist in corporate planning and in the formation of business ethics. The essence of being a responsive organization in the modern world is to move from coping with external demands to anticipating how demands can best be met within the technical and economic context of the organization (Post and Kelley, 1988).

Scouting the terrain

What companies believe to be the nature of the marketplace is likely to influence their strategic business plans. The same can be said of businesses that use issues monitoring to assess the public policy environment. Greater sophistication has been used in an effort to refine strategic management information systems. In addition to straightforward polls and surveys, futurists, for example, have used social scientific techniques to offer valuable insights into the ways issues can be identified, monitored and analysed. The key to making this activity effective is understanding a corporation's culture, its organizational and political structures and the nature of public policy issues analysis. Companies can then determine what issues to monitor and analyse as they refine their public policy and strategic plans. This process requires more than periodic public opinion surveys.

SUMMARY

The importance of anticipation – forward-thinking skills inside the organization – and outside-in thinking skills in relation to the role of new and diverse stakeholders, should not be underestimated. The push towards globalization and the requirement for organizations and institutions to understand and respond to the sophisticated demands of consumers and constituents emphasize the critical connection between business and society in the decades ahead.

While practical experience demonstrates that barriers exist to understanding, resourcing and managing the impact of change in the future, we are convinced that the implications of failing to examine the farthest reaches of the lighthouse loom – how issues emerge, mature and are resolved at a political, regulatory, economic, social or technological level – can deprive an organization or an industry of its ability to continue to sustain a viable existence. Equally, evidence exists to suggest that organizations can gain influence and commercial advantage through positively shaping the progress of trends, conditions and events which spawn issues. The rationale for anticipation, planning and progression to minimize risk and capitalize on opportunities in the issues arena are explored in the next chapters.

3

Planning an issues management programme – an issues management model

You can't build a reputation on what you are *going* to do.

Henry Ford

Issues generally evolve in a predictable manner, originating from trends or events and developing through a sequence of identifiable stages that are not dissimilar to the cyclical development of a product. Because the evolution of an issue often results in changes in public policy, the earlier a relevant issue can be identified and managed in terms of a systematic organisational response, the more likely it is that the organisation can resolve conflict and minimise cost implications to its advantage. For this reason, understanding the cyclical development of an issue is critical to effective issues management.

Hainsworth, 1990

Meng (1987) identifies six possible groups or publics that make issues:

associates, employee associations, the general public, government, media and special or general interest groups. Their influence on organizations may vary from controlling the operations of a company to forming internal and external coalitions to increase the potential influence of an issue. So, when issues are ready for decision, organizational response can be critical. Meng characterizes issues into several types: demographic, economic, environmental, governmental, international, public attitudes, resources, technological, and values and lifestyles.

An issue originates as an idea that has potential impact on some organization or public and may result in action that brings about increased awareness and/or reaction on the part of other organizations or publics (Hainsworth, 1990). In a model developed by Hainsworth (1990) and Meng (1992), this process can be described as a cycle made up of four stages: origin, mediation and amplification, organization, and resolution. In Figure 3.1, the vertical axis of the diagram represents the level of pressure exerted on an organization by a developing issue; the horizontal axis represents the various stages of development. At each stage of evolution

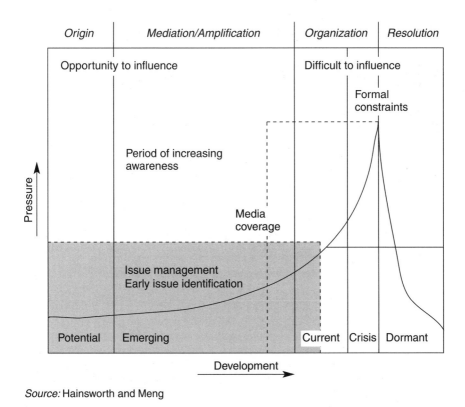

Source: Hainsworth and Meng

Figure 3.1 *Issue lifecycle*

pressure mounts on the organization to respond because of the increasing importance of the issue. An issue can fail at any point in the process for any number of reasons, but issues that continue to mature appear to consistently evolve from one stage to the next.

ISSUE LIFECYCLE

Stage 1 – origin: potential issue

An issue arises when an organization or group attaches significance to a perceived problem (or opportunity) that is a consequence of a developing political/regulatory, economic or social trend (Crable and Vibbert, 1985). From a management perspective, trends must be identified from which issues at some points may emerge. Trends probably first become identified and articulated by academics or specialists participating in working groups, policy and planning units, who may become concerned with some problem, situation or event that has potential impact and demands response from an institution, organization, industry or other group. If a response is forthcoming, it frequently results in counter-responses from those benefiting from the status quo and those desiring change.

An issue begins to gain definition when an organization or group plans to do something that has a consequence for another organization or group (Grunig and Hunt, 1984). Awareness and concern on the part of a group brings about a resolve to 'do something'. Lines become drawn and conflict emerges (Crable and Vibbert, 1985).

So, what we see in the early *potential* stage is a defined condition or event which has the potential to develop into something of importance. The types of issues which exist in this phase, however, have not yet captured significant expert or public attention, although some specialists will begin to be aware of them.

From our own experience in the healthcare sector, an example could be a trend in the increased incidence of a disease or knowledge of forthcoming research that highlights adverse side effects of a drug. At this stage, however, the issue often lacks sufficient form or substance to justify deliberate external intervention, for example by competitors who seek to shape or redirect it. Issues that make it past Stage 1 are alive, have a momentum of their own, and are capable of being modified as they move towards resolution.

In Stage 1, groups or individuals generally begin to establish a certain level of credibility in areas of concern and seek out support from other influencers and opinion leaders who are involved to some degree in that particular area of interest. At this point it is common for those involved to feel a bit uneasy as they begin to recognize that, in some situations, a point of conflict could exist.

The constant scanning of this process and early identification of potential issues is important and should be an integral part of the corporate planning process itself.

(Nagy Hanna, 1985)

Stage 2 – mediation and amplification: emerging issue

As groups emerge and lines become drawn, a process of mediation and amplification occurs among other individuals and groups who may have a similar viewpoint and may be expected to react in a similar way. Initially, this takes place within the relevant specialist media of interest groups, industries, professions and others with comparable opinions, values or concerns. As momentum builds within the mass media, the issue becomes amplified into a public issue that may become part of the public policy process.

The *emerging* issue stage indicates a gradual increase in the level of pressure on the organization to accept the issue. In most cases, this increase is the result of activities by one or more groups as they try to push or legitimize the issue (Meng, 1987). Using our healthcare example, this may involve competitors of a pharmaceutical company using published data to gather support from opinion leaders and influencers such as the media to gain medical community and, ultimately, public/patient acceptance of *their* interpretation of the issue.

At this stage in the issue's development it is still relatively easy for the organization to intervene and play a proactive role in preventing or exploiting the evolution of the issue. However, it is often difficult to determine the urgency of the issue, and we have often found the issue slipping away at this point as management attention evaporates in favour of more immediate and pressing matters. Although it is hard to know whether the issue will remain moderate or increase in intensity, stay confined to a particular area or become pervasive, it can be folly simply to pursue the status quo. We have seen this in recent public health scares and in increasingly persistent and professionally organized grass roots campaigning on animal welfare and environmental issues.

A dominant factor in the development of the issue in this phase is media coverage. Frequent editorial, initially specialist/trade and then broader general/business, begins before the issue reaches the shaded area in Figure 3.1. Before the issue reaches the next stage, those involved usually try to attract media attention as a means of progressing the issue. Sporadic in the beginning, this coverage will eventually become regular and is a critical factor to be considered in the advancement of the issue (Meng, 1987). Time and time again we have been involved in situations where regular competitor assessment, early media scanning and the decision to communicate with the media have happened too late.

According to Hainsworth the process of mediation is critical and has the effect of accelerating the full development of the issue. It is therefore essential that companies which are targeted conduct regular and effective monitoring of the commercial, regulatory and social environment in order to identify Stage 2 issues and begin to formulate action plans to deal with them.

Stage 3 – organization: current and crisis issue

Mediation brings varying degrees of organization. Positions solidify. Groups begin to seek a resolution to the conflict that is either acceptable to their best interests or at least minimizes potential damage.

In the context of the public policy process, publics or groups should be viewed as dynamic. They are often groups of individuals with varying degrees of commitment who face a similar problem, recognize that the problem exists and unite in some way to do something about the problem (Hainsworth, 1990). These groups are not static and their level of organization, funding and media literacy can vary enormously. At one end of the spectrum, they may be informal networks of people sharing only one passing interest in the resolution of the conflict, or they may be highly organized, well connected and funded with an intense and focused commitment.

As these groups work out their viewpoints and objectives and seek to communicate their respective positions, conflict achieves a level of public visibility that is likely to push the issue into the public policy process (Hainsworth, 1990). In turn, increased public attention motivates influential leaders to become a part of the emerging conflict and pressure mounts on institutional bodies to seek a resolution to the conflict.

An example of this process was the establishment of the Snowdrop Campaign in the UK in 1996 which called for a ban on hand guns in the aftermath of the Dunblane massacre. The impact of an individual can be equally effective. In early 1997, a village resident campaigned successfully against his local parish council in Yorkshire, England to protect 56 yards of hawthorn hedge from being removed to develop a bowling green, with knock-on implications for the protection of 40,000 miles of hedgerow in the UK.

In the *current* phase, the issue has matured and is displaying its full potential upon those involved. It becomes very difficult to affect the issue as it has now become enduring, pervasive and increasing in its intensity. The different parties involved recognize its full importance and, in response, place pressure on regulatory institutions to become involved.

As the issue lifecycle diagram illustrates, in no time at all the issue ramps up from *current* to *crisis* status to reach a formal institution such as a regulatory authority which has the power to intervene and impose constraints on the organization or industry as a way to resolve the situation. This was clearly demonstrated by Exxon Corporation's perceived failure to move swiftly enough to clean up the *Exxon Valdez* oil spill in Alaska in 1989, which led to stiff public policy requirements for ocean-going oil tankers to be built with two hulls.

Similarly, looking at our pharmaceutical industry example, there could be demands for additional safety data through costly new patient trials, blacklisting of specific drugs restricting patient indications, major changes in prescribing information, company-funded patient education programmes and, ultimately, product withdrawal. Options available to the organization to affect or influence the issue are now limited – it is in crisis response mode.

In 1982, Eli Lilly was the target of international media attention and protracted, costly litigation associated with the withdrawal of the anti-arthritic drug, Opren. With claims that the drug caused unpleasant side effects, including persistent photosensitivity, the company was forced into significant out-of-court settlements valued at millions of pounds.

Hundreds more alleged victims of the banned drug sought compensation some ten years later, but the courts ruled that the majority of claimants had initiated their actions too late. The issue continued to be the focus of adverse media commentary, citing elderly arthritic sufferers attempting to seek compensation from an unsympathetic pharmaceutical giant.

Arguably, if Eli Lilly had moved more quickly to present an efficacy and safety database that could refute the severity of the claims being made against Opren and mobilized supportive opinion leaders to present a balanced case via the media, the company could have avoided such long-term negative consequences.

And, as we shall demonstrate more than once over the following pages, industry quickly forgets the lessons it could have learnt from previously mismanaged situations.

Since the Opren case, there have been many examples of similarly mismanaged situations. Norplant, a contraceptive implant launched by Hoechst Marion Roussell (HMR) in 1993, is just one of them.

CASE STUDY: NORPLANT

At its launch, Norplant was hailed as a revolution in contraception. Over 50,000 women in the UK had the implants, which were designed to stay for five years, removing the inconvenience normally associated with contraception. They were fitted by GPs who received special training from HMR.

Two years after the product's launch a Norplant Action Group was formed after a small number of women began to experience side effects. Some 400 women joined the group. Although small in number when compared with the total number of women using the product, warning lights should have been flashing on the company's risk radar screen.

HMR was then astonished to find 275 women bringing a class action against the company. At this point, it tried to open a regular dialogue with the women but failed to put across clear messages in support of Norplant quickly enough to the media. Even though the statistics were in HMR's favour (women experiencing problems with implants represented less that 0.5 per cent of UK users), it was too late to stem the tide of critical media coverage of Norplant.

The coverage led to public loss of confidence in the product and prompted the British Medical Association (BMA) to step in. In spite of agreeing with HMR that the problem had arisen because a small number of doctors had not under-gone the training and had incorrectly inserted the rods, the BMA issued a general warning to all GPs not to use the product with new patients. This led to a spate of headlines claiming that 'GPs advise against Norplant'. Unsurprisingly, a rush of women visited their GP to have the rods removed, followed by a rapid decline in new users.

Although the BMA apologized to HMR for issuing the wrong message, the damage was done. By 1996, sales were down 100 per cent and in 1999 the product was withdrawn, in spite of strong support from family-planning agen-cies and doctors.

With some justification, a spokesman for HMR at the time said, 'In effect, a major therapeutic advance, fully approved by the UK Medicines Control Agency and widely welcomed by doctors and users, has been killed off for non-medical reasons by an unholy alliance of bureaucrats, lawyers and the media.'

Nonetheless, early on in the process HMR failed to see the incoming iceberg on the radar screen, even if it was only a blip on the horizon, failed to move fast enough when it got closer, and was ultimately torpedoed by the very people who were supposed to provide the rescue.

Stage 4 – resolution: dormant issue

Once issues receive the attention of public officials and enter the policy process, either through changes to legislation or regulation, efforts to resolve the conflict become protracted and costly, as illustrated by the tobacco industry. The object of the public policy process is the imposition of unconditional constraints on all parties to the conflict – either to their advantage or to their disadvantage (Hainsworth, 1990).

So, once an issue has run the full course of its lifecycle, it will reach a height of pressure that forces an organization to accept it unconditionally. The pervasiveness of anti-smoking legislation in the United States can be viewed as an example of this stage.

The following case study demonstrates this cyclical development of an issue and the implications of a slow organizational response.

CASE STUDY: MONSANTO WRECKED BRAND AND LOST OPPORTUNITY

Monsanto's plans for the introduction of genetically modified (GM) crops in the UK and more widely in Europe in the mid-1990s met a strong backlash from consumers, environmentalists, regulators and retailers.

Concerns about insufficient testing of GM organisms rapidly became a subject of national media debate. Despite refutations by senior scientists of health risk claims, the issue made front-page news in most national papers. The issue was picked up by the European media – particularly in France, Germany and Italy.

Monsanto continued to roll out its promotional plan, including a $1.5 million advertising campaign, and did not acknowledge stakeholders' concerns about GM products. It left the UK government, European Commission and retailers to respond to rising pressure, intensifying protests, boycotts and regulatory demands.

This resulted in a plummeting share price, and led to its merger with Pharmacia & Upjohn. Hostility to GM foods and Monsanto's attitude also led to the ruination of the UK and wider European markets for other GM producers: 24 of the top 30 European food manufacturers are now 'GM free'.

The story of Frankenstein food

Monsanto's biotechnology division had been very successful in the United States. The company had met little resistance from farmers or food producers to the concept of genetically modified food and its stock was high on Wall Street.

However, throughout the early 1990s, international environmental campaign groups Greenpeace and Friends of the Earth had been campaigning against the introduction of GM crops. In the United States, these campaigns remained marginal and were not viewed by Monsanto as a material threat. The dominant news story was Monsanto's commercial success and imminent expansion into Europe. In 1996, the European Commission approved imports of GM foods and the development of research and supply sites for GM foods.

In spite of growing concern among environmentalists and consumer groups following the EU's approval, it was not until early 1998 that Monsanto's strategy received sustained, hostile media and public attention.

Growing pressure on supermarket chains from environmental groups and consumer associations to label GM products were dismissed by Monsanto. Of key importance was the fact that the company did not acknowledge the different concerns held by European consumers and proceeded with the same strategy it had used in the United States.

Monsanto's attitude contributed to the decision by the frozen-food chain Iceland to announce the removal of GM products from its own-brand goods. Iceland's decision immediately raised questions about the policy of other retailers and increased political pressure in Europe to regulate the sale of GM products and give consumers choice.

Monsanto responded to concerns in the European media with a misguided $1.5 million advertising campaign, including television advertising in the UK. It failed to address growing concerns about the long-term implications of GM and was seen by campaigners and consumers to be aggressive and dismissive.

The growing public and media perception of Monsanto as a company unwilling to address important questions about GM was compounded by its announcement at the beginning of 1998 that it planned to introduce a genetically modified potato. The announcement triggered a wave of critical media coverage.

In a *World in Action* programme screened in April 1998, one of the scientific researchers, Dr Arpad Pusztai, gave an unauthorized comment on the preliminary, unpublished results of tests in which modified potato had been fed to rats. He suggested that immune system damage was possible. Despite refutations of Dr Pusztai's claims by senior scientists at the Rowett Institute Laboratory where he worked, fears about the health effects of genetically modified organisms became the front-page story in many national newspapers.

In October of that year, a summit of international consumer groups accused Monsanto of 'bio-colonialism' and dismissed its claims that biotechnology could help the developing world. By now, the growing concern had reached investors and led to a fall in its share price of 11 per cent. This, allied to the mounting criticism of GM products in Europe, led to the collapse of Monsanto's planned merger with American Home Products. As a result, Monsanto came under increasing pressure from Wall Street to separate off its biotechnology function as the scale of opposition caused panic among shareholders. A report from financial specialists J P Morgan advised Monsanto to restructure.

Early in 1999, Monsanto's chairman, Bob Shapiro, confidently predicted that Europe was ready for the introduction of biotechnology and would provide a gateway for the company to markets in the developing world and the British Commonwealth.

This statement appeared to be at odds with the increasing resistance from European consumers and regulators. In February 1999, the UK's Health and Safety Executive successfully prosecuted Monsanto for its release of GM oilseed rape into the British countryside and the company was fined £17,000.

Oblivious to all, the company continued to roll out its plan and take an aggressive and uncompromising line with any opposition. In April, it failed to win its High Court action against the direct action group Genetix Snowball for destroying the company's crops.

Monsanto left the British government and European ministers to respond to public concerns, despite the fact that pro-GM politicians, including the British Prime Minister Tony Blair, were blatantly failing to stem the tide of negative perceptions towards GM food.

Throughout the summer of 1999, environmental activists kept the issue of GM fears in the news with high-profile direct action tactics. The head of Greenpeace, Lord Melchett, was arrested for uprooting GM crops and the subsequent court hearing was widely covered by the media. In other European countries, particularly Italy, protest centred on retailers that stocked GM products. The media debate intensified when Prince Charles aired his highly critical views on genetically modified organisms in an exclusive interview with the *Daily Mail* newspaper.

The situation in Europe resulted in further falls in Monsanto's share price, and increasing pressure from investors contributed to its merger in July 1999 with Pharmacia & Upjohn. Hostility towards GM foods and Monsanto's attitude also led to the ruination of the UK and wider European markets for other GM producers: 24 of 30 top European food manufacturers pledged that their own products would become 'GM free' over the course of the year.

The battle in Europe was undeniably lost for Monsanto. At Greenpeace's 1999 annual conference, Monsanto's US chairman Bob Shapiro encapsulated the realization of the mistakes made, 'because we thought it was our job to persuade, too often we have forgotten to listen'.

The impact of negative sentiment about GM products was captured by a Deutsche Bank report in August 1999 advising institutional investors to sell their shares in companies involved in the development of GM organisms. It drew attention to Monsanto spending $1.5 million on a wasted advertising campaign and the 11 per cent fall in the value of its stock over the previous six months. The Deutsche Bank report to investors also noted that European consumers had been through a number of food scares and 'hearing from unsophisticated Americans that their fears are unfounded may not be the best way of proceeding'.

It has proved impossible for the Monsanto brand to shake off its pariah status in Europe. In the summer of 2000, the Pharmacia Corporation announced proposals to sell off Monsanto's biotechnology subsidiary.

The outcome

Monsanto's strategy was for Europe to become a major supply and research base for GM products. The company intended simply to replicate its success in the United States. But in the United States, limited protest against GM had not impeded the company's continued expansion. Monsanto had dismissed its opponents as insignificant because they had inadequate scientific knowledge. It therefore rolled out its expansion strategy in Europe in the face of growing negative sentiment, confident that resistance would subside.

The UK government, European Commission, farmers and retailers were left to handle the public reaction. As a result, the company was seen to ignore the concerns of European consumers and opposition became entrenched. Commentators, politicians and even environmentalists who had been willing to support aspects of the GM programme were isolated and retracted their support. Anti-GM sentiment came to dominate Monsanto's attempted expansion into Europe.

CASE STUDY: THE PILL PANIC, A LESSON IN OVER-CAUTION

The safety of contraceptive pills has been debated since they were first marketed in the 1960s. Over time, new formulations have been developed to try to remove potential negative health effects. Second-generation pills, introduced in the 1970s, contained less synthetic progesterone than the first pills, but being chemically similar to the male hormone testosterone, caused side effects in some women, including nausea, headaches, irritability, acne, weight gain and water retention.

Third-generation contraceptive pills, which contain a different form of synthetic progesterone, were introduced in the early 1990s to reduce these side effects. However, some studies indicated that third-generation pills were more likely to cause a thrombosis than second-generation pills. The research found that second-generation pills were associated with a lower incidence of thrombosis than previously thought, not that third-generation pills posed an increased risk.

By the mid-1990s, government and public attitudes towards risk were changing. This was particularly the case in the UK, where the debilitating disease CJD had been linked to the BSE crisis, and public trust in the government to ensure public safety was negligible. Therefore, when the World Health Organization (WHO) issued findings in July 1995 that the second-generation progestogen, levonorgestrel, was only half as likely to be associated with thromboembolism as the third-generation progestogens desogestrel and gestodene, the story hit the headlines. Increased media coverage of the 'danger' associated with third-generation pills ensued, and individual cases of thrombosis were publicized to evoke public concern.

Following accusations of a BSE cover-up, the UK government was keen to be seen to be protecting public health and taking action. As a result of the political climate and mass media focus on the issue, the government accelerated a pan-European study on the subject, and the UK Committee on Safety of Medicines (CSM), an advisory governmental body, conducted its own study from the UK GP database. On the findings of these three unpublished studies, on 18 October 1995 the CSM faxed a letter to 190,000 GPs, pharmacists and directors of public health alerting them that third-generation pills posed a higher risk of thrombosis. The CSM announced that the 1.5 million women in the UK taking third-generation pills should be encouraged to use second-generation pills or other forms of contraception.

At the same time as the CSM mailout, a statement was made to the press and broadcast media. The government was keen not to be perceived to be covering up information, so it issued a warning before GPs had the chance to digest the results of the research. Although women were advised not to stop taking the pill until they sought medical advice from their GP, the message conveyed in the media was one of increased risks. This is unsurprising, as the release contained no numerical information on what the increased risk represented in real terms. (Table 3.1 outlines the actual risk.)

Furthermore, the manner in which information was conveyed to journalists – an emergency announcement at the end of a routine press briefing on another subject – emphasized its importance and urgency. The scare and controversy filled the pages of newspapers for days, and alarmed women across the country.

The absence of an adequate briefing to GPs amplified the panic. Many GPs were angry that although they should have been alerted by the CSM, they heard the news from the media, as did their patients, some of whom stopped

Table 3.1 *Risk of non-fatal thromboembolism per 100,000 women per year (19 October 1995)*

Women not using oral contraceptives	5–11
All women using low dose combined oral contraceptives	30
Women using combined oral contraceptives containing desogestrel or gestodene	30
Women using combined oral contraceptives containing levonorgestrel or noresthisterone	15
Pregnant women and women post-partum	60

using the pill straight away. Sales of the seven brands of the pill plummeted, as an estimated 41 per cent of women stopped taking them. Figures from the Prescription Pricing Authority PACT report showed that contraceptives containing desogestrel and gestodene, which had accounted for 55 per cent of usage and 70 per cent of cost in October 1995, had fallen to 12 per cent and 23 per cent respectively by June 1996.

The panic led to thousands of unplanned pregnancies, and has been blamed for almost 3,000 extra abortions in England and Wales in the first quarter of 1996, a rise of 6.7 per cent on 1995 and the highest figure since 1991 (Office of National Statistics). The British Pregnancy Advisory Service reported that 61 per cent of women requesting termination of pregnancy during this period claimed to have failed to finish their current course of oral contraceptives. Maternity units around the country also reported higher than expected birth rates of up to 25 per cent.

The pill panic increased the risk of thrombosis among women, because the risk of thrombosis is twice as high for pregnant women than for women taking third-generation pills. The highly publicized twofold increase in risk for women taking third-generation pills rather than second-generation pills amounted to a doubling of a very small number, which may have caused, according to the original estimates, an extra two fatalities a year (BBC, 1997).

Ann Furedi, director of the Birth Control Trust at the time, said, 'Our research shows this was a needless panic. Other countries, having assessed the same data, concluded there was no need for immediate action. The action of the Committee on Safety of Medicines resulted in the misery of unwanted pregnancy for many women in the UK and undermined the attempts of medical authorities in other countries to present a more objective assessment of the risks and benefits of the pill. We are not arguing that information should be held back from women – simply that it should be presented in an accurate, balanced way.'

Analysis of the WHO data by the European Drug Safety and Advisory Committee in November 1996 concluded that no action was necessary other than informing women of the possible increased risk. The European Commission ruled that third-generation pills posed no higher risk to public health than other brands of oral contraceptives. As a result, only Germany and Norway followed the UK lead in advising women against taking the pills.

The actions of the UK government seriously undermined the actions of other national medicine control agencies that had chosen to interpret the new

studies more cautiously. For example, in Cyprus, where the UK CSM announcement was widely reported in the press and discussed on television, it is claimed
that around 10 per cent of the women who were on third-generation pills
stopped taking them (Ministry of Health, Nicosia, 1996). In the United States
there was less concern over third-generation pills as they were not used widely.
However, the culture of litigation meant that many doctors were wary of
prescribing third-generation pills for fear of being sued.

The lesson that the Chief Medical Officer of Health drew from this panic in
his annual report (Department of Health, 1997) was that 'there is an important
distinction to be made between relative risk and absolute risk'. Clearly an
unquestioning adoption of the precautionary approach can cause more harm
than good. (Source: Larkin 2003.)

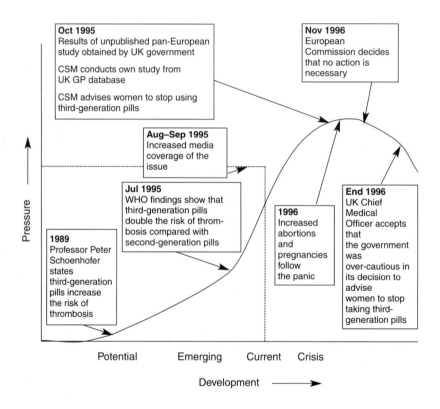

Figure 3.2 *Contraceptive pill issue lifecycle*

CASE STUDY: 'IN THE GOO' – INDUSTRY FAILING TO LEARN THE LESSONS

Nanotechnology, the manipulation of atoms and molecules, could be a defining technological discovery of our generation. However, despite being one of the best-funded new technologies in the world, nanotechnology is little known outside scientific and business circles.

However, when headlines of 'Grey goo' (about nanoscale mechanical robots reproducing uncontrollably) were screaming from the front pages of the press everywhere, the spectre of the great GM debate once again raised its head. But nanotechnology scientists and industry proponents attacked the media for generating hysteria about the future impacts of atom-scale manipulations. The threat of 'Grey goo' was quickly brushed under the carpet by industry as a technical impossibility. But some informed commentators would argue that the concerns are not unfounded, and industry is, once again, ignoring the very real and present dangers that nanotechnology poses. At best, having failed to learn the lessons of the recent debates on mobile phones, MMR and GM food, the industry is failing to address public perception of risk in an open and proactive manner. Once again the media and activists are setting the agenda, with industry appearing reactive and secretive.

As with mobile telecommunications, demand for this technology exists and scientific advances will enable demand to be met relatively soon. But failure on the part of industry and the science community means that the general public is not ready for this exciting scientific development.

CASE STUDY: INTEL

The case of the faulty chip

Before long the majority of households in Britain will have a personal computer, a domestic appliance to be trusted much like a washing machine or fridge. Consider, then, the sense of betrayal if the computer gets it wrong. Intel, the company that makes 9 out of 10 of the microprocessors that go into PCs, went through that nightmare in 1994. Pentium, the company's new high-performance microprocessor chip, occasionally failed to come up with the right answer in complex division calculations. The errors were rare but costly, resulting in a write-off of £306,000,000 and a dented reputation.

The academic and the internet

At Lynchburg College, Virginia, in the United States mathematics professor Thomas Nicely discovered the Pentium bug. His moment of fame came as he completed a complicated long division early one morning in June 1994. He always liked to double check his sums by hand but for some reason this time it simply wasn't working out.

According to Professor Nicely: 'Intel's tech support desk said they had never heard of it. They said they would speak to an engineering group and return my call later; in fact we did exchange calls for a period of six days or so but they never came up with any explanation or acknowledged that the error actually occurred.'

So, Professor Nicely did what any self-respecting American mathematician would do and raised the alarm to users of the internet. He found he was not alone.

He continued: 'Within two or three days I started getting reports back that nearly all of their machines made the same error and that they came to the same conclusion as I did. It was an error in the floating point unit of the Pentium chip.'

The timing could not have been worse for Intel. The company had decided to target the lucrative home computer market with a major international advertising campaign promoting the versatility of an 'Intel inside' PC for educational, recreational and business use. The Pentium was Intel's newest and fastest chip and the advertising campaign was aimed straight at the business customers who now bought computers for their homes. Intel was becoming a consumer company – its transformation was one of the big technology success stories of the 1990s.

The corporate response

Intel's first reaction to the saga, however, looked more like a backward step. The company offered customers replacement chips but only if they could prove they did sums affected by the bug. In December 1994, however, IBM forced Intel's hand by saying the bugs were worse than reported and suspending shipments of all IT products containing Pentium microprocessors.

According to the editor of a leading UK computer magazine: 'IBM are a blue chip company and people pay a premium, corporations especially, for their machines. IBM were simply protecting their reputation as a quality supplier and at the time they were quite right in saying not enough was known about the bug.'

A senior IT systems specialist at Thorn EMI added: 'Once we determined that the faulty chip might occasionally do its sums wrong, we wouldn't know when it would happen again because it was dependent on particular combinations and particular sums. But the very fact that it might happen was enough to shake our confidence in the machines and I really couldn't afford to run with machines that potentially might get their sums wrong.'

The impact of public pressure

For Intel it was time for retreat and the company finally agreed that anyone with a Pentium-based machine could have a new chip. The cost amounted to £306,000,000.

In Silicon Valley, California, there was no doubt in people's mind that Intel was losing the public relations battle. The company was being forced by media

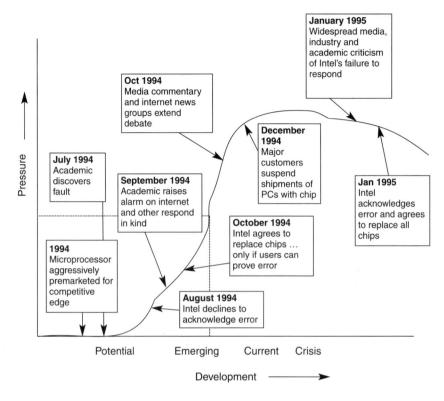

Figure 3.3 *Intel issue lifecycle*

and industry pressure into an expensive U-turn that left a golden reputation tarnished. It was a real object lesson in how an issue ignored can turn quickly into a crisis.

Professor Kevin Keller of Stanford University summed it up: 'The two keys are to be swift and to be sincere in how you handle it and I think in both cases they [Intel] were a little bit lacking.'

When he was asked by reporters how much damage the incident had caused to the company, Andy Grove, Chief Executive Officer of Intel, acknowledged the company had failed to understand the psychology of the market. Although Intel was renowned for quality and reliability, 'some place we crossed over the line to where there are millions of consumers out there who think they are better able to judge quality than we are and we were insensitive to that'. The whole issue is summarized in Figure 3.3.

Interestingly, in early 1996 when Intel was charged with misleading customers by advertising an inaccurate, higher transaction processing speed for its latest Pentium microprocessor, the company moved extremely quickly to make a public apology and change its promotional materials.

THE IMPORTANCE OF EARLY ACTION

The principal goal of issue identification is to place initial priorities on emerging issues. They can be classified by type (social, economic, political, technological), response source (industry, corporation, subsidiary, department), geography, span of control and salience (immediacy, prominence). Factors such as degree of impact and also the probability that the issue will mature within a reasonably predictable period of time also need to be considered.

Using the Chase/Jones Issues Management Process Model, once emerging issues have been identified and prioritized, the *issue analysis* stage begins. The aim here is to determine the origin of the issue which is often difficult as few emerge neatly from one source. The authors recommend that existing qualitative and quantitative research should be examined *before* committing to new research and that experience – past and present, internal and external to the organization – should be tapped into. Analysing the present situation will determine the current *intensity* of the issue. Applied research about the relationship of the issue to the corporation should be targeted towards opinion leaders and media gatekeepers. This initial research and analysis stage will help to identify what influential individuals and groups are saying about the issues and provide management with a clear idea of their *origin* and *evolution*.

Needless to say, in practice we have found great reluctance to spend money on this type of research as part of the benchmarking and planning process. Where possible, we try to develop arguments in terms of impact on financial performance and risk to maintaining an organization's licence to operate. These are often more powerful messages in the boardroom than damage to credibility and reputation!

A review of the company's present position (if it has one) and its strengths and weaknesses in positioning itself to take a role in shaping the issue will help to give focus for the action planning stage.

The third stage, called rather cumbersomely *issue change strategy options*, involves making basic decisions about organizational response. The Chase/Jones model cites three options to deal with the change:

Reactive change strategy refers to an organization's unwillingness to change with the emphasis on continuing past behaviour, for example by attempting to postpone the inevitability of public policy decisions. This reluctance to change rarely leaves room for compromise on legislative matters.

Adaptive change strategy suggests an openness to change and a recognition of its inevitability. This approach relies on planning to anticipate change and offering constructive dialogue to find a form of compromise or accommodation.

Dynamic response strategy anticipates and attempts to shape the direction of public policy decisions by determining how the campaigning over the issue will be played out. This approach allows the organization to become a leading advocate of change.

After choosing one of these approaches to responding to each issue the organization should decide on policy to support the selected change, which is the fourth stage – *issue action programming*. This requires coordination of resources to provide the maximum support for reaching goals and objectives.

CASE STUDY: 2004 OLYMPIC SCANDALS – WHERE NOW FOR WORLD'S GREATEST SPORTING EVENT?

The two major issues that came to a head at the 2004 Athens Olympic Games highlight fundamental (and common) flaws in handling issues and averting a crisis. Firm responsible action to rectify acknowledged faults and effective, early communication to maintain control and avoid uninformed hypothesizing are vital. Neither appeared to happen in the case of host bid cities' vote-buying, and the action was purely reactive on doping. Consequently the issues are perceived to be endemic, with the authorities unable – or unwilling – to address them and not in control of the situation.

Any organization that seeks the moral high ground, actively promotes its transcending of political and religious disagreements, and embeds in its charter such concepts as 'respect for universal fundamental ethical principles' and 'encouraging the establishment of a peaceful society concerned with the preservation of human dignity' needs to be whiter than white. The International Olympic Committee (IOC) has a slightly unusual challenge in protecting such a composite reputation as 'the Olympics'. The perception of the Olympic Games is the sum of many parts, including an administrative body, the pre-eminent global sporting event, the slightly nebulous concept of the 'Olympic Family', and the distinctly nebulous ideal of the 'Olympic Spirit'. The Olympic Spirit is intangible and influenced by a large and disparate group of organizations and individuals over which the IOC can have little direct control – most notably the athletes. So where now for the Olympic dream?

Drug testing

The IOC has put itself in a strong position on drug testing recently. It has aligned itself firmly alongside the World Anti-Doping Agency (WADA) and its president, Dick Pound. It has pulled renegade national Olympic associations and athletics federations (such as the US federation) into line, and rigorously and consistently applied the letter of the law to all athletes, regardless of status. In the past, exceptions appeared to have been made for headline stars.

The IOC cannot physically stop individual athletes taking performance-enhancing drugs. What it can do – and needs to be seen to do – is provide the strongest deterrent. New drugs tests that are able to detect previously undetectable drugs (such as THG) seem likely to see an increase in the number of positive tests. The IOC should not shirk from this or apologize, but should welcome the results as 'cleaning out the cancer of drugs from sport'. No pain now, no gain in the future.

The messages from the IOC in Athens were absolutely right. They insisted that a number of high-profile doping scandals do not tarnish the Olympic Games, but rather mean the anti-doping programme is working. It stressed that the IOC priority is its determined fight against doping, and that the more athletes caught will lead to the ultimate objective of a 'clean Games'. However, if anything, it is not mitigating the public and media 'shock' factor because communications always occur after the test revelations and at the Games, immediately reflecting on the actual sporting event.

As the pre-eminent sporting organization, the IOC should be seen to take a leading role in the fight against doping – and this means being active between Games in concert with other administrative bodies. Very little proactive activity from the IOC occurs in the intervening period between Games – an activity that would allow the IOC to manage expectations, explain its positive messages, and be perceived to be 'in control'.

Vote buying

It now seems apparent that the host city bidding process is just an invitation to corruption. The IOC must be seen to be as tough and steadfast in its desire to end corruption as it is to end doping. But the timeframe for results needs to be shorter, because the IOC has the ability to directly control and monitor its own members and systems.

Vote buying was an issue that the IOC was believed to have addressed and resolved, with radical measures designed to eradicate internal corruption after the 2002 Salt Lake City appointment scandal. Drastic and sweeping changes were made to the organization and personnel, which were generally believed to have created a 'clean IOC'. The new revelations in the BBC *Panorama* exposé have undermined that new-found trust, and give the impression that corruption will be forever endemic in the host city bidding process.

An issue never 'dies' after seemingly being resolved – the legacy remains with that organization or individual, and is incredibly potent if the issue raises its head again. With the IOC it seems that power corrupts; particularly when such vast sums of money are involved, and the IOC needs to be seen to act upon the system that puts its members in such positions. The processes, not just individuals, need to change.

The IOC should consider further overhauls of the selection of IOC members, the host city election procedure, and policing the ethical veracity of the Election Commission members. It should be seen to acknowledge the potential for corruption, but be perceived as super-vigilant and unyielding in its punishment of offenders. Monitoring and policing the process needs to made be highly visible to sceptical and critical stakeholders – particularly the world's media – on an ongoing basis if the Olympic Family is to avoid being perceived as distinctly dysfunctional.

Finally, the requirement for research to evaluate the actual versus intended results of the programme is desirable. We say 'desirable' when it should be 'essential' but, again from practical experience, few companies are willing to do it properly and we have a way to go before enough damning evidence forces better take-up!

It should be remembered that the longer the issue survives, the fewer choices are available and the more it costs (see Figure 3.4).

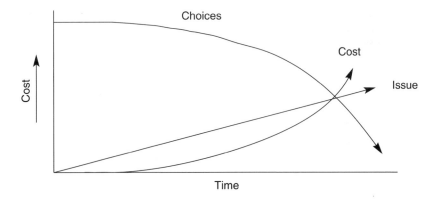

Figure 3.4 *Costs and choices*

SUMMARY

Effective issues management response is based on two key principles: early identification and organized response to influence the public policy process. Issues management is a proactive, anticipatory and planned process designed to influence the development of an issue before it evolves to a stage which requires crisis management. Early action also allows for flexible and creative thinking 'outside the box'.

It is important to remember that issues are constantly being modified and redefined throughout the whole process. Next year's issue is often seeded this year. A brief flurry of media coverage in the UK in 1995 over the potential risk of phthalates – 'gender-bending chemicals' – in infant formula milk preparations could well herald a period of growing public concern over the impact of these synthetic chemicals on human reproduction and the environment in general. The tobacco industry in the United States provides another example, with the rights of smokers evolving into the rights of non-smokers.

Furthermore, defeat on an issue in one area can be seen as success in another. When tobacco companies had to place a warning label on their products, the *loss* in the legislative arena eventually provided a *win* in the judicial arena because when sued, companies were able to argue that consumers had been warned. Exerting an influence on the development of identified issues before they bring negative consequences means that an organization should actively represent its interests in the public policy process, by broadening the debate and informing those groups of importance. This *advocacy* participation in the public policy process is central to issues management (Jones and Chase, 1979).

4

CSR: the new moral code for doing business

You cannot escape the responsibility of tomorrow by evading it today.

Abraham Lincoln

INTRODUCTION

Corporate social responsibility (CSR) is an emerging, as yet poorly defined, process used by some as a fashion statement through glossy reports and websites, and by others as a potential framework for demonstrating a more responsible approach to doing business.

Over the past two decades, the pressure upon business to become accountable and perform a social and environmental role has increased dramatically. Incidents such as the Union Carbide accident in Bhopal, India, in 1984 and the Chernobyl nuclear power station disaster in the Ukraine in 1986 helped put corporate responsibility for environmental hazards on the international agenda. Western industrialized governments responded to such incidents, and established legal and regulatory frameworks for corporate accountability.

Globalization has had an extraordinary impact on its emergence. Throughout the late 1980s and 1990s, the new, knowledge-based economy generated millions of new jobs and a rash of innovative products and services for Western consumers. The offset of this has been to expose a wide range of labour, human rights and environmental abuses, and to create a dysfunction between meeting people's needs, protecting planetary resources and enhancing corporate profits – the perfect trigger for the anti-globalization demonstrations of 1999, 2000 and 2001. The result has been that even companies in sectors with high levels of environmental risk have introduced ways to reform their business by looking and listening.

Globalization has gone hand-in-hand with business short-termism and a total focus on maximizing shareholder value – a strong emphasis on immediate results and a loss of faith in long-term strategic management.

CSR (or sustainable development, which is a closely allied concept) is generally regarded as the opposite of short-termism. It is argued that sustainable development looks at the needs of future generations rather than a focus on short-term delivery with scant regard for the consequences. It appears to run contrary to established market forces and modern business practices. However, there is a growing business imperative to embrace social responsibility, and it is emerging through consequences to the bottom line.

THE GROWING BUSINESS IMPERATIVE

Whether or not organizations are enthusiastic about embracing greater social and environmental accountability, there seems to be a growing business imperative to do so. This can be defined in four categories of commercial penalties and incentives:

1: Socially responsible investment (SRI) and shareholder targeting

SRI and shareholder targeting are developments that are beginning to receive serious attention from financial analysts and institutional investors. Banks, term assurers and asset managers are screening their shareholdings in favour of companies that demonstrate commitment to social and environmental programmes, and against those that engage in activities deemed detrimental to society and the environment. With institutional investors potentially deterred by the 'hassle factor' of picking non-SRI stocks, a company's ability to conform to sustainable development models will potentially have share price implications. The growth of ratings agencies is likely to mean that companies will find their financial position rated on CSR issues as well as conventional criteria, whether they like it or not. It is likely that in the future regulators will make companies hold capital against such risks.

SRI is an investment strategy that takes into account a company's ethical, social and environmental performance as well as its financial performance. SRI has supplanted 'ethical investment' as the criterion for judging responsible business, and has widened to include environmental and social issues. A range of vetted products, including unit trusts and pensions, are now on offer from most large banks and assurance companies.

Today, SRI is a dynamic and rapidly expanding sector of financial services in North America, parts of Europe, and Australia. It is estimated to be worth more than $2 trillion in the United States and around £25 billion in the UK, the largest market in Europe. The Dow Jones Sustainability Group Index has outperformed the Dow Jones Index by 36 per cent over the past five years. In the UK, changes to the Pensions Act now require pension funds to declare how far they take social, environmental and ethical considerations into account when choosing stocks for investment, and other European countries are considering introducing similar legislation.

The initial emphasis of SRI funds was on negative screening – specifically excluding companies engaged in particular types of activity. However, negative screening has partly given way to screening on the basis of companies' positive activities and looking for best practice in what were once seen as controversial industries. Many fund managers now look to invest in companies that make a positive contribution to the economy and to society. A survey of the 23 top European ethical and green unit trusts' adoption criteria revealed that screening under positive measures is rapidly becoming as significant as negative screening:

Table 4.1 *Criteria for negative and positive SRI screening*

Negative criteria	%	Positive criteria	%
Alcohol	74	Community involvement	70
Animal testing	96	Employee welfare/rights	70
Armaments	100	Environmental management	65
Environmental damage	91	Environmental policy	74
Gambling services	83	Environmental products	65
Nuclear power	96	Environmental reporting	65
Oppressive regimes	74	Packaging reduction	61
Pornography	91	Sustainable forestry	61
Tobacco production	100		

Source: Regester Larkin

Strict screening can exclude whole sectors, such as chemicals, from investment, but some new funds are adopting a 'best of sector' or 'light green' approach, and investing in (mostly larger) companies shunned by traditional ethical funds. This has enabled companies in the energy, automotive and agrochemicals sectors to warrant inclusion in some funds. For example, car manufacturer Volkswagen, chemicals company BASF and mining company Rio Tinto are included as sector leaders in the Dow Jones Sustainability Index.

Harnessing the importance of SRI through shareholder activism is now considered by some environmental groups to be a much more significant tool than consumer boycotts. In 1999 concerned investors in the United States introduced more than 200 resolutions on a wide range of issues relating to environmental health and corporate governance matters. In one case, Home Depot, a large lumber and hardware store, announced it would stop selling forest products from environmentally sensitive areas and would give preference to timber certified as sustainably produced, just three months after 12 per cent of its shareholders asked the company to stop selling wood from old-growth forests.

Organizations like Friends of the Earth and Amnesty International are now consulted by fund managers, partly to clarify screening for ethical funds, but also to ensure that future pressures on companies' behaviour are adequately appreciated in financial-led investment decisions. This has developed particularly since the response in Europe to genetically modified products, which led to the near collapse of Monsanto and its subsequent acquisition by Pharmacia Upjohn. Monsanto had previously been strongly commended on Wall Street because of its rapid expansion in the United States. However, NGO pressure in Europe became so intense that it began to affect the US share price. Campaigners targeted all stakeholders, including shareholders. This led Deutsche Asset Management to recommend that institutional investors should sell Monsanto shares quickly. The resulting drop in share price made the company easy prey for takeover at the end of 1999. In spite of being one of the most innovative companies in the agrochemical and biotechnology sectors, the Monsanto brand never recovered from the legacy of this attack.

2: Regulation, reporting and liability

The last 10 or so years have seen an astonishing proliferation in corporate codes of conduct, often linked to reporting initiatives. New voluntary governance and reporting standards such as AA 1000, the Global Reporting Initiative, FTSE4Good and ISO 14001 are adding pressure to the need for greater transparency, better integrated internal issue management controls and a much wider commitment to corporate governance.

The 'old world economy' companies (oil, minerals, automotive, industrial) were the first to embrace CSR reporting. Ford Motor Company developed a number of metrics designed to measure and work towards reducing fuel consumption and emissions, and committed itself to report progress. In addition, the banking sector is now reporting on assets under 'green' management (UBS), the pharmaceutical industry on animals used in research (Novartis) and manufacturing emissions (Roche), and the technology sector on end-of-life recycling (Fujitsu) and lead-free components (Sony).

However, some exponents fall into the category of 'greenwash' – PR smokescreens designed to delay or deter regulatory measures. Nike has a code of conduct based on the International Labour Organization core conventions, but this counts for little to those who see Nike paying demonstrably inadequate wages to workers in their global supply chain. Nike, along with others such as Reebok, Liz Claiborne, Sara Lee and The Gap, established the Apparel Industry Partnership with a view to developing an agreed code and approach to certifiable external verification, but these companies were widely seen by critics to be conducting a PR exercise. And the idea of a gambling and leisure group, a cigarette manufacturer, a fast food retailer, an alcohol supplier or an arms dealer producing CSR reports appears completely counter-intuitive to many. Others yet are simply determined to keep their heads down, trying not to draw attention to themselves.

Regulation (often enforced through financial instruments), reporting and liability not only have a bottom-line impact, but take the initiative away from organizations in determining how broad social and environmental goals can be achieved. A greater emphasis on transparency and information access is now expected by stakeholders, and regulators are writing these requirements into the rule books. Pioneers of social responsibility reporting are already actively engaged in setting out reporting standards in an effort to retain the initiative ahead of proposed regulation.

If companies do not act in a socially responsible manner, they are likely to face, and lose, expensive lawsuits. For example, the tobacco and asbestos industries lost class action lawsuits following the allegedly inadequate action the industries took to minimize the health risks of their products. Today legal action is targeting the mobile phone and electricity industries, which are facing potentially tougher, precautionary regulation and the threat of lawsuits in the United States concerning alleged health effects of electromagnetic frequency emissions from power lines, base stations and handsets.

The complexity of regulation is growing, with the penalties for wrongdoing getting tougher. Directors can go to prison for 'eco-crimes' and, potentially, for any major health, safety or environmental failure.

Table 4.2   *A more inclusive framework for reporting*

Old system	New system
Shareholder focus	Stakeholder focus
Paper based	Internet based
Standardized information	Customized information
Company-controlled information on performance and prospects	Information available from a variety of sources
Periodic reporting	Continuous reporting
Distribution of information	Dialogue
Financial statements	Broader range of performance measures (not just financial)
Past performance	Greater emphasis on future prospects
Historical cost	Substantial value-based information
Audit of accounts	Assurance of underlying system
Nationally oriented	Globally oriented
Essentially static system	Continuously changing model
Preparer-led regulations	Satisfying marketing demands

3: Competitive advantage

As demands for environmental and social responsibility in business have developed, they have also become more mature. Concerned consumers look at the corporate face behind the brand, and this influences purchasing decisions. At the same time, there is public acceptance that not every company can be the perfect eco-friendly business. Society needs products like oil and chemicals – but there is demand for companies in these sectors to reduce their negative environmental and social 'footprint'. Consequently, there is an emerging emphasis on CSR best practice and leadership within sectors of industry, opening the way for individual companies to gain competitive advantages.

4: Reputation opportunity costs

The opportunity costs of damage to reputation – loss of existing investment and innovation in marketing; difficulty with recruitment and staff retention; advertising that is undercut by public perception – merit serious consideration. The need to safeguard reputation is already implied in the substantial budgets dedicated to marketing, compliance, recruitment, public affairs and communications. As society becomes less tolerant of companies that do not conform to social and environmental standards, the risks to reputation are much greater. Even more importantly, however, 'doing the right thing' by adopting and integrating a values system into the organization actually does generate financial value. People want to bring their own values to work, as employees, and to have relationships with companies – as customers, suppliers or investors – that relate to their own behaviour, expectations and methods of working.

CSR is concerned with many aspects of a company's impact, from sourcing to service delivery or product disposal, and can affect a host of cost-based as well as reputational aspects of a business. The commercial and reputation risk management case for CSR is demonstrated in the risk to shareholder value from poor management of supply chain issues,

Table 4.3 *CSR impacts*

Negative impacts	
Aspect of CSR	**Impact on**
Concern with social and economic impacts	Operating efficiency
Human rights	Innovation Operating efficiency
Positive impacts	
Aspect of CSR	**Impact on**
Ethics, value and principles	Risk profile Brand value and reputation
Focus on environmental process	Risk profile Access to capital Operating efficiency Shareholder value
Community action	Brand value and reputation
Workplace conditions	Human and intellectual capital Operating efficiency Revenue

Source: Buried Treasure – Uncovering the business case for corporate sustainability, 2001

inadequate environmental management, human rights abuses and poor treatment of employees, suppliers or customers. Human capital has become more important than physical capital, and so the threat to important relationships has become critical. Concerned investors will apply pressure to those that are not managing such risks and reward those that are.

The proliferation of financial and regulatory instruments in support of sustainable development is starting to engineer market forces in some countries to the extent that companies need to take a serious look at adoption. Failure to do so risks criticism for lagging behind and a detrimental impact on reputation. A perception of moving slowly in response to new societal and consumer trends and demands can now be damaging in the financial markets.

WHAT CONSTITUTES GOOD SOCIALLY RESPONSIBLE CORPORATE BEHAVIOUR

In response to growing public interest in what constitutes acceptable corporate behaviour, the 1999 Millennium Poll, supported by the Conference Board and the Prince of Wales Business Leaders Forum, polled 25,000 people in 23 countries to gather information about society's expectations. Some of the key findings included:

- People in 13 out of 23 countries think their country should focus more on social and environmental goals than on economic goals in the first decade of the new century.
- In forming impressions of companies, people around the world focus on corporate behaviour and social responsibility ahead of either brand reputation or financial factors.
- Two in three people polled wanted companies to go beyond their historical role of making a profit. In addition to paying taxes, employing people and obeying the law, they want companies to contribute to broader societal goals.
- Actively contributing to charities and community projects doesn't satisfy people's expectations of corporate social responsibility.
- Half the population in the countries surveyed are paying attention to the social behaviour of companies.
- Over one in five consumers report either rewarding or punishing companies in the past year based on their perceived social performance, and almost as many again considered doing so.
- Opinion leader analysis indicates that public pressures on companies to play broader roles in society will likely increase significantly over the next few years.

Friends of the Earth set out guidance for companies seeking to make the CSR transformation under three themes – eco-innovation, social accountability and political responsibility:

- *Innovate for sustainability*: seek out new practices, new products and services, and new technologies that meet people's needs and improve quality of life on minimal material and energy use. This means improving product efficiency and durability, taking responsibility for products over their full lifecycle, and finding ways to replace products with locally delivered services.
- *Prioritize resource productivity*: make 'bottom-line' savings by turning management attention, research and development from labour saving to resource saving through waste avoidance, recycling, reuse and adopting the principles of industrial ecology. Set targets in line with environmental space limits or factor-10 objectives (methods used to quantify the changes in environmental resource use necessary to deliver sustainability; both suggest cuts by up to 90 per cent in economies like the United States and Europe).
- *Spread best practice through supply chains*: ensure that suppliers and subcontractors adopt the same high environmental and social standards as the company – to help spread good practice to small- and medium-sized enterprises.
- *Promote sustainable consumption*: use product development, marketing and advertising strategies to support 'sufficiency' rather than encouraging over-consumption and the spread of products that replace sustainable practices such as breast-feeding.
- *Invest in people*: adopt high, non-discriminatory labour standards and family-friendly working practices, and invest in the knowledge and skills of the workforce, to enhance their quality of life and their productivity.
- *Account to all stakeholders*: report comprehensively and transparently on environmental and social impacts – with independent verification. Respond accountably to the demands and interests of employees, customers, communities and other stakeholders – not just to investors.
- *Play fair in politics*: use lobbying power and influence transparently, in favour of a high level playing field for fair competition with high environmental and social standards. Support green tax reform and effective regulation for environmental protection and corporate accountability, including legal and criminal liability for defaulting companies and their directors.

NEW BUSINESS VALUES

Ethics and values – the basis for good behaviour – are increasingly regarded as the building blocks of sustainable development or corporate social responsibility. The definition of this has evolved to embrace eco-efficiency, business ethics, investment strategies, human rights and a wider social agenda.

The early adopters were PR people who saw value in better communication around environmental impact, and environmental engineers, thinking in terms of inputs, outputs and impacts, who started to recognize that by cleaning up emissions and reducing toxic waste streams, a better overall business solution could be achieved. The debate, however, has shifted from public relations to competitive advantage through good business practice, and reaches from the factory fence into the boardroom.

The development and implementation of CSR policies should not simply be viewed as an additional burden on costs. The fact that companies are coming under increased pressure to be acceptable winners in a wider social context creates opportunities for 'early adopters' to demonstrate best practice and achieve competitive advantage. The companies that have already put down CSR navigation markers are being called 'forward looking' and accredited with 'visionary management' by management peer groups and business commentators.

Consumer pressure, fuelling regulatory pressure, helps to explain why we are seeing more companies revisiting or establishing their business principles to create standards and values that integrate and bind an organization together. Business for Social Responsibility suggests that the reasons why organizations are doing this include:

● A wish to create a corporate culture 'touchstone', with business principles creating the glue or moral backbone of the organization.
● The provision of a focus for evolving internal conversations, with an initial 'straw man' version drawn from existing policies, codes and principles being used to stimulate internal debate and engagement.
● A means to embed values throughout the organization, with the ability to integrate them into strategic planning, decision-making processes, business practices, management systems, employee performance assessment and succession planning.

Issues raised in the CSR discussion have provided a useful starting point for some companies to restate the business case for longer-term strategic planning and investment in reputation. The relaunch of BP in 2000, under the banner 'Beyond Petroleum', is an example of utilizing social and environmental issues on the sustainable development agenda to set out forward-looking priorities that situate BP firmly within the sphere of new, cleaner technologies and potential future markets.

According to John Elkington, author of *The Chrysalis Economy: How citizen CEOs and corporations can fuse values and value creation* (2001), sustainable business success in this century will depend on stewardship of the following six values:

- *Ultra-transparency* – assuming everything is public through to the ethics of privacy.
- *Open governance* – to bridge the gap between global capitalism and global governance systems.
- *Equal opportunity* – between today's generations and tomorrow's.
- *Multiple capitals* – human, social and natural.
- *Real diversity* – as reflected in the immense variety of our present ecosystems.
- *Shared learning* – invention and innovation.

Effective environmental and social stewardship makes business sense. In a rapidly changing world where issues are readily highlighted but solu-

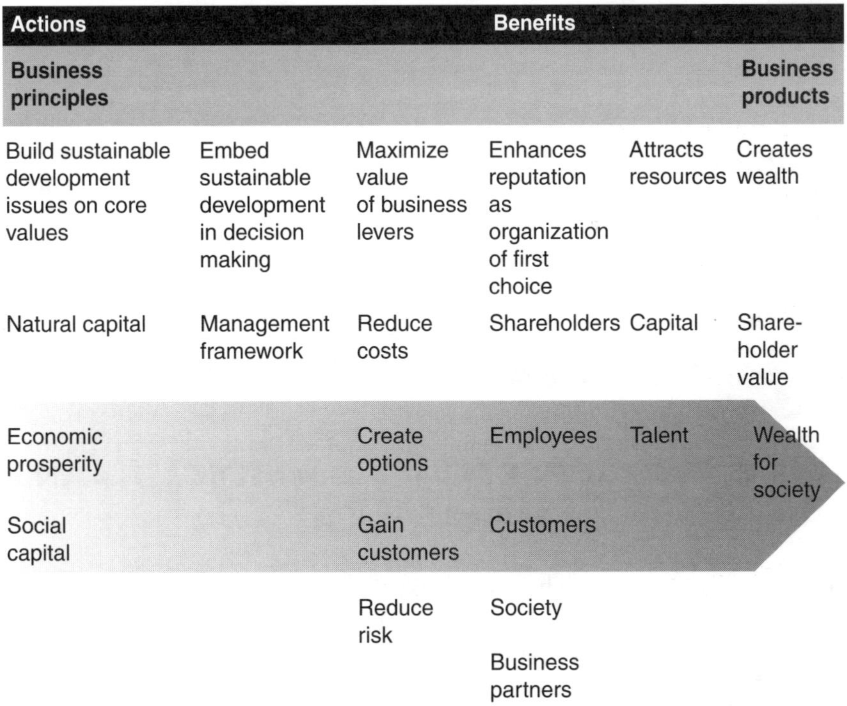

Actions			Benefits		
Business principles					**Business products**
Build sustainable development issues on core values	Embed sustainable development in decision making	Maximize value of business levers	Enhances reputation as organization of first choice	Attracts resources	Creates wealth
Natural capital	Management framework	Reduce costs	Shareholders	Capital	Shareholder value
Economic prosperity		Create options	Employees	Talent	Wealth for society
Social capital		Gain customers	Customers		
		Reduce risk	Society		
			Business partners		

Figure 4.1 *Shell's view of the business case for sustainable development*

Source: Shell International, 2000

tions are sometimes harder to discern, it is difficult to know where to go and how far to travel. Good stewardship isn't just about adhering to policies. BP considers that it is the outcome of three things:

- *behaviour* – how the company lives up to its policies;
- the *impact* of the company's operations and products;
- the company's overall *contribution to society*.

As part of this process, BP will consult with, listen to and respond openly with its stakeholders, work with others to raise standards, openly report on performance, and recognize those who contribute to improved HSE performance.

Shell highlights the importance of greater engagement and transparency, exploring new ways to assure performance, focusing on reliability of health, safety and environmental data management systems, and providing a clearer indication of what is verified and how. (See Figure 4.1.)

So a combination of legal, regulatory and moral pressure is leading to a changed perception of the goals of business, and growing acceptance of the idea that responsible business entails social and environmental performance and reporting. Some corporations have found opportunities within this changing landscape: to develop reputations as leaders of best practice in product stewardship and environmental reporting; to overcome, as BP, Ford, DuPont and Toyota are attempting to do, the legacy of damaging reputational crises through improved stakeholder communication and engagement; and, like Ikea, the world's largest furniture store, to seize competitive advantage by offering alternatives to questioned practices which are helping to position the company as a credible socially responsible investment. But the jury is likely to be out for some time. Nike's admission in its first corporate responsibility report that it 'blew it' by employing children in Third World countries certainly isn't convincing Oxfam's NikeWatch or the Clean Clothes Campaign.

CSR BEST PRACTICE POLICY DEVELOPMENT AND MANAGEMENT

The Association of British Insurers (2001) has stipulated the checklist in Figure 4.2 for CSR best practice within an organization. From our experience of working with a number of companies across the CSR delivery chain, we believe the principles of socially responsible policy development and management are intrinsically aligned to a successful issues management programme. The four-phased approach we recommend (see Figure 4.3) is mutually supportive, with each stage feeding into the other three.

Declare top management committee to CSR

⬇

Develop corporate principles and codes of practice

⬇

Implement and embed through cascading systems

⬇

Establish/implement green/ethical procurement

⬇

Reduce HSE 'footprint' of operations and products

⬇

Set targets for CSR performance

⬇

Prescribe criteria for own pension fund investment

⬇

Engage with all stakeholders and communities

⬇

Report on risk and progress towards targets

Figure 4.2 *ABI checklist for CSR best practice*

Phase 1: Assessing and planning

Establishing leadership and commitment:

- Identify the business case for and key benefits of a sustainable strategy.
- Secure senior management commitment.
- Appoint a board-level sponsor(s) (executive or non-executive, but allow for an independent audit and assessment function).
- Develop and obtain approval for a framework for management.
- Review existing compliance and governance through internal and external auditing.
- Review business principles and values.

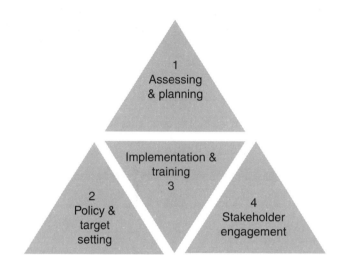

Figure 4.3 *A four-phase approach for CSR*

Phase 2: Policy and target setting

Addressing feedback and policy review:

● Assess feedback; complete a gap/risk analysis associated with policies, procedures, compliance.
● Validate or revise business principles and values.
● Define/agree policy framework: a) against compliance; b) against appropriate accreditation scheme(s) or internal audit procedure.
● Agree strategy, priorities and actions required for implementation.

Phase 3: Implementing policy and training

Consider the most appropriate ways of securing understanding and buy-in across the organization, for example:

● Management workshops to explain purpose, benefits, generate involvement, validate approaches and roll-out (including target setting, KPIs and communication toolkit).
● A 'train the trainers' scheme to facilitate outreach.
● A seminar programme and supporting intranet or printed toolkit for middle management/functional teams to outline benefits, policies, targets and programme for internal and external communications implementation.

● Identify a 'CSR ambassador network' to promulgate rationale, process and solicit employee ideas and initiatives that reflect creativity and innovation in support of business and reputation performance goals.

Phase 4: Stakeholder engagement

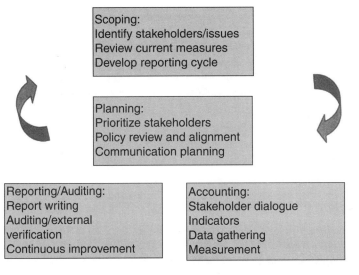

Figure 4.4 *Stakeholder engagement*

● Scope, plan, account and report.
● Integrate with compliance and risk management processes.
● Prepare and develop for accreditation requirements.
● Agree process for external reporting and validation.
● Commit to continuous refinement and improvement.

SUMMARY

CSR does offer a route for creating more flexible and anticipatory reputation risk management processes by sensitizing the business to risks associated with unfamiliar patterns of social change. It is also a means to influence stakeholders which can help to shift the risk burden from one of passive response to one of more active engagement and management.

CSR supports reputation risk management strategies by:

- managing short-term risk by acquiring quality information through dialogue;
- accessing valuable marketplace and social trends data;
- moving towards consensus and away from conflict through better stakeholder engagement;
- influencing views and behaviour inside and outside the organization, with associated performance benefits;
- enhancing value through socially responsible investment.

(*Source*: adapted from Zadek, 2001)

The evidence base is growing, and shows that successful companies are those that can operate in relative harmony with the needs, aspirations, and most importantly values of their stakeholders. When this works well, it can enhance reputation, performance and shareholder value. However, it isn't simply enough to articulate corporate values in an annual report or code of conduct. Nor is it about making financial 'contributions', which will always be interpreted as '£100 towards the new scout hut'. Ethics and values must form an integral part of corporate culture and that must apply consistently across all operations, locally and internationally, to become a living and breathing organism.

Mark Goyder, Director of think tank Tomorrow's Company, insists that CSR must be embedded into the DNA of an organization. As one business leader has said, 'It is one thing to produce a set of universal principles, quite another to ensure they are implemented practically and sensitively across different cultures.' However, he continued, 'our commitment to contribute to sustainable development holds the keys to our long-term business success'. So values must be considered as an intangible business asset, talked about across the business as a source of competitive advantage, as a basis for good corporate reputation and as a reinforcer of effective risk management. Good business and social responsibility will inevitably move forward hand in hand.

5

An issue ignored is a crisis ensured

In the kingdom of the blind the one-eyed man is king.

Desiderius Erasmus

CASE STUDY: DECOMMISSIONING THE BRENT SPAR – IMPLICATIONS FOR A GLOBAL INDUSTRY

In 1995, Shell UK, a leading oil producer, decided to dispose of the Brent Spar, a redundant North Sea floating storage and tanker loading buoy, in Atlantic deep water. The company undertook and independently commissioned numerous environmental and risk assessment studies, the principal findings of which were released for public consultation. Shell also scrupulously observed all national and international legal and regulatory requirements.

Shell was eventually forced to choose what it and others widely regarded as the second-best environmental option, taking the Spar onshore for break-up, because of intense pressure exerted by Greenpeace and some European governments.

The pressure was not characterized by any significant scientific evidence refuting Shell's case – many leading independent scientific experts supported Shell's recommendations. The consortium of Shell, the operator and Esso, a subsidiary of Exxon, was defeated by a single-issue pressure group which skilfully secured the support of influential politicians and administrators in Europe by shaping public opinion. As a result, the oil industry may face an expensive and environmentally questionable requirement to return all North Sea installations to shore when redundant, contradicting existing international disposal agreements.

The rationale for deep water disposal

The Brent Spar was commissioned in 1976. It is a vertically floating buoy, 141 metres high and fixed to the sea bed. The buoy consists of oil storage tanks at the bottom, capable of holding 300,000 barrels of crude oil, 12 buoyancy tanks towards the middle and a topside containing offshore tanker loading equipment and accommodation for 30 people.

Rising maintenance costs prompted a review in 1991 to conclude that the work necessary to refurbish the facility, to extend its operational life, could cost over £90 million. The buoy would also have to be out of commission for about three years during the work. Given the age of the structure, the presence of a pipeline system for the export of crude oil from the field and the cost of refurbishment, the Spar was taken out of commission in September 1991.

Thirteen methods of abandoning or re-using the Spar were put forward for consideration and six were identified as viable options. These included horizontal or vertical dismantling and onshore disposal, in-field disposal and deep water disposal. Of these, horizontal dismantling and deep water disposal were considered in detail.

The assessments were designed to determine the Best Practicable Environmental Option (BPEO), taking into account factors such as technical feasibility, risks to workforce health and safety, environmental impact, costs and public acceptability. Shell also had to take into account likely additional stress to the structure when upended and the fact that two main storage tanks had been accidentally ruptured some 25 years earlier and repaired only to maintain structural integrity and not ongoing use.

In October 1991, undamaged crude oil storage tanks were emptied, process pipe work was flushed through with sea water, buoyancy tanks were emptied, all valves were shut to prevent flooding and loose equipment removed. An analysis showed that an estimated 100 tonnes of oily sludge contained about 9.2 tonnes of oil and a number of heavy metals, with the remainder composed of a mixture of sand and scale. The walls of the storage tanks were, reportedly, coated with an estimated 41.3 tonnes of hydrocarbons in the form of a thin layer of oil and wax. Shell said that scale is commonly found in oil processing facilities and that it may be contaminated by small amounts of naturally occurring radioactive salts from the oil reservoir. The company believed that its impact was minimal with no implications for health or the food chain.

The BPEO demonstrated that the most appropriate action was to dispose of the Spar at an authorized deep water disposal site, as it was the option of least technical risk, minimized workforce exposure to accidents, would have a small but insignificant impact on the environment and was economically the most attractive. Onshore disposal would be a much more technically complex and hazardous operation in safety and occupational health risk terms. Shell summarized its position in a press release in June 1995:

> Extensive studies and an independent report confirmed deep water disposal of the Spar as the simplest operation, posing low risk to health, safety and the environment. It would not be environmentally hazardous and would have a negligible effect on the deep sea environment.

Organizations involved in the 30 studies included the University of Aberdeen, Global Maritime, Metocean, McDermott Engineering, Smith Engineering, Aker, Heerema and Amec.

The decision was taken after consultation with the Scottish Office and other UK government departments, and was endorsed by the UK Department of Trade and Industry. The proposed disposal was in accordance with all relevant UK and international laws and conventions and approvals were received on 17 February 1995.

The Greenpeace allegations

In late May 1995, Shell exchanged correspondence with Greenpeace. A letter from Uta Bellion, Chairman of Greenpeace International, addressed to Cor Herkstroter, Chairman of the Committee of Managing Directors of the Royal Dutch/Shell group, commenting on Shell UK's 'appalling plans to dump the Brent Spar', claimed that it was:

> laden with over 100 tonnes of toxic sludge and more than 30 tonnes of radioactive scale. It contains a lethal cocktail including lead, arsenic, mercury, and PCBs which, if allowed to enter the marine environment, would present a considerable threat.

Allegedly, the dumping was 'wholly inconsistent with the best international practice in disposing of oil installations' and that in the Gulf of Mexico, where 'dumping of redundant oil installations is prohibited', Shell practises 'far less environmentally damaging methods of disposal'. Shell UK was charged with showing 'utter contempt' in its treatment of the environment. Greenpeace claimed the credit for publicizing Shell's disposal plans and that the decision to dump the Spar was based on economic, not environmental criteria.

In response, Dr Chris Fay, Chairman and Chief Executive of Shell UK, replying on behalf of Cor Herkstroter, described the 'widely-publicised assertions repeated in your letter' as 'misinformed and unjustifiably alarmist'. He continued:

> You claim that Shell UK has rejected the best available solution, putting economic performance before the environment, because of the alleged laxity of UK regulatory standards. Neither could be further from the truth.

The UK regulatory regime was among the most scrupulous in the world. The letter stated:

> On every count, the procedures, principles and standards which underlie the Brent Spar disposal plan authorised by the British Government represent current best international oil industry practice in respect of the care, rigour and independence of the analysis of the options, the responsible balancing of environmental, safety and health considerations and the extent and openness of consultations with interested parties, including fishermen and environmentalists, which preceded the Government's approval of the disposal plan.

Dr Fay stressed that Shell UK was not predisposed to the offshore disposal of redundant installations simply to save costs. UK government policy, consistent with best international practice, took into account the individual characteristics and circumstances of each disposal on a case-by-case basis. He continued: 'The responsible option in this case, on environmental, safety and health considerations, is carefully managed deep water disposal'. However, he added that the balanced case-by-case approach could lead to onshore recovery and scrapping for many subsequent disposals of redundant British installations.

Shell denied totally that Greenpeace activity had ensured that the disposal plan had become public knowledge, not least because discussions with interested parties had started in 1994. Fay's letter stated:

> We understand that all the governments which are parties to the Oslo Convention governing international standards for the protection of the marine environment were notified months ago of the proposed disposal plan for the Brent Spar.

The Greenpeace comment that Shell UK was prepared to treat the environment with contempt highlighted the contrast between, as Dr Fay put it, 'those of us who are engaged in the painstaking process of seeking responsible balanced solutions and those, like yourselves, who focus only on the problems'.

The chain reaction begins

The emerging issue of the Brent Spar quickly established a momentum of its own when, on 30 April 1995, Greenpeace activists occupied the Spar amid considerable media interest. In less than a month, from 30 April to 23 May, the UK government had issued a licence for deep water disposal, the German government had lodged a formal protest to its UK counterpart – in spite of making no comment during the earlier compulsory consultation process – and, finally, the activists were removed from the Spar amid one of the most visually striking and intense international broadcast stories of the year. Public interest in this so-called 'David and Goliath' debate, now amplified by a global print and electronic media, quickly brought about top level political resistance as the issued moved cross-border.

At the Esbjerg North Sea Conference in early June, several European countries called for all defunct oil installations to be disposed of onshore, leaving the UK and Norway isolated in arguing for a case-by-case approach.

On 10 June, Shell UK started to tow the Spar to an approved deep Atlantic site – 6,000 feet deep and about 150 miles off the west coast of Scotland. At the same time public perception, through widespread editorial fuelled by Greenpeace, was of a location much closer to the mainland with the potential to create enormous environmental damage to the marine ecology.

Public opinion in continental northern Europe became increasingly vociferous in its opposition to Shell's action and by mid-June, eager to demonstrate his green credentials during elections in Germany, Chancellor Kohl protested about the disposal plans to Prime Minister Major at the G7 Summit in Nova Scotia. In a very short period of time a potential issue that was not widely considered to be of particular importance in the UK had escalated to become one of international public scrutiny and militant action.

In Germany, a boycott of Shell products and picketing of Shell forecourts started and within days some 200 service stations were damaged, with two facilities fire-bombed and one raked with bullets. On 20 June, John Major defended Shell's position on decommissioning the Brent Spar in the House of Commons, only to discover afterwards that in The Hague, the parent company of Shell UK had already decided to abort the decommissioning plan in the face of intense public opposition. As the success of the Greenpeace campaign was acknowledged across the world, Shell was condemned by UK government ministers and the media for its U-turn and the Prime Minister referred to the company as 'wimps'. Michael Heseltine, then UK President of the Board of Trade, said that it was a total embarrassment for Shell and that the company 'should have kept its nerve and done what they believed was right'.

In a press release issued on 20 June, Shell UK effectively confirmed that it was succumbing to pressure. Admitting that the new decision was not taken on a reassessment of the technical factors, the company said that it still believed the deep water disposal of the Brent Spar was the best practicable environmental option.

The *Financial Times* concluded in an editorial on the subject:

> If democracy means the successful exploitation of popular anxieties by a militant minority, then so be it. However, Shell's rout is hardly a victory for rational policy-making, let alone for the environment.

In the aftermath of the Brent Spar incident, commentators have argued that Shell's failure to successfully present its case to a wide audience base not only damaged a reputation for commercial enterprise and environmental vigilance built over many years but created serious financial consequences for the company (for example, through voluntary relinquishment of tax relief) and for the oil industry as a whole if offshore disposal were to be disallowed. The impact of greater public scrutiny, not least surrounding the environmental and social credibility of Shell's operations in Nigeria, has further implications for the business.

Could the surrender have been averted?

The answer has to be 'Yes' and here are our maxims for an effective response.

1. Manage the response

Managing the response to an emerging issue as it gains momentum through the lifecycle curve needs clearly defined roles and responsibilities and the committed time and focused attention of senior management. Without this focus at the absolute top of the organization, reputation and performance are quickly threatened.

In a BBC *Newsnight* interview on 20 June, following Shell's announcement to abandon deep water disposal, the interviewer, Jeremy Paxman, challenged Dr Chris Fay over the company's management competence in handling the issue and argued that a company shouldn't fail with the full might of government behind it. In response Dr Fay said: 'Am I expected to react every day to the misinformation that the media takes in and spend all my time arguing against that misinformation while the media doesn't seem to want to take hold of the total story?' Clearly, responding to every potential issue isn't feasible nor is it good management practice. However, when key issues do emerge, it is critical for the chief executive to decide at the earliest possible stage when to get directly involved and what resources need to be allocated to manage the task. In the case of

Brent Spar, the chief executive did not make these decisions early enough.

Because of the consequences of failing to manage and respond to public opinion, senior management must have appropriate systems and resources in place to be able to focus – full-time if necessary – on the management of the issue.

2. Understand the public view

The increasing demands of public scrutiny place new pressures on organizations to be alert, aware and ready to shape or respond to potential public debate. It is often about harnessing and managing emotion.

Shell assumed that because it had followed all the international regulatory agreements and had secured the cooperation of the British and other governments (at least initially) there was no need to seek approval from a wider audience. Indeed, Dr Fay quite reasonably stated that it was 'the first example where governments have openly protested against an option which has been carried out in a lawful and proper manner'.

The speed and amplification techniques of a modern, global media and the growth and sophistication of single-issue campaign groups make them extremely capable in reaching and relating to public emotion. These factors create a new imperative for institutions and corporations to monitor and assess public perception and behaviour on any matter that could affect, either directly or indirectly, operational performance.

3. Make the case – clear and simple

Shell had difficulty explaining detailed scientific analysis succinctly, meaningfully and swiftly. By the time that some allegations were refuted more were made. In contrast, images of Greenpeace members aboard the Brent Spar being attacked by plumes of water fired from nearby vessels made instant news and more interesting broadcast viewing than scientific experts 'dryly' assessing the merits of the proposed decommissioning plan.

As we described in Chapter 1, there is growing evidence of the public's ability to challenge reassurances about risk made by government and industry. Reliance solely on the availability of scientific or technical data without communicating clear messages that distil key findings in a manner that responds to potential public concern about a particular risk is simply not enough to prevent or win the debate. Furthermore, research into memory loss indicates that we forget two-thirds of what we absorb in a day and 98 per cent in a month. Clear message points repeated over time help to make sense of complex issues for most of us.

The avoidance of complex language and statistics is essential. Instead, the use of analogies to emphasize the low degree of potential risk to the environment, coupled with basic facts, message points and illustrations are effective mechanisms for

91

making a clear and compelling case. This approach can be used, for example, to demonstrate the remoteness and depth of the disposal location, the potential for marine life to colonize the structure over time and the health and safety benefits of offshore disposal.

This type of approach isn't about talking down to people but it is about focusing on a few key points, and constantly and consistently communicating those points to secure understanding and, ultimately, support from the majority of those either interested or directly involved.

4. Find out who you are up against and how they are likely to behave

Shell appeared to have no knowledge of the planned campaign by Greenpeace and was seemingly taken by surprise when correspondence started to fly and activists attempted to occupy the Spar.

*The whole point of an early warning system is to monitor, anticipate and assess the likely origin and evolution of potential issues. This involves gathering information on the agendas and activities of **all** relevant audiences, however peripheral in the beginning. In the case of issues relating to public health, safety and environmental protection it is essential that organizations pay particular attention to special interest groups. Building a profile of the working methods and organization of such groups through examining the characteristics, style and approach to campaigning, membership recruitment, funding, promotional activities and current agenda setting, will provide valuable intelligence for planning purposes.*

5. Work with the media

Shell seemed unable to counter the powerful visual icons offered by a very media-aware, single-issue pressure group. Conveying detailed environmental analysis in a 'sound bite' context is a tough challenge but possible to do through some of the techniques described earlier. This needs to be coupled with a clear understanding of the working practices and demands of the media. Shell failed to make this distinction and put its faith in sound science rather than sound bites. There was a clear opportunity to communicate the low potential risk of offshore disposal, the complexity in health and safety terms of onshore disposal and the fact that, for example, many of the heavy metals contained in the Spar are produced in much higher volumes by nature.

Shell was not slow to disseminate material to the media but the latter showed little sustained interest in the story until Greenpeace first occupied the Spar on 30 April. It is inevitable that because of our increasing scepticism and lack of trust in big things, ie corporations and institutions, sections of the media may be biased in favour of campaign groups. In particular, the concept of a 'David and Goliath' combat provides mouthwatering potential for sensational editorial. There is also a tendency by the media to call for and critically scrutinize a company's arguments and supporting data to a much greater degree than that of a pressure group.

Some analysts criticized Shell for not taking a more positive stance with the media earlier. However, the company could argue with some justification that seeking a higher profile might have attracted disproportionate attention to a complex issue. The right balance is often difficult to determine until it is too late.

Finally, as the issue was developing, a perception evolved that Shell representatives were seldom seen or heard on radio or television. Producers turned to other 'experts' which helped to inject some independence into the story but implied, however unjustly, that Shell was keeping a low profile.

The need for regular availability of no more than two or three designated spokespeople for communication with the media is essential.

6. Sing from the same hymn sheet

Faced with managing an issue, a company must never appear divided. *Perceptions matter.* The perception was that Shell did not speak with one voice. When public outrage developed in Germany, the local company attempted to distance itself from its UK counterpart, claiming that it had no influence there. One comment attributed to the German chief executive was that the first he knew about the proposed deep water disposal plan was when he saw the Brent Spar on television! Later, according to a press report, Shell Germany apologized to the public for paying more attention to scientists and authorities than to customers' wishes.

Similarly, Shell in the Netherlands did not want to be seen supporting London, and a senior Shell executive in Austria was quoted as saying that the sinking of the Brent Spar was intolerable.

Although sometimes difficult to institute across international and highly decentralized organization structures, it is imperative that policy guidelines are introduced and adhered to in such a way that there is always a single, consistently communicated position on an issue, with authorized spokespeople assigned to represent that position.

7. Remember – issues transcend borders and politics

Issues that involve an international industry and regulatory environment rarely stay local. Transmission of information and opinion through a host of newly available electronic media cannot be geographically constrained.

Similarly, changing political systems and agendas demand constant review and assessment no matter how removed from equivalent national institutions. Shell in London acknowledged that it was astonished by the depth of German feeling on environmental issues relating to oceans. Why? Any international organization should be tuned into policy making in all the markets in which it operates, particularly in those that could be affected by a potential change or development like the Brent Spar.

This also applies to monitoring the methods of working and campaign activities of special interest groups. Shell decided that it would not discuss issues with Greenpeace until the illegal occupation of the Spar was ended. However reasonable such a stance may have been, it was a turning point.

Talking to an organization may give it added status, but it can help to publicly demonstrate a commitment to listen and potentially negotiate a resolution of conflict.

Appropriate early warning systems and internal information networks, which can operate across borders, are essential ingredients to the effective strategic planning and issues management functions within the organization.

Conclusion

The *Financial Times* noted:

In hindsight, Shell failed to detect the extent of public concern in continental Europe or to win adequate support for its argument that the best place for the Brent Spar was in a deep trench in the Atlantic. As a result, years of careful cultivation by Shell of an environmentally friendly image have been thrown away.

It is always easy to criticize corporate response with the benefit of hindsight and it is important to note how rigorously Shell followed every procedure with regard to agreed international regulatory policy and environmental best practice.

Shell, alongside other large companies, could be forgiven for questioning the validity of international agreements sponsored in the framework of the law. If governments accept the rules, ignore the deadline for comment on projects devised in strict accordance with the requirements and then reverse their stance because of local protest, where does that place the credibility of such agreements?

Ruminating on the consequences of Shell's decision to do a U-turn on the planned disposal, Shell UK's director of public affairs wrote:

Businesses will now have to include in their planning not just the views and rational arguments of all concerned – whether opponents or supporters – but will also have to come to grips with an area of deep seated emotions, subconscious instincts and symbolic gestures.

The Brent Spar issue is summarized in Figure 5.1.

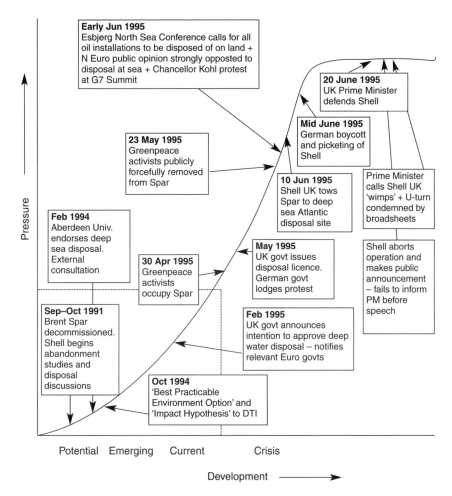

Figure 5.1 *Shell Brent Spar issue lifecycle*

CASE STUDY: MAD COWS AND ENGLISHMEN – THE STORY OF BSE

Introduction

The only simple factors in the mad cow disease drama were the initials BSE and CJD. The existence of a probable link between bovine spongiform encephalopathy (BSE) and Creutzfeldt–Jakob disease (CJD), a rare and fatal brain disease in humans, was revealed in March 1996. CJD has an incubation period of between 10 and 50 years and the average age of its victims had been 63. Researchers in Edinburgh, however, identified a new variant whose victims had an average age of 27. It seemed likely that BSE had crossed species to affect humans.

It was clear that some cattle would have to be slaughtered and burnt to prevent infected meat from entering the human food chain. But confusion reigned. There was no agreement on how many cattle should be culled, whether this should include animals less than 30 months old, who should compensate farmers, and the magnitude of the potential human epidemic. One scientist claimed Britain could face up to 500,000 cases of CJD; others thought the risks were minimal. Some experts said BSE would be eradicated within two years, others suggested it was endemic.

Relations with Brussels, none too cordial at the best of times, were further soured by EU bans on British beef and bickering over the size of the cull. Beef sales in Britain recovered after the initial panic, but remained sharply lower on the Continent. The number of slaughtered cattle by 2001 was well over 2 million, with the annual cost to UK agriculture estimated to be £326 million. So far 100 people are estimated to have died from CJD in the UK.

Most experts now agree that BSE was spread by cattle eating Meat-and-Bone Meal (MBM), which contained infected brain tissue of other grazing animals. How scientific information was assessed and communicated by politicians and the media to an increasingly anxious public and responded to by a major industry potentially on the verge of financial ruin has been critical in the shaping of European sensitivities to all subsequent food-related issues.

The story unfolds

The beginning of the BSE crisis can be traced back to the 1970s, following changes made to the processing of sheep offal into cattle feed, designed to make MBM meal more appetizing.

In September 1979, the British government received a warning from the Royal Commission concerning the dangers of passing animal diseases to humans via infected foodstuffs. This was followed by advice from the Institute for Animal Science and Health in the Netherlands, that meat rendering at low temperatures could have dangerous implications for the spread of disease across species barriers. Unlike their continental counterparts, British renderers had, in some cases, used temperatures lower than 100°C, thus increasing the risk of infection.

BSE was officially diagnosed by the UK Central Veterinary Laboratory in November 1986. The findings were not made public until 5 June of the following year when the Chief Veterinary Officer (CVO) informed government ministers of the disease. Studies commissioned to identify possible causes of the disease concluded in December 1987 that cattle feed made from MBM was the only viable cause of BSE. Papers published in scientific journals over the following months began to raise concerns over the potential impact of BSE on human health.

As soon as other European countries suspected that animal meal could be the source of the disease its use was banned, with France and Ireland taking the added precaution of destroying all animals in any herd with a case of BSE.

In July 1988, six months after the cause of the disease had been identified, the British government ordered a ban on the use of scrapie-infected sheep offals in cattle feed. This was followed in August by legislation requiring the slaughter of all BSE-infected animals and the destruction of their milk. A compensation scheme was introduced providing farmers with 50 per cent of the market value of each infected cow.

Faced with an uncertain and potentially catastrophic financial future, it is alleged that some farmers marketed cows with early signs of BSE and continued to use old cattle feed in the absence of rigorous monitoring of the bans. It was not until seven months later that the government increased compensation to 100 per cent, to prevent further infected meat entering the human food chain.

In May 1989, Dr Hugh Fraser, a leading scientist at the Institute of Animal Health carrying out government experiments on BSE, was interviewed on BBC Radio 4's *Face the Facts* programme. He said: 'there are suspect tissues from certain categories of cattle which it would be prudent, I think, to remove from human consumption' and identified pies and pâtés as sources of suspect tissues most likely to carry the disease. Following his interview, the Ministry of Agriculture instructed scientists at the Institute not to talk to the media about BSE.

The calm before the storm

In November 1989, the government announced a ban on the use of certain specified bovine offals (SBOs) thought most likely to carry BSE. This action was explained as a precautionary measure, but designed to maintain consumer confidence in British beef. The working party on BSE, established by the government in 1988 to investigate possible human implications of the disease, concluded the following year that it seemed unlikely that BSE could cross the species barrier. The possibility of a 'species jump', however, could not be ruled out – the implications of which would be 'extremely serious'. Despite doubt among members of the scientific community, the CVO said on national television, 'We don't believe there are any implications [from BSE] for humans at this time'.

As early as February 1990, however, the Institute of Environmental Health Officers submitted a report to the Ministry of Agriculture outlining problems with the implementation of the offals ban. Abattoirs were not rigorously enforcing the new restrictions and SBOs were still getting into the human food chain. The Ministry did not respond to the report.

In September 1990, renewed fears about the ability of BSE to 'jump species' were caused by the announcement that a laboratory transmission had caused the disease to develop in a pig. The then Agriculture Minister, John Gummer, responded to negative media comment with a photo-call depicting himself and his 4-year-old daughter eating beefburgers made with British beef. In a subsequent television interview, Gummer stated that his priority was first and foremost to 'make sure the public knows that it is perfectly safe to eat British beef'.

In 1991, reports in the national media about the possible spread of BSE reached new levels following the discovery that a domestic cat had died from the disease. The cat's death was assumed to have been caused by eating pet food made with infected offals, prior to the 1988 voluntary ban on the use of SBOs by major pet food manufacturers. The CVO dismissed the incident by saying 'this is only one cat death out of seven million cats in the UK and there is no reason for cause for concern at all'.

The year 1991 also saw the first evidence that the government's feed ban was not working with the announcement of the first case of BSE in cattle offspring born after the ban was implemented.

Debate over the dangers to humans continued with the government issuing countless assurances that British beef was safe despite growing doubt among the scientific community. In October 1992, as reports of BSE continued to increase, the CVO again appeared on national television to say: 'there is no need to be alarmed and so far as the public is concerned, there is no risk at all from consuming beef in this country'.

The issue rumbled on over the next three years as unannounced checks on abattoirs began to highlight failings in the implementation of the offals ban. With the absence of new findings or government initiatives, media and public interest began to decline.

The year 1995 saw the issue ratchet up the lifecycle curve at alarming speed:

● In September, new evidence demonstrated a possible link between BSE and the rare human brain disease, Creutzfeldt–Jakob disease (CJD). James Ironside, an experienced neuropathologist at the Western General Hospital in Edinburgh, discovered a new variant of CJD that had recently caused the death of two young people. There were significant differences in the formation of this strain of the disease and a more familiar type of CJD traditionally only found in older people. Ironside believed his discovery could somehow be linked to BSE.
● In October, *The Sunday Times* reported that more than one million infected cattle may have entered the food chain.

● At the end of November, Sir Bernard Tomlinson, another eminent neuropathologist, stated that he would not be eating burgers, pies and other processed meats due to uncertainty over whether BSE could be transmitted to humans.

A case of too little too late

The government embarked on a damage limitation exercise as hundreds of schools began to take beef off their menus and beef sales fell by 25 per cent. British Agriculture Minister, Douglas Hogg, stated, 'British beef has never been safer', arguing that safety measures imposed by the government had prevented any infected meat entering the food chain. But confusion arose when he simultaneously extended the existing offal ban to include food from the spinal cord and mechanically recovered meat, immediately raising concerns that the existing ban had not been adequate.

Even in a December television interview, the Health Minister, Stephen Dorrell, persisted: 'Science suggests that there isn't a link and secondly, even if science was wrong on that subject, we've removed from the human food chain the organs that could conceivably be linked to a transmission'.

By the end of 1995, the CJD surveillance unit had examined the brains of six young people whose death had been caused by the new strain of CJD; the number of deaths rose to eight by the end of the following February.

An urgent briefing was arranged on 8 March to communicate the findings of the surveillance unit to members of the spongiform encephalopathy advisory committee (SEAC). Two weeks later a ninth case of variant CJD was discovered. The CMO and CVO were immediately informed. Discovery of a tenth case within days led scientists to believe that exposure to BSE was the most likely cause.

On 19 March, the British Prime Minister called a crisis cabinet meeting after being informed that leading scientists believed exposure to BSE may cause CJD in humans, thus challenging a decade of government reassurances about the safety of beef.

The potential financial implications for the UK economy were daunting – the prospect of having to destroy Britain's 12 million cattle was estimated as costing between £10 and £20 billion. The outlook for the beef and associated processing industries was devastating with the potential for businesses failing, significant job losses and a host of other major economic, political and social implications.

The following day, the Health Minister announced to the House of Commons that new scientific evidence relating to recent cases of CJD in young people indicated BSE might be transmissible to humans: 'The [spongiform encephalopathy advisory] committee have concluded that the most likely explanation at present is that these cases are linked to exposure to BSE before the introduction of the Specified Bovine Offals ban in 1989.'

The government pledged commitment to take on board the advice from SEAC and other leading scientists, and stated that original controls on the slaughter and processing of beef introduced in 1988 would be tightened and rigorously monitored. The Health Minister stressed the risk of contracting the disease remained 'extremely low'. By this time, however, intense media speculation over the risks of a human epidemic fuelled public anxiety further; editorials stated that the government's handling of the beef crisis was characterized by 'dither and delay'.

France was the first country to react, introducing a total ban on British beef imports, worth £220 million, and was quickly joined by other European countries. Thousands more British schools took beef off the menu and sales prices plummeted. The European Union endorsed a worldwide ban on exports of British beef on 27 March.

At the same time, many restaurants, including major fast food chains, removed all beef dishes from their menus. McDonald's took out full page advertisements in the national media informing the public that the company was using alternative sources to British beef.

In an attempt to calm the panic over BSE, the Ministry of Agriculture announced that all British cattle over 30 months old would be destroyed at the end of their productive lives, reducing the risk of infected meat entering the food chain. But because the disease had been seen in animals younger than 30 months, the policy was widely criticized by EU members, the media and the public, as a costly half-measure that did not remove the risk of BSE entering the food chain.

The crisis rapidly became political following the EU ban, with the British government criticizing the EU for its 'knee-jerk' reaction which further undermined consumer confidence. In retaliation, the Prime Minister announced, on 21 May 1996, that Britain would embark on a policy of non-cooperation with the EU, effectively freezing certain legislative procedures until agreement over the criteria needed to lift the ban could be reached. The EU remained unimpressed; member states were far more concerned about protecting their own beef markets which had seen a 25 per cent drop in demand. The Agriculture Commission pledged financial support in the form of compensation to British farmers as a gesture to help resolve the crisis. By the end of August 1996, the EU and UK governments had invested £2.65 billion in propping up the European beef industry.

Regardless of compensation, the financial and emotional impact on farmers, meat processors and butchers throughout the UK soon became apparent. Charles Runge, chief executive of the Royal Agricultural

Society of England, explained the panic: 'A lot of people who have contacted me are not so much angry as bloody frightened. They see their livelihoods being taken away from them for reasons they don't understand.'

The cull set in motion by the government became a source of constant media criticism highlighting the complex logistical problems that were already posing enormous difficulties for destruction and disposal of carcasses. Questions remained over the real effectiveness of the slaughter programme. Some experts claimed it was 'too little too late', bearing in mind the potentially long incubation period before symptoms of the disease were identified and ongoing uncertainty over the risks of BSE crossing species barriers. In May, *The Sunday Telegraph* argued: 'this chaotically ill-organised plan to incinerate all cattle over 30 months old flies in the face of all scientific advice' and suggested that to cull those herds known to be infected with BSE would have been a far more sensible option.

Additional legislation introduced in August 1996 attempted to demonstrate a tightening of the defence against the spread of BSE by making possession of animal feeds made partly from farm animals a criminal offence. Media interest began to wane from the early summer and sales recovered, with British beef reappearing on supermarket shelves.

The EU, nevertheless, remained adamant that the ban on imports from the UK could not be lifted until the cull was widened. New scientific evidence indicated that BSE could pass from mother to calf, highlighting the need for a much more comprehensive slaughter programme.

By September 2001, an estimated 100 people had died from CJD. Nearly 2 million animals had been slaughtered at an estimated cost to the Treasury of £4.6 billion.

While latest research indicated the likelihood of a CJD epidemic was remote and that BSE would have almost run its course by 2001 regardless of the cull, scientists acknowledged that it would be at least 8 to 10 years before clear evidence on the risks of BSE was known; a cure for CJD would take much longer.

Our verdict

As we explained in Chapter 1, communicating about risk has special requirements.

With scientific evidence about the risk of contracting CJD from BSE so unclear, it was not easy for government ministers to tread the narrow line between complacency and alarmism. In retrospect, however, the government committed a number of basic mistakes, which could have been avoided early in the issue lifecycle.

1. A stitch in time

The British government failed to impose and monitor controls as soon as BSE had been identified. It was unforgivably slow to respond in identifying and slaughtering sick cows and to pursue the causes of the outbreak more rigorously.

2. Half-measures won't work

It was a mistake early on to pay farmers only half the market price for infected cattle. There were persistent rumours of farmers rushing cattle suspected of having BSE to slaughterhouses rather than settling for half-payment.

3. Start as you mean to go on

The government's repeated tightening of controls on the beef industry over the last 10 years to try to ensure that infected beef did not reach consumers implies that it would have been more prudent to impose stricter controls right from the beginning. By 2001, over 2 million cattle had been slaughtered.

4. A clear strategy avoids knee-jerk penalties later

More thought should have been given by policy makers to defining a clear strategy before announcing in March 1996 that the possibility of a link with human brain disease seemed greater than had first been thought. The government should not have sprung the announcement as a surprise on its bemused European partners. By denying that neighbouring countries should have a right to act to protect their own beef industries, significant negative feeling developed across the EU towards the UK.

5. Don't assume the public is ignorant

The biggest error was one of communication. Government ministers insisted, over and over again, that there was absolutely no risk to human health from BSE. While there was no certainty either way, such confident reassurance was imprudent and, subsequently, compounded public cynicism and anxiety. The stunt in 1992 by John Gummer, then agriculture minister, of feeding a beefburger (unsuccessfully) to his 4-year-old daughter in front of television cameras, now looks ludicrous.

6. Act swiftly, decisively and responsibly

While elected governments have a duty to represent the best interests of a diverse electorate, including industries which play an important role in providing products and services to consumers, in matters of public health those same governments must demonstrate an ability to act swiftly and decisively to protect the public from both real and perceived risk.

7. Politics shouldn't come before public health (but what's new!)

A combination of threats from Brussels, restless backbenchers and panicky headlines led the government to make policy decisions driven by pressure and panic, for example:

- the decision to cull cows over 30 months old, together with a further 147,000 under that age but deemed to be at risk, when research findings published in 1996 indicated that such action would have no tangible effect on the eradication of BSE;

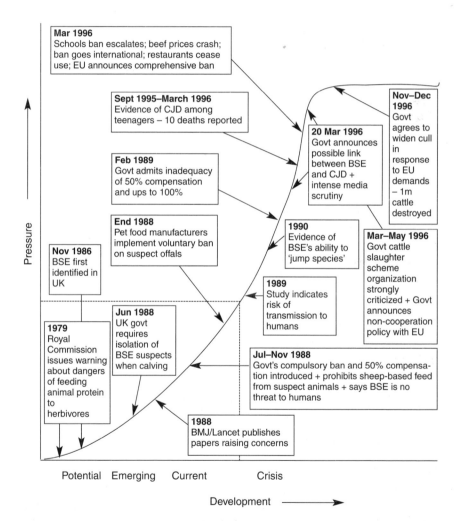

Figure 5.2   *BSE issue lifecycle*

- the attempt to shift blame to the EU for introducing and maintaining a ban on British beef, by retaliating with a policy of non-cooperation on inter-governmental decision making.

8. Find credible, independent and trustworthy spokespeople

A key lesson from this and other public health risk issues over the years relates to the need for government institutions to establish a method for delivering scientific information to the public untainted by the suspicion of political or commercial calculations. Any links between government departments, which normally represent the interests of farmers and other producers, and advice to consumers should be removed.

As far as possible, scientific advice on health and safety issues should be communicated to consumers by scientists, capable of distilling complex data in clear risk–benefit terms, and not by politicians.

The BSE issue is summarized in Figure 5.2.

Did the government show that it had learnt any lessons from the BSE issue when faced with subsequent national emergencies: flooding, the fuel crisis and the foot and mouth epidemic? Absolutely not!

After the fuel crisis, one minister was quoted as saying, 'We pulled the levers and nothing happened'. But in July 2001, Prime Minister Tony Blair announced the formation of a crisis management unit in the cabinet office to deal with national emergencies. The 'civil contingencies secretariat' is allocated the tasks of providing an early warning system for impending disasters and of drawing up a strategy for dealing with them – and also, presumably, of preventing the prime minister from appearing unprepared and powerless again. The secretariat is also charged with undertaking routine 'horizon scanning' to look for potential crises.

CASE STUDY: DRUG PRICING IN SOUTH AFRICA – THE BUSINESS PERSPECTIVE IS NOT THE ONLY PERSPECTIVE

Protection of patents and prices has been a constant challenge for the pharmaceutical industry, particularly concerning the costs of essential drugs, such as HIV/AIDS medication. The issue came to the fore in October 1997, when the South African government introduced the Medicines Control Act to make all medicines more affordable. The government was concerned that over 4.5 million people in South Africa were infected with the HIV virus, and the vast majority of those infected did not have access to effective treatment.

In February 1998, 39 pharmaceutical companies, coordinated by the Pharmaceutical Manufacturers Association of South Africa (PMA), responded to the Medicines Control Act by bringing a lawsuit against the South African government to prevent the implementation of the Act. The argument was that patents, and therefore drug prices, must be protected for research and development purposes. The US government and European Community were initially sympathetic to the pharmaceutical industry's position.

From September 1998, the case was suspended while the pharmaceutical companies negotiated with the South African government to stop the Act. These negotiations were unsuccessful, however, and the case was resumed in March 2001. However by this time the political, public and media reaction was very different. The pharmaceutical industry had failed to anticipate how the issue was to develop.

In 1998 the South African AIDS advocacy group, Treatment Action Campaign (TAC), was formed and began to mobilize global support against the pharmaceutical companies. TAC worked within South Africa to politicize the AIDS problem as a poverty issue, and used the established networks of the European and US AIDS campaigners to raise the profile of the campaign.

The international NGOs Oxfam and Médicins Sans Frontières (MSF) also latched on to the drug pricing issue, helping to make the case more visible, and an international issue as opposed to a local one. MSF and Oxfam both have valuable political and campaign group networks, and used their websites to convey the latest information on the campaign. The NGOs publicly condemned the 'profiteering' practices of the industry while emphasizing the terrible consequences of AIDS. Emotive news reports in Europe and the United States showed young African children dying from AIDS after being passed the disease from their mothers.

The public profile of the AIDS pandemic in the developing world rose dramatically during this period, coinciding with a series of new initiatives in the developing world to address the problems of AIDS in poorer countries. By the time the court case was resumed in March 2001, the AIDS pandemic topped the agenda of the United Nations, World Health Organization (WHO) and the Group 7 countries.

The trial became a subject of industry, government and media debate in Europe and the United States. The pharmaceutical companies continued with the case in spite of rising pressure, intensifying protests (GlaxoSmithKline was nicknamed 'Global Serial Killers') and boycotts. MSF and Oxfam posted a 'Drop the Case' petition on their websites and in the six-week period after the court case was resumed, over 250,000 people from 130 countries signed it, including various members of governments and celebrities.

The issue escalated to such an extent that in April 2001, two of the largest pharmaceutical companies, GlaxoSmithKline and Merck, asked Kofi Annan, the UN Secretary General, to help negotiate a settlement. A joint working party to govern the Act was established and the court case was dropped. The settlement allowed the South African government to implement the Medicines Control Act if the government agreed to abide by the World Trade Organization's Trade-Related Intellectual Property Rights Agreement (TRIPS). This was widely reported as a climb-down by the industry, and as a victory against the pharmaceutical companies' profiteering.

The pharmaceutical industry clearly took too long to acknowledge public concern. The issue ignited a discussion in Europe and the United States about the cost of drugs in the developed and developing world. The pricing policies of Bayer were also called into question after the September 11 terrorist attacks increased international demand for the smallpox vaccine, Cipro.

The pharmaceutical industry also made the mistake of dealing with the issue of drug pricing in South Africa from a strictly business point of view. When dealing with emotive issues such as AIDS, it is a huge mistake not to show care and humanity. Furthermore, the industry should have assessed the significance of the issue as it developed. The terrible consequences of AIDS were publicized more and more by NGOs and the media as the case developed, removing any sympathies that the international community may initially have had.

Before the South African drug pricing case arose, the pharmaceutical industry did not have a particularly good social and environmental record. Therefore when the issue escalated, the industry did not have credit to draw from its reputation bank.

The rise of socially responsible investment (SRI) has now placed considerable pressure on the pharmaceutical industry in particular. Following the WHO guidelines, institutional investors are placing increasing demands on companies' behaviour towards diseases of the developing world. The industry picture is that market prices in the developing world do not support the average $500 million research and development costs of new drugs. However, large pharmaceutical companies' R&D has long since overtaken academic research in the discovery of new medicines. The power to affect change rests with them – but the perception remains that they are profit-driven over finding cures.

AIDS, malaria and tuberculosis are the world's biggest killer diseases – accounting for 6 million deaths per year (30 per cent of the worldwide total) with the highest rates in the poorest countries – yet little is done to resolve this by those with the power to do so. Massive pressure is now being brought through institutional investors to change this. It is not a time for the industry to make charitable gestures dressed up in CSR greenwash. This is not a contribution to the scout hut. The pharmaceutical industry has to embed developing world diseases drug discovery into its R&D business. Opportunities exist in managing this issue, not least in the potential size of markets opening up in India and China, but it requires effective and considered reputation management.

If the industry wants to stop its drug pricing policies from being called into question in the future and be in a credible position to defend associated business risks such as black market trading and intellectual property rights, it clearly needs to establish a more caring and responsible image.

CASE STUDY: CFCs – FINDING AN ESSENTIAL BREATHING SPACE

Seventy million patients throughout the world rely on medicines delivered by a metered dose inhaler (MDI) to treat their asthma and other respiratory diseases. Few have been aware that their pocket-sized delivery system remains one of the last sources of chlorofluorocarbons (CFCs) escaping into the atmosphere and contributing to the depletion of the ozone layer.

In 1987, an international agreement was reached under the auspices of the United Nations Environment Programme (UNEP), which called for a freeze on production of selected CFCs and for all signatories to begin to phase out their use.

Industries using CFCs were presented with a legislative framework which would eventually lead to a total ban and significant financial implications associated with current and future manufacturing processes.

A group of leading pharmaceutical companies affected by these changes decided to act in concert to minimize risks to commercial performance and potential public criticism. The issues centred on the industry's ability to respond to the new regulations in order to help protect the environment, while at the same time ensuring continued and safe supply of asthma medication throughout the world. The consortium's programme of work continues but this case study illustrates how industry can successfully handle complex issues to the benefit of a wide range of audiences.

The background

CFCs are synthetic substances and were developed by General Motors in the 1920s for use as coolants in automotive air conditioning systems. Because CFCs have many useful properties and are non-toxic to humans, industry quickly found multiple uses for them – in refrigeration, air conditioning, foam blowing, aerosol propellants and technical cleaning solutions.

In 1974, however, an American scientist predicted that it was possible for CFCs to destroy the ozone layer. In the absence of firm evidence, governments were slow to respond until in 1977 the US administration introduced a ban on non-essential aerosols. Western European countries responded with a voluntary 30 per cent reduction in aerosol CFCs and, in some countries, a ban on most aerosol uses was introduced. In spite of growing pressure from special interest groups, public policy makers did not consider concerted legislative action was necessary based solely on scientific theory.

By 1985 all the proof that was needed emerged through dramatic satellite pictures that revealed a white hole over the South Pole. The discovery by a British scientist provided a focus for debate and study across the world and quickly generated public interest.

Scientists gathered conclusive evidence of the link between CFCs and ozone depletion and started to predict how cumulative use would affect the atmosphere.

At a time of growing interest in environmental issues, the media amplified scientific and special interest group arguments about the need for atmospheric protection. This helped to create an emerging issue of importance for public debate and potential public policy formulation.

The emergence of this new risk issue posed serious questions for environmental and health policy. If the protective ozone layer was reduced further, greater levels of ultra-violet radiation would reach the Earth's surface causing increased risk of cancer and potential ecological imbalance – and on a global basis. The question was no longer *should* CFCs be banned but *when* and *how*.

The United Nations provided an umbrella organization to bring national governments together to decide on a course of action. Under the terms of the 1987 Montreal Protocol on Substances that Deplete the Ozone Layer, all CFC production except for designated essential uses was to be phased out throughout the developed world.

Concern focused primarily on large industrial uses of CFC compounds in refrigeration, air conditioning and foam manufacture. However, the implications of the agreement were also profound for the pharmaceutical industry.

Over the last three decades, CFC emissions from MDIs have amounted to less than 1 per cent of the total and these inhaler devices provide probably the safest and most effective delivery system for treating millions of asthma sufferers worldwide. However, each inhaler contains about 15 grams of CFC – enough to destroy one tonne of ozone, the equivalent needed to protect about 1,600 square metres of the Earth's surface. Without these devices millions of people suffering from respiratory disease would be affected, but with them, the long-term impact on the Earth's atmosphere could be significant.

To the pharmaceutical industry, the medical and commercial imperatives presented by CFC phase-out were clear:

- the total worldwide market for asthma medicines is worth several billion pounds; a substantial percentage of this involves the regular use of MDIs;
- if CFCs were to go, alternative propellants had to be found;
- if a new propellant could be found for asthma inhalers, switching patients to a new inhaler could not happen overnight; the logistics of replacing 450 million devices used each year would be enormous;
- significant financial, medical and social differences existed between managing the potential change in developed as opposed to developing countries;
- many patients would be reluctant to change from a tried and tested device they depended on for treating a life-threatening disease;
- most patients and doctors were unaware that CFCs were used in asthma inhalers;
- explaining that the use of CFCs in inhalers was safe while acknowledging that the same CFCs were responsible for destroying the ozone layer would not be easy.

While it was inconceivable that the Protocol would deny patients access to the use of inhalers without an appropriate alternative, the pharmaceutical industry was now facing the fact that by the late 1990s the use of CFCs would be completely phased out.

The industry had to recognize and accept the environmental realities. The need for change was clear and so the pharmaceutical companies involved in asthma treatment agreed that they needed to be a partner in the change process.

How action planning got under way

Nine major companies agreed to act together and formed The International Pharmaceutical Aerosol Consortium – IPAC. The priorities for IPAC were to:

- communicate the industry's commitment to change;
- inform influencers and decision makers about the risks of asthma;
- ensure the Montreal Protocol's Technology and Economic Assessment Panel (TEAP) agreed with the industry consensus that the preferred method of drug administration for treatment of asthma is by the use of inhalers;
- find a candidate for a replacement propellant, test it for medical use and seek regulatory approval for market introduction as soon as possible;
- make representations to public policy makers to secure essential use exemption for MDIs, while reformulated products were developed, tested and brought to market;

- agree an appropriate strategy for an orderly transition process for replacement products to minimize public health risks.

The IPAC approach offered benefits both to member companies and to Protocol coordinators. Working in unison would help to speed the whole process of developing an approved replacement for CFCs. Participants would pool research and development expertise and resources, as well as share the considerable costs. In addition, the consortium created one voice for the industry – vital for success in putting forward a coherent and valid case to the many groups participating in such a complex, unfolding debate.

However, there were also a number of potential barriers for the consortium, namely:

- lack of informed knowledge about the importance of medical inhalers;
- country-by-country competition to lead the race to totally phase out CFCs would require national legislation to ensure an exemption clause;
- special interest groups were likely to campaign aggressively for a 'no exemptions' outcome;
- recycling CFCs, an option favoured by some groups, could run the risk of contamination; support for this process had to be countered;
- the proliferation and complexity of other related legislation would make the communication process particularly challenging.

Defining a potential solution

The first step was to establish a representative task force with clear guidelines on methods of working, roles and responsibilities, and resource allocation. Importantly, a secretariat was established employing an environmental law firm and administrative support to ensure rigorous coordination and implementation of agreed actions.

A network of working groups was established on a geographic and institutional basis for information gathering, analysis, response strategy coordination and implementation. This framework was essential to ensure organized, informed and targeted communication; to reduce duplication of effort; and to track, target and mobilize important groups (scientific, environmental, medical, special interest and other influencers and policy makers) at UN, EU, member state and regional levels.

The principal focus of IPAC's work had to be finding a suitable replacement and gaining regulatory approval. Without this all other activity would be pointless. Two sub-committees were set up to investigate alternatives to CFCs – HFA-134a and HFA-227. Pre-competitive cooperation on research and development was agreed.

It was essential for patient welfare, however, that in the rush to resolve the CFC problem policy makers did not inadvertently ban essential medical uses. Research conducted by IPAC members among doctor and patient groups indicated only a 20 per cent awareness that asthma inhalers contained CFCs. The same research showed that awareness was even lower among the decision makers who would actually shape the policies designed to phase out CFCs. So there was a real danger that a crucial life-saving device could be overlooked in the complex policy formulation process.

On the basis that it takes up to 10 years to test, validate and gain approval for a new medical treatment, IPAC realized that a CFC-free inhaler would not be ready to beat the deadline. Even if one were available sooner, the low level of awareness of the issue would make it virtually impossible to switch all patients to the new inhaler in such a short timeframe.

IPAC was faced with two options: convince the policy makers to extend the deadline for CFC phase-out, or make the case for an exemption for essential CFC uses for which there is currently no viable alternative.

As environmental issues were high on the public policy agenda in developed countries during the pre-recessionary period of the mid/late 1980s, and given that the threat to the ozone layer had been scientifically proven and was the subject of widespread concern, the second option was chosen as the consortium's position. Once IPAC had agreed this course of action, a clear strategy and action plan was required to secure the exemption.

Getting the issues management programme under way

All relevant decision makers and influencer groups needed to be made aware of the issues at stake and understand that:

- asthma affects 70 million people worldwide and is a life-threatening disease for which there is no cure; patient care must be protected;
- IPAC supports the environmental objectives of the Protocol;
- IPAC is working to a non-CFC inhaler solution;
- the non-CFC alternative will take time to develop;
- an exemption is therefore required for certain medical uses of CFCs;
- limited quantities of CFCs must be available for this purpose.

The Protocol was being negotiated with all member countries of the United Nations. Within each country a wide range of people had to be reached, not just the decision makers but also those responsible for advising on and drafting environmental, scientific and healthcare policy. Because of IPAC's medical case, it was essential that government health departments, medical opinion leaders, doctor and patient support groups understood the implications. It was also important that they could be mobilized to actively support the consortium's case in the face of critical opinion from special interest groups, parts of the media, competitors and other industries with vested interests.

Messages were agreed and tested by IPAC centrally. They were kept simple and to the point. It was important that IPAC was not perceived to be objecting to the central tenant of the Protocol – the need to protect the ozone layer. It was also crucial that the industry was not seen to be dragging its feet or being self-serving at the expense of patient welfare.

To support IPAC member companies in their contact programmes, a comprehensive package of written and visual materials was produced designed to address as many audiences as possible with minimal adaptation by audience and country. A key document and positioning statement, titled *An Essential Breathing Space for Patients*, presented a clear and concise version of the case for an exemption.

External lobbying and issue management specialists were employed. The secretariat advised on presenting case materials to the committees of the Montreal Protocol and coordinated, tracked and evaluated consortium activities and their impact as the programme evolved. This provided invaluable information for refining and focusing communication in such a way that opinion could be influenced so that necessary behavioural changes happened. In-country working groups of member company and consultancy staff reported on a regular basis to the secretariat. They were responsible for highlighting key developments, both positive and negative, and seeking input on successful programming in other geographic and institutional areas.

One working group was given responsibility for overseeing the activities of the various technical, scientific and legal committees established by UNEP. Another working group coordinated all contact with the European Union. Other groups targeted in-country communication with particular emphasis on mobilizing as much independent third-party support as possible.

The use of a hub-and-spoke organizational structure with a strong central focus for policy formulation and review in the secretariat helped to minimize bureaucracy. The use of electronic document management was also an important time-saver.

The consortium was, ultimately, successful in achieving its initial objectives. An exemption was won for the continued use of CFCs beyond the general deadline of the Montreal Protocol. In addition, European Union regulatory approval was received to develop an HFA-134a-based propellant.

More recently, IPAC has submitted a policy document to committees within the Protocol designed to use market forces to facilitate the transition to non-CFC MDIs, minimize CFC emissions during the transition and provide maximum protection to patients. New CFC-free inhalers have now been developed. A key part of the consortium's ongoing work will be to retain the exemption in conjunction with coordinating the transition to new products through intensive information and education programmes. Dr Stuart Smith, then head of Corporate Communications at 3M UK plc, an IPAC member, highlighted some of the critical success factors influencing the programme:

- Spot the issue *early* while the policy situation is still fluid.
- Ensure that the issue is *actually worth managing*. In this case there were clear business reasons and a moral obligation to the millions of people who rely on their inhalers every day of their lives.
- Develop a strong case based on *research* and supported by influential *independent endorsers.*
- Where possible, take your case forward with other companies as a *consortium*, or with other stakeholders as a *coalition* of interest.
- Ensure that you have access to the right *expertise* when you want it and excellent campaign *coordination* and *administration*.
- Remember, in Woody Allen's immortal words, 'the world is run by the people who show up'.

The CFC-inhaler issue is summarized in Figure 5.3.

CASE STUDY: FORD AND FIRESTONE – A MANAGEMENT AND COMMUNICATION FAILURE

Ford and tyre manufacturer Firestone disastrously handled a product recall in the United States in 2000/2001 after it emerged there was a fault with the Ford SUV Explorer. Because of the poor way the issue was managed and communicated, both companies are still suffering the repercussions of their actions.

Ford and Firestone were slow to initiate an initial product recall of SUV tyres in the United States, despite evidence from overseas suggesting that there was a problem. A recall of 6.5 million Firestone tyres was first initiated in the United States in August 2000; however, Ford and Firestone had been aware of tread separation problems on Ford Explorers in Saudi Arabia three years before. In 1999, at Ford's direction, Bridgestone/Firestone developed tyres with a nylon cap for countries with hot climates and rough roads; and Ford replaced Firestone tyres in

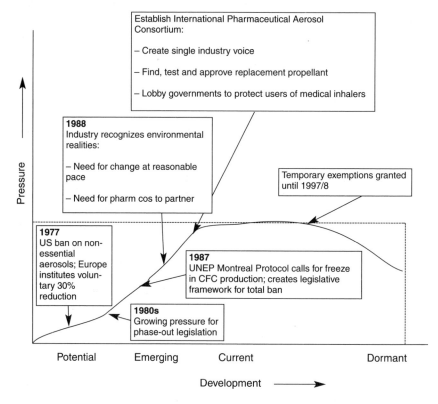

Figure 5.3 *CFCs issue lifecycle*

Saudi Arabia in August 1999, in Malaysia and Thailand in February 2000 and in Venezuela in May 2000. Tyres had been replaced on nearly 50,000 vehicles outside the United States before any action was taken. This led to criticism from the media, NGOs and the public that Ford and Firestone were putting profits before customer safety.

Neither Ford nor Firestone understood the risk potential of the initial incidents overseas, and when faults began occurring in the United States, the problem was not linked to what had happened elsewhere – each problem was treated in isolation. If both the companies had considered how risks can be amplified across countries they might have identified and acted on the risks faster.

By the time the US National Highway Traffic Safety Administration (NHTSA) opened its preliminary investigation into Firestone tread sepa- rations in May 2000, the agency had received 90 complaints involving 27 injuries and four deaths. Both Ford and Firestone initially adopted a unified response. It was agreed that Firestone tyres produced at its

Decatur plant in the United States were causing the problem, and this led to a 6.5 million tyre recall in August 2000.

Accidents continued to occur after this product recall, and Ford and Firestone began blaming each other for the fault. Ford emphasized a tyre problem and Firestone pointed to customer error, heat exposure and design flaws with the SUV Explorer. The lack of agreement between the two companies dominated the media coverage, leading the public to believe that neither company was putting customer safety first. As neither company was willing to take responsibility, it appeared that both were just trying to mitigate legal exposure.

Firestone's Japanese parent company, Bridgestone, became involved in the communications response in the early stages of the incident. Although this was perceived to be the right response in Japan, the American public and media felt it inappropriate that the foreign parent company was attempting to reassure them. Bridgestone should have left Firestone to handle the communications.

Although the CEO of Ford, Jac Nasser, managed to communicate Ford's concern and care towards its customers, some of his actions led the public to believe that his words were insincere. Although Nasser managed to do two television commercials reassuring customers that SUV Explorers were safe, he then refused to testify at Senate and House Commerce subcommittee hearings on the tyre recall in September 2000, stating he was 'too busy' to attend. Nasser forgot that in crisis situations, it is essential that your actions match up with your words.

Ford and Firestone's poor handling of the crisis led to a dramatic fall in share price and profits for both companies; and the end of a long-term commercial partnership at a time when both were struggling within highly competitive markets. The recall also led to an internal crisis within both companies; Firestone and Ford both restructured their organizations following the crisis. Masatoshi Ono stepped down as CEO of Bridgestone in October 2000, and Nasser resigned as CEO of Ford in October 2001.

Over 200 lawsuits have been filed against the companies. On 9 January 2001, American victim Donna Bailey brought a court case against Ford and Firestone and was awarded $100 million in damages, making the case the largest vehicular liability crisis ever. In November 2001, Bridgestone/Firestone agreed to pay $51.5 million to settle claims by American state attorneys.

The Ford and Firestone case also led to new legislation in the United States. On 11 October 2000, the House and Senate passed the Transportation Recall Enhancement Accountability and Documentation (TREAD) bill. The bill ensured that the Department of Transportation would receive the information it needed to detect defects, including information about foreign recalls, and increased penalties for manufacturers that fail to comply with the statute and its regulations. All car manufacturers in the United States now have to report any recalls that they issue in any part of the world, and need to report warranty information. (Source: Larkin, 2003.)

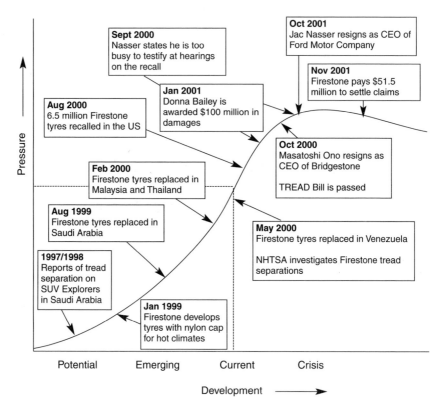

Figure 5.4 *Ford and Firestone issue lifecycle*

6

Implementing an issues management programme

> Not everything that is faced can be changed, but nothing can be changed until it is faced.
>
> James Baldwin

A similar, complementary process to the issues management model described in Chapter 3 can be defined for the role of management decision making at each phase and is shown in Figure 6.1. The *awareness* phase maps on to the first stage in the issues lifecycle – *potential issue*. Here, the emphasis in the management team is on listening and learning. Those involved need to be alert, open, low-key, inquisitive and challenging. Full use should be made of background information, research and ensuring monitoring infrastructures are in place.

The *exploration* phase indicates an increased urgency over the importance of the issue. Specific responsibilities need to be assigned, organizational awareness is raised and the analysis and opinion formation process begins. Based on working with a number of pharmaceutical companies, an example structure and allocation of responsibilities is shown in Figure 6.2. Typically, in this type of organization, representation should come

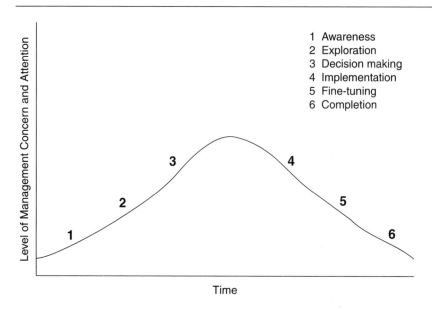

Figure 6.1 *The management process*

from medical, safety, regulatory, planning, legal, marketing and communications functions with authority to take specific action. Characteristics of any task force are:

● seniority to make decisions, allocate resources and direct programme implementation;
● breadth of disciplines represented and appropriate access to information for decision-making purposes;
● easy access for arranging meetings and 'networking' information; flexibility and informality in working methods;
● ability to combine analytical and creative skills with rapid, focused decision making and action;
● minimal paper flow to avoid bureaucracy, slow response and leakage of sensitive information.

Broader awareness of the issue in the company is raised at this stage and the analysis and opinion formation process begins.

At the *decision-making* stage the company has to consider action. The management team must objectively assess and decide upon the alternatives presented while still encouraging broad thinking and creativity in the formulation of an action plan.

The *implementation* phase involves taking the necessary steps to make management decisions work in practice, while *fine-tuning* allows for the

Roles and Responsibilities:

Task Force
(chair and secretariat)

Communications	Marketing/Sales	Medical	Regulatory	Legal/Planning
● media contact and intelligence gathering ● media training ● briefing documentation ● media briefings/workshops ● article drafting and syndication ● crisis communications support	● sales force briefing and training ● product education (doctor/patient) ● competitive analysis ● doctor mailings ● medical meetings management ● sales and marketing support materials	● review/analysis of data ● opinion leader networking ● study definition/commissioning ● data presentation at symposia, medical meetings, workshops, regulatory working groups, etc	● liaison with authorities ● submission of data ● licence approval status/monitoring ● analysis/assessment of approval processes	● impact assessment ● liability implications ● strategy review ● counsel

Figure 6.2   *Example task force for a pharmaceutical company*

measurement and evaluation of current actions and results so that adjustments or enhancements to the action plan can be made.

Completion is the wind-down period which should decrease senior management involvement. Key activities involve appropriate delegation and ensuring implementation of any resulting change management within the organization.

Effective issues management can help to build competitive advantage and sales, particularly in new and emerging markets; it can exploit opportunities or protect corporate policies where there is the potential for major social change. The pressures of market dynamics, competitor activity and resource availability can make it difficult to anticipate, initiate or plan for important issues.

Kerry Tucker and Bill Trumpfheller (1993) have created a five-step plan to help establish an issues management system, which we have found works well in practice.

1. Anticipate issues and establish priorities

This first fundamental step can take many forms, from drawing up a very basic set of assumptions through to a highly elaborate issues anticipation system. Setting up an internal task force, based on the approach outlined in the previous section, is a crucial starting point. Brainstorming sessions and database analysis should focus on responding to questions like:

- What immediate and medium-term competitor, social or regulatory factors do we need to contend with?
- What changes do we anticipate in the marketplace and wider political and social environment over the next 12 months and beyond?
- What factors are likely to affect the way we are working?
- What special events are likely to take place and have an impact on our ability to sustain and develop our markets?

Once these issues are identified, priorities can be set and decisions can be taken on how much time and resource to devote to them.

2. Analyse issues

Develop a formal brief or analysis of the issue, looking at the opportunities and threats against a series of different scenarios. This should cover what could happen if the issue is ignored, and an assessment of how key audiences are likely to be affected by the issue. There should also be a summary of the direction in which the issue is likely to be heading. This will give management a broad view of the issue and its effect on a number of areas such as product marketing positioning, financial performance, corporate reputation and the potential for regulation or even litigation.

3. Recommend an organizational position on the issue

The analysis from the previous step should provide a database to develop a position designed to create support from the greatest majority of individuals and groups affected. The database is built from answers to the following questions:

● Who is affected?
● How do the affected groups or individuals perceive the issue?
● What are their likely positions and behavioural inclinations?
● What information/data can we gather to support our case?

4. Identify groups and opinion leaders who can advance your position

These groups and individuals should emerge from asking:

● Who makes decisions on the issue?
● Who is likely to support our position?
● Who is likely not to?
● Who can we target successfully to make the biggest difference in advancing our position?

If possible, research should be undertaken to validate assumptions made about groups during the analysis stage. Opinion leaders, closely followed by influential industry or employee associations, consumer and other special interest groups and informed media, can be powerful allies in dealing with a range of audiences, and criteria for selecting them include:

● Who do members of our target groups look to for advice on the issue?
● Who will the (customer, consumer) community and the wider public trust on the issue?
● Who has the credibility to best advance our position on the issue?
● Who is likely to be open to our position on the issue?

5. Identify desired behaviours

This is an easy point to overlook, according to the authors. Advancing specific behaviour relating to the company's position drives development of the rest of the planning processing, namely: communications and marketing strategy, goals, objectives, messages, tactics, resource allocation and budgets.

Finally, evaluation of progress needs to be incorporated into plans to ensure that key milestones are met, the course of the issue is charted, and adjustments made if necessary.

Our experience from dealing with current and historic issues across different industry sectors endorses the value of implementing the following types of activity as early as possible, both to gain the initiative and protect against adverse developments.

Task force set-up

- Identify an appropriately experienced/resourced task force to define and manage issue response strategy.
- Maintain a flexible, creative approach to considering competitive counter-measures, regulatory change and positive corporate positioning initiatives.
- Think positively and proactively throughout – it is easy to be drawn into a defensive strategy from the outset and lose the opportunity to secure or regain the advantage of opinion leader, media and public support.

Intelligence gathering and analysis

- Invest in and establish an early warning intelligence gathering network to monitor, collect and review relevant research/data.
- Constantly assess competitor/regulatory activity and refer to similar, practical experience from other companies for guidance on approach.
- Obtain and monitor relevant peer review/specialist publications as early as possible for assessment and action where appropriate; track trade and broader mass media.

Issue champions

- One way of managing resourcing requirements for information gathering and analysis is for each issue to be assigned to an appropriately experienced individual within the organization. These in-house experts – issue champions – should act as authoritative, up-to-the-minute sources of information to assist task forces and other management in the planning and coordination of related activities.

Background briefing materials

- Prepare background information relevant to desired positioning, eg key messages, corporate/product/service back-grounders, Q&A, reference contact and research databases, core presentation kits, etc.

Research databases

- In industry sectors where there is the potential for risk to public health, safety or the environment, it is essential to build and maintain technical and scientific databases of information relating to, for example, the long-term safety of a drug, the rigour of hygiene monitoring systems in food processing, the frequency of routine safety checks and actual incident occurrence at manufacturing facilities, the use of independent expert safety audits and impact assessments to encourage best practice techniques for minimizing the risk of chemical or oil spillage, etc.

Relationship management

Build equity *early* through developing and managing influential relationships with:

- supportive academic and other opinion leaders;
- informed journalists;
- peer review journal editorial boards;
- regulatory authorities;
- industry and employee associations;
- policy units;
- political groups at local, national and international levels;
- local and other special interest groups.

Do this through informal contact and briefings; information distribution; educational programmes and research sponsorships, etc. These groups communicate informally and formally together, so it is important to understand the linkages between them and the potential for common agendas on issues relating to an organization's positioning. Try to assess their perceptions/opinions on potential issues by classifying them into positive/neutral/negative groupings.

Opinion leader development

- Contact and build relationships with potentially supportive opinion leaders who may become influential, independent endorsers of the company's desired positioning.
- Consider the use of tactics such as research and publication sponsorship, invitations to attend symposia, chair or present data at meetings, round-table discussions where appropriate.

Information/education programmes

- Build support at grass roots level through the organization of community meetings, correspondence, roadshows and provision of training/education aids to encourage more effective understanding and interest. Similar activities should be considered for customer and supplier groups.

Regulatory affairs

- Be prepared to proactively respond to potential regulatory questions relating to organizational, product and service performance.
- Prepare responses and develop relevant information updates that can be regularly mailed to appropriate authorities.
- Organize a meetings programme to build relationships and neutralize potential critical reporting.

Media management

- Work with the media (specialist, general at regional/national and international level as appropriate) proactively by establishing contact, ensuring spokespeople are available, issuing press statements, letters to specialist publications, bylined articles, media briefings and workshops.
- Monitor editorial coverage and individual journalists or publications for interest/bias; classify into positive/neutral/negative editorial stance on an ongoing basis and immediately following major announcements.
- Train appropriate spokespeople – corporate, technical and marketing, and supportive independent opinion leaders where possible.

The 'glocal' approach

- Act local but think global... in managing issues. Consider implications for other operating companies, the industry as a whole, to decide whether a coalition approach is likely to be more effective, etc.
- Be aware that as the impact of an issue declines in one market, it can easily cross national borders and quickly activate in other countries where local political or competitor agendas may trigger new threats.

Checklists can help

- A checklist to assist in planning an issues management programme is provided on the following page.

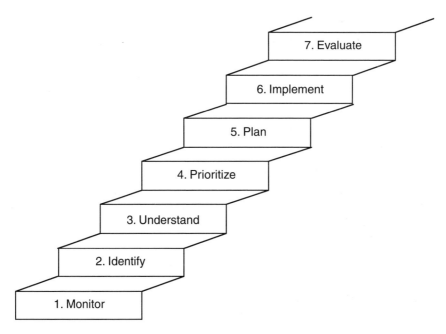

Figure 6.3 *Stepwise diagram*

Table 6.1 *A summary of the seven steps of issue management*

Step 1 – Monitoring • Analyse the business environment. • Scan and monitor what is being said, written and done by public, media, interest groups, government and other opinion leaders. • Consider what may impact on the company or its divisions. **Step 2 – Identification** • Assess from the business environment those elements that are important. • Look for a new pattern emerging from what most	**Step 5 – Strategy decision** • Create a strategic response and define the content of the message. • Identify the target groups. • What are the company's strategic options? • What resources are needed? • What specific actions should be taken? By whom? When? With whom? • Develop issue management communication plan – consider timing. **Step 6 – Implementation** • Implement the policies and

people take for granted.
- Identify the issues that impact on the company and are gaining widespread support.
- What is the type of issue and where is it in its lifecycle?

Step 3 – Prioritization
- How far-reaching will an issue's impact be (product, sector, company, industry)?
- Assess what is at stake – Profit? Reputation? Freedom of action?
- What is the probability of occurrence?
- How immediate is the issue?

Step 4 – Analysis
- Analyse the most important issues in some detail.
- Determine their probable impact on the company or its divisions as precisely as possible.
- Establish issue support teams if appropriate.
- Identify/rank stakeholders.

programmes approved by management.
- Communicate the response effectively with each target group in a credible form.
- Advocate the company position to prevent negative impacts and encourage actions with beneficial effects.

Step 7 – Evaluation
- Assess results.
- Evaluate the success of policies and programmes to determine future strategies.
- Capture learnings from failures and successes.

EXAMPLES OF ISSUE MANAGEMENT MODELS AND PROCESSES

There are many different company models for the practice of issue management principles. There is no one-size-fits-all approach; in fact, the best practice is often to mirror the organizational processes elsewhere in the organization to ensure that issue management procedures are successfully embedded in a company culture. The following three example models have been well and truly inculcated into the DNA of their respective organizations (one for as long as 20 years), and address three key areas of issue management: the issue manager ('champion'), the issues management process, and the involvement of senior management. (*Source: Corporate Public Issues and their Management*, January 2004.)

Memorial Health: the role of the issue manager

Issue management is most often launched and championed by a single individual within an organization, preferably a full-time equivalent position. This person learns the fundamentals of issues management, observes how others approach the discipline, and then recommends the appropriate process and initial participants. The champion, or 'steward', selects an initial issue to address, and with ratification from senior management, activates the issue management process.

The process steward's maintenance responsibilities include:

- Identify emerging issues.
- Monitor prospective issues.
- Help set issue priorities.
- Help set accountabilities and 'issue owners'.
- Ensure appropriate resource allocation.
- Create issue consistency by identifying and eliminating conflicts among issue plans.
- Provide a 'one-stop-shop' macro overview of issues across the organization.
- Deliver and collect issue intelligence.

The issue process steward responsibilities model at Memorial Health was developed nearly 20 years ago and remains pertinent today. It is summarized in Figure 6.4.

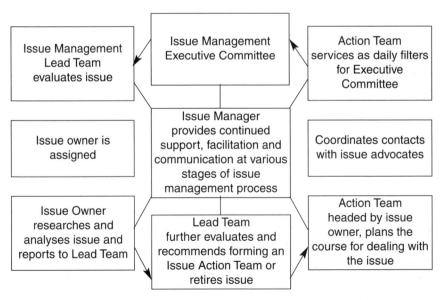

Figure 6.4 *Memorial Health issue management model*

Weyerhaeuser Company issues management process

Some people process information verbally. Others prefer a visual point of reference. The reality is that everyone suffers the constraint of limited time, so to create an awareness and understanding of how issue management works at a company it is useful to be able to map the process. That way, the individuals who have key roles and responsibilities on any given issue can easily see the intended end product and their role in achieving it. Senior management can also more easily grant resource allocation and evaluate progress against issue goals.

At paper and wood products firm Weyerhaeuser, where issue management has been continuously practised since the 1970s, the process finds a balance between being simple and comprehensive. See Figure 6.5.

DaimlerChrysler Group: weekly issue management process flow

The most senior officers of a company are responsible for being sure they are fully apprised of the results of the issue management process. They are also responsible for providing the necessary resources to achieve those results. DaimlerChrysler's weekly global issues call concludes with a key issue briefing that is sent to the board of management. Through this process, top management is regularly supplied with fresh and relevant insights on the issues that have merited task force assignments, as well as those that are likely to build steam and may therefore require resources for a more thorough treatment. See Figure 6.6.

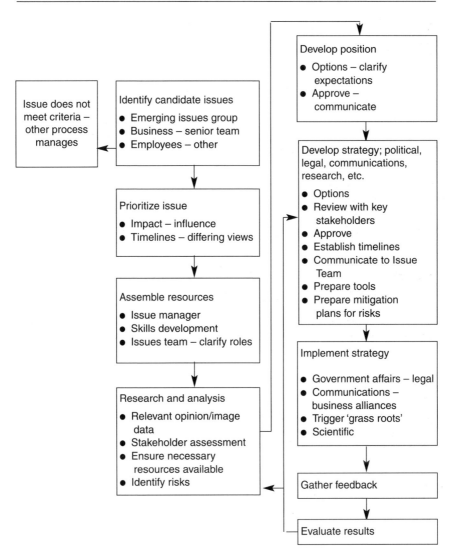

Figure 6.5 *Weyerhaeuser issues management process*

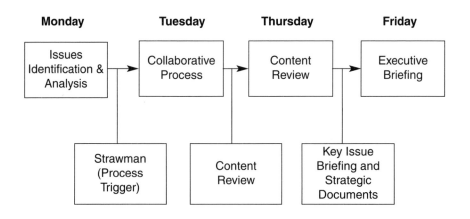

Figure 6.6 *DaimlerChrysler issues management process*

SUMMARY

While there is never a single generic approach that will work for every issue, this type of framework will help to anticipate, identify and plan a response to potential issues in a methodical and innovative way. Information should always be carefully focused, and briefing papers should have specific objectives that concentrate on realistic outcomes. Defining action in the context of potential bottom-line implications is a good discipline for maintaining this focus.

Part 2

Crisis Management

7

So it hits the fan – now what?

> If you can keep your head when all about you are losing theirs, it's just possible you haven't grasped the situation.
>
> Jean Kerr, humorist

In business as in life, crises come in as many varieties as the common cold. The spectrum is so wide it is impossible to list each type. Product-related crises alone range from outright failures as in the case of the widget which resulted in millions of cans of Carlsberg-Tetley bitter being withdrawn from the market in 1995, to unanticipated side effects illustrated by cases of asbestosis and thalidomide. Accidental or deliberate contamination experienced by Lucozade, Perrier and Tylenol and enforced obsolescence as in the case of PCBs are yet two more categories.

However, it is major crises such as aeroplane and ferry disasters involving tragic loss of life which lead to greatest public interest. It is this type of crisis which leads to the most visible and measurable erosion of public confidence. The public perception of the risk of such events – fuelled by the disproportionate amount of negative publicity – is often out of kilter with the statistical evidence. For example, in the United States it would take two 747 crashes per week to equal the number of people killed on US highways in the same period, but automobile crashes rarely make the headlines in the way aeroplane crashes do.

Advancing technology, which the public has often come to believe to be foolproof, forms yet another category. This category includes the 1967 Apollo spacecraft fire in which three astronauts died, the 1979 'incident' at the Three Mile Island nuclear reactor, the 1986 Challenger space shuttle tragedy, and Chernobyl in April of the same year.

More recently the world was stunned to learn of the fatal Concorde crash.

CASE STUDY: SUPERSONIC DISASTER

On 25 July 2000, Air France Concorde flight AF4590 crashed minutes after take-off, killing all 109 people on board, as well as four people on the ground.

Eyewitnesses watched as the Concorde pilot fought to keep the aircraft airborne and then crash into a hotel in the town of Gonesse on the outskirts of Paris. News and images of the first-ever Concorde crash in its 25-year history were flashed around the world.

Immediately after the accident, Air France grounded its entire Concorde fleet pending a full enquiry by the French accident investigation bureau, the BEA. British Airways, by contrast, grounded a flight immediately after the accident but waited until 25 August before suspending all its Concorde flights indefinitely – after the Civil Aviation Authority advised that it would be withdrawing Concorde's airworthiness certification following discussions with the BEA.

In the days following the disaster, Air France was put under intense media pressure to communicate what had happened in the accident. The company used its website to release press statements, with two press releases being posted on the day of the crash. These included telephone incident numbers and a message of sorrow and condolence from the company. Air France continued to issue press releases on its website on a daily basis after the accident.

The airline acknowledged there would be demands for financial compensation and arranged to pay relatives of the victims an interim amount in advance of a full legal settlement. It also recognized how important it was to involve senior Air France personnel. The chairman, Jean-Cyril Spinetta, visited the crash scene on the day of the accident and flew to Hanover to attend a memorial service with the affected families two days later.

As a consequence of these actions – fast and open communication with the media and sensitive handling of relatives of those who lost their lives – the airline suffered minimal reputational damage. The immediate grounding of the fleet illustrated how seriously Air France regarded the incident and its commitment to put the safety of its passengers first. After an initial steep decline, the airline's share price quickly recovered.

By contrast, the share price of British Airways took longer to recover amidst criticism that it was ignoring passenger safety by not grounding its fleet earlier.

Following the accident Air France and BA set up an Anglo-French working group, which met every month to plan the reinstatement of Concorde's airworthiness certificate. The public collaboration of the two airlines helped to prevent further potential reputational damage through their coordinated and unified responses before, finally, the aircraft was withdrawn from service.

On other occasions, significant tragedies can have such an impact that the extent of the fall-out affects entire industries, not just single organizations. They can be man-made events or natural disasters but an explanation will always be demanded and blame sought. The 9/11 terrorist attack on the World Trade Center was one such example. Another, more recently, was the devastation of the Asian tsunami in 2004.

CASE STUDY: THE ASIAN TSUNAMI AND THE TRAVEL INDUSTRY

On 26 December 2004 the world witnessed the worst natural disaster in living memory. At around 1 am (GMT) a massive undersea earthquake occurred just off the coast of Indonesia. The quake, the most powerful for 40 years, triggered a series of deadly tidal waves, which fanned out across the Indian Ocean. At the time this book went to print the latest estimate was that 280,000 people in coastal areas from Somalia to Sumatra were killed and many millions left homeless or destitute.

Coastal areas in the northern Indonesian province of Aceh, the closest inhabited area to the quake epicentre, took the full force of the tsunami. The nearby Indian-controlled Andaman and Nicobar islands were also hit. Waves measuring 10 metres in height slammed into towns and villages without warning. Initial reports from Aceh did not even hint at the monstrous scale of disaster, speaking of unexplained flash floods damaging bridges and roads.

Tourists enjoying the delights of southern Thailand's beach resorts saw a wall of water approaching at high speed. As the tsunami swept in, foreign holiday-makers and locals alike were trapped. Many drowned in hotel rooms, others were dragged out to sea. The deadly waves lost little of their power as they raced across the Indian Ocean, so when they reached eastern Sri Lanka, just a couple of hours later, they crashed into coastal areas with overwhelming force. As the tsunami moved inshore, reducing buildings to rubble, it also hit a passenger train. The carriages were packed with more than 1,500 people, most of whom drowned as the train was ripped off the tracks.

The low-lying Maldives are just four metres above sea level and as the deadly waves continued their rampage across the Indian Ocean they flooded the archipelago. Locals and tourists, many of them newlyweds enjoying their honeymoons, were left clinging to palm trees to try to avoid being swept away. Between six and seven hours after the earthquake occurred, the waves it triggered arrived on Africa's east coast. Surging seas destroyed homes and poisoned water supplies. Worst affected there was Somalia, where fishing boats were engulfed by the waves and crews lost.

The scale of the Asian tsunami disaster shocked the world and instigated an unprecedented relief effort. Government aid to the affected countries reached US$3.5 billion and was matched by massive public donations across the world as funds were raised to assist the survivors and the devastated region. It was a terrible tragedy that touched every nation. The immediacy of the disaster as news of the tsunami broke was amplified in many Western countries by the sheer numbers of nationals present in those popular tourist destinations at that time of year. As the story unfolded in the UK, significant attention was turned towards the thousands of British tourists on holiday in the region. The scale and complexity of the disaster presented an unprecedented challenge to travel companies and the industry at large.

How did the travel industry react?

Travel companies are among the best-equipped and most prepared organizations to handle a crisis. The examples of Thomas Cook and Exodus in this book bear testament to the importance placed by tour operators on successful and responsible crisis management and the commitment made to ensuring procedures are in place and well tested. The reputation of the company is of preeminent importance in an industry that hinges on the care it shows its customers. On the occasions of tragic accidents, how the company acts and is seen to act is vital. However, the tsunami disaster presented an unusual scenario; one unlike anything the tour operators would likely have considered in their preparedness planning.

This event was not an incident that exclusively involved one operator: it was a natural disaster on an unimaginable scale that left no company unaffected. Rather than one company having to manage its own crisis, the tsunami was indiscriminate and the vast majority of the travel industry in the UK was implicated.

As each travel company involved swung its individual operational recovery plans into action to locate and address the needs of its customers, the question of communicating around the crisis was a different matter. The tsunami was a catastrophe that impacted no one company in isolation; it had involved thousands of British holidaymakers and it was an entire travel industry that was responsible for their well-being. The industry needed to unite, with one voice communicating the efforts being taken across the travel industry.

Being able to talk with one voice was something that the travel industry was well placed to achieve. Even without having a premeditated plan of action for such an eventuality, the industry was able to draw on its trade associations and the way it organizes itself in other areas.

The Association of British Travel Agents (ABTA) quickly assumed the role of spokesperson and the Federation of Tour Operators (FTO), which represents the large tour operator groups such as First Choice, Tui, Kuoni and MyTravel, co-ordinated a consistent operational response. Utilizing structures already in place, the industry was able to move dynamically to manage the crisis operations and communications.

Coordinating the response

More than 10,000 British tourists were stranded in the areas affected by the tsunami. While many, particularly in Thailand, were independent travellers and backpackers, the majority were on package holidays with tour operators.

Consequently, they benefited from the support that the tour operators were able to provide both on the ground and in co-ordinating disaster recovery plans from the UK.

As news of the consequences of the tsunami broke, the entire travel industry quickly became focused on common goals to:

- locate and identify all holidaymakers;
- ensure that all concerned relatives and friends are kept abreast of the latest information;
- arrange the rapid repatriation of tourists back to the UK and provide for the needs of those choosing to remain on holiday; and
- contact all tourists due to fly out to the affected areas with information on what to do, including the offer of full refunds or alternatives for cancelled holidays.

The FTO is blessed by having a relatively small number of member companies whilst at the same time representing a very large volume of the travel industry. Because of this it was able to make decisions very quickly to help a large number of holidaymakers. The FTO became the liaison with the Foreign and Commonwealth Office (FCO), which was co-ordinating the search for and identification of British nationals as well as the relative information help-line in the UK. With specific advice from the FCO on the state of different areas in the affected region, the FTO was able to formulate operational plans for the recovery of stranded tourists very quickly. The focus was, and had to be, the welfare of those and future travellers, regardless of monetary cost to the industry. But the industry also needed to be *seen* to be doing this. ABTA represents the widest membership in the industry and it became responsible for communicating via the media and reassuring the public.

In much the same way as the attack on the World Trade Center presented uncharted territory for the news media, so did the Asian tsunami disaster. A rapidly evolving scenario, with poor communications links to the directly affected areas yet continual updates in information, combined with widespread shock and emotional reactions to the events from the public, left the media to plough a route through a minefield fraught with sensitive hurdles.

The initial reaction of the rolling 24-hour media in particular reflected that of the wider public – shock, and an inability to comprehend the sheer magnitude of the disaster that had unfurled. However, increasingly the media began to ask the question, 'how could this disaster have been averted?' As sources of blame began to be explored it was important that the travel industry protected its reputation.

The first ABTA knew about the disaster was at 4.30 am on 26 December when Keith Betton, the head of corporate affairs, was woken at home by the BBC. Within 30 minutes contact had been made with the Foreign and Commonwealth Office to establish their understanding of the situation. After this several early radio interviews were given to provide an initial reaction. By 8.30 am the first live TV interviews were being given as the public woke up on Boxing Day to the news. At this point a number of travel pundits were already being used by the media to predict doom for the industry, so ABTA interviewees were made readily available to put things in perspective. An early challenge was to predict the number of Britons in the affected area and some were putting that at nearly 100,000. ABTA moved quickly to place a more accurate estimate of between 10,000 and 20,000 – the true figure was quickly disseminated and became widely used by all the media.

The key messages on the first day were sympathy for those caught up in the tragedy, support for the FCO efforts, and an assurance that tour operators were doing everything possible to help those tourists affected. Over 125 media calls were handled and 16 national broadcast interviews were given over the course of that day.

On the second day ABTA provided live studio interviews to the BBC *Today* programme, BBC Breakfast, BBC News 24, Sky News and Talk Sport – all before 9.30 am. These were the crucial outlets and an estimated 10 million people were reached with this breakfast update on what the industry was doing to bring home holidaymakers. In total around 100 media calls were handled on day two. In addition, a special edition of the association's member update *ABTA Today* was emailed to all member companies giving them details of how to download the latest advice and news from the ABTA website. Even though it was still a bank holiday, travel agencies were being opened to handle requests for information from the public – it was vital to have the consistent communication of the information contained on the ABTA site. The media were also encouraged to use the latter as their official source of information.

On the third day, stories of the first returning passengers were being reported. These were generally positive towards the rescue effort, although the Foreign and Commonwealth Office came in for criticism for the inability of the helpline to handle the sheer quantity of calls from the public. ABTA chose to support the FCO as a demonstration of the different factors involved all sharing a common goal – the welfare of those involved in the disaster and concern for their relatives and friends.

The financial markets re-opened following the Christmas break on 29 December and a new business angle from the media was added to the mix. What were the short- and long-term implications for the travel industry? At this stage individual tour operators such as First Choice were in a position to communicate specifically on their own business implications, while ABTA continued to address the broader efforts of the travel industry regarding the disaster recovery.

Much of the media coverage was happy to point out that package holidaymakers had a distinct advantage with the support of their tour operators and the 'duty of care' for their customers. While independent travellers were effectively on their own, the repatriation efforts of tour operators were non-discriminatory. The media warmly embraced the fact that the 'rescue flights' by the tour operators were collecting all stranded tourists regardless of who they booked with or if they were independent travellers.

The reputation of an industry enhanced

As Keith Betton commented, 'one would never hope for such a disaster in order to show the travel industry in a good light, yet it is a brutal fact that events such as these throw the industry into the spotlight.' It is an obvious consequence of the devastation to the region that there will be a short-term impact on tourism and that this will impact the travel industry. However the compassionate, committed and united approach taken by the travel industry in the UK was widely and positively received. An interesting reflection of that is how the share prices of the big tour operators were unaffected when the markets re-opened. It is a resilient industry and the goodwill generated by the behaviour of its members in such a disaster will continue to benefit it in the future.

BUSINESS CRISES

Business crises are often created by mismanagement of the company – injudicious expansion or diversification – evident in cases such as Brent Walker, Next, Saatchi & Saatchi, Blue Arrow/Manpower and Ferranti International. Fraudulent behaviour has led to the demise of some major businesses in recent years of which Barings, Enron and Arthur Andersen are key examples. Increasingly, business crises are the result of the failure to have in place an issues management system which enables companies to spot greater forces at work such as the underlying economic tides of the 1980s boom and the early 1990s recession which the late billionaire Sir James Goldsmith of Cavenham Foods did and George Walker of Brent Walker did not.

But the business tribulations of recent years are hardly unique. In 1637, speculation in Dutch tulip bulbs peaked at today's equivalent of more than £500 per bulb and the market collapsed under its own weight, presenting financial nightmares to speculators and their backers.

In 1861, the infant Pony Express in the United States met its sudden demise when Western Union inaugurated the first transcontinental telegraph. In 1906, the San Francisco earthquake devastated the city and its banking community – except for A P Giannini, whose small Bank of America continued making loans during the crisis and went on to become one of the world's largest banks – showing that sometimes a crisis can be turned into an opportunity. In 1912 the 'unsinkable' *Titanic* sank.

William Shakespeare showed a keen business sense when he wrote:

There is a tide in the affairs of men,
Which, taken at the flood, leads on to fortune:
Omitted, all the voyage of their life
Is bound in shallows and in miseries.

CASE STUDY: SAYONARA CITIBANK

Having your 'licence to operate' withdrawn is one very serious and 'final' consequence of poor issues and crisis management. Perceived occasionally as a drastic measure, governments often baulk at the prospect and prefer to pursue fines or regulation as a means of resolution. Its slim likelihood and the 'pinprick' effect of fines to the bottom line have often led big business into a sense of complacency as far as governance is considered. But complacency is a dangerous state of mind. In 2004, Citibank found this out to its cost.

On 17 September, Japan's regulators ordered Citigroup to close its private banking offices in Japan. The world's biggest bank by stockmarket capitalization was to be shut out of the world's second-biggest market for wealthy clients, where it has around 10,000 such customers and once held high hopes for boosting profits.

In issuing its sanctions against Citibank Japan, the country's Financial Services Agency (FSA) cited improper transactions and a flawed system of controls that allowed abuses to take place. It accused the private bank of selling securities and derivatives at 'unfair' prices to its clients, many of whom appeared to have been rich but unworldly, without explaining the risks. It also claimed that Citibank ignored warnings to teach its salespeople better practices and to keep a closer eye on them. On top of that, the FSA took Citibank to task for letting a client open an account that 'could be suspected of being associated with money laundering' while giving too little thought to what it was doing, and for lending money to clients who used the proceeds to manipulate share markets.

The bank, the FSA went on, had constructed 'a law-evading sales system that disregards the laws and regulations of Japan', and had done so 'in a management environment in which profits are given undue importance by the bank headquarters'. This followed continued failure to improve internal controls, despite regulatory warnings going back three years and a scolding by the FSA in May.

Douglas Peterson, who took over Citigroup's Japanese arm in May of the same year, was faced with the need to overhaul the bank's local practices and rebuild its reputation. Citigroup did not try to play the charges down, and chief executive, Charles O Prince III, issued a memo to employees highlighting 'the serious consequences of failing to comply with regulatory requirements and of violating our business standards'.

Citigroup still runs its century-old retail bank in Japan, which had enjoyed a reputation for convenient service and for financial soundness. It also has a corporate bank, which provides cash management, currency trading and other transactions for business clients, plus it has a securities joint venture with Nikko Cordial. However, all three business were left concerned with the knock-on consequences – that Japanese clients would shy away in response to Citigroup's tarnished reputation. While the Japanese private banking unit probably only contributed 0.5 per cent of Citigroup's profits, it is these wider ramifications that worried analysts.

Merrill Lynch, in a report published the week after the Japanese FSA announcement, warned that Citigroup could have difficulty in growing private-banking markets in other Asian countries, such as China and India – the new 'tiger' economies. It also suggested that the bank might attract scrutiny from regulators outside Japan, noting the FSA's remarks about pressure from head office in New York. The report downgraded the bank's shares to neutral from a buy, with a charge that 'aggressive profit incentives [are] overriding judgement'.

There is a threat that Citigroup's aggressive, profit-driven culture has created a 'monster' beyond the control of management. Financial analyst Howard Mason explained: 'Citi has become so large that it is simply not possible to mandate behaviour. The challenge now is to create a culture to inculcate a shared set of values that guide employee behaviour.' It will take more than a memo to affect a case of 'turning an oil tanker'. Prince's memo stated that 'Citigroup's culture must be synonymous with integrity', but as another analyst said, 'these people grow up with claws and fangs'.

Regulators in the United States, UK and across Europe are circling Citigroup, and there is a real threat to the bank's financial goals. As Mason said, 'It may well be that Citi can't achieve its growth ambitions because it cannot safeguard itself properly from regulatory and reputation risk.' Certainly more than a memo is required.

Of course, when looking at different corporate crises, hindsight is the best of all management tools. As *Management Today* (1994) has pointed out, a major corporate crisis never fails to provoke – from journalists, investment managers and fellow businessmen – a chorus of exemplary wisdom after the event.

The writing was on the wall months ago, the pundits will claim. You only had to walk down any high street to see it. Surely you could see the board was incompetent, the management deceitful, the auditors complacent, the advisers gutless, the banks irresponsible.

Why didn't 'they' stop George Walker from buying the William Hill chain of betting shops from Grand Metropolitan for £689 million, later pinpointed by Walker himself as the deal that broke the Brent Walker empire? Why didn't the colleagues and advisers who read the draft of Gerald Ratner's 1991 speech to the Institute of Directors stop him from describing his products as 'total crap'?

The answer is that Walker was overwhelmingly persuasive, that the banks were slavishly keen to back him, that analysts were prepared to argue that a chain of betting shops, with their abundant cashflow, represented a brilliant addition to the Brent Walker portfolio, and that no one at the table had a crystal ball.

In Ratner's case, his upmarket audience thought the joke was funny and true. It was the next day's tabloids, notably the *Sun*, which devoted five pages to the story, a story which tore Ratner apart for his mocking insincerity towards the customers who had made him his fortune.

HOW THE MIGHTY FALL

No company, no matter how financially successful, powerful or reputable, is immune to crises. Very often, organizations ignore the warning signals which are so obvious in hindsight. Here are three examples in the 'accident' category.

CASE STUDY: CHALLENGER SPACE SHUTTLE TRAGEDY

In the early 1980s NASA officials, fearful they could not otherwise obtain congressional funding, mounted an energetic public relations campaign which depicted the shuttle as 'all things to all people'. The agency promised the shuttle would lift scientific payloads into orbit, provide the Pentagon with access to the 'high ground' of space, and offer an efficient, economical means of launching communications satellites which would be a highly profitable enterprise. The shuttle's promoters viewed the future through glasses as rosy as those worn by the Soviet engineers who employed nuclear power at Chernobyl to steamheat the suburbs of Gorky and Odessa.

Faced with spiralling costs and ever-lengthening delays, NASA cut back its training programme, cannibalized parts from other spacecraft and deferred spending half a billion dollars on safety. There was an increasingly wide gap between the facts and the shuttle's glowing public image.

In spite of numerous warnings from NASA engineers – in fact impassioned pleas, unusual for technical people – that the shuttle could not take off in certain temperatures, NASA officials increasingly chose to believe in the image which, in turn, drifted ever further from reality. The odds of a fatal shuttle crash were estimated variously at one in a hundred to one in a hundred thousand. The Challenger mission, the programme's 25th, proved these odds had been incredibly optimistic.

The justification for NASA's trust in its flawed spacecraft was reduced to the fact that it hadn't blown up yet. As at Chernobyl, the accumulation of an impressive safety record in the past came to be taken as a guarantee that nothing could go wrong in the future.

'The argument that the same risk was flown before without failure is often accepted as an argument for the safety of accepting it again,' noted Richard Feynman, the Nobel Prize-winning physicist who served on the presidential commission. But, Feynman added, 'when playing Russian roulette, the fact the first shot got off safely is little comfort for the next'.

It was Feynman who cut through reams of bureaucracy on the O-ring question (which caused the space shuttle failure) by simply immersing a piece of O-ring material in a bucket of iced water during a break in the committee hearings and noting it grew brittle. The trouble with NASA's belief in its own press clippings, Feynman said, was that nature had not read them. 'Reality must take precedence over public relations for nature cannot be fooled,' he concluded.

The Challenger disaster set back the NASA programme by decades.

CASE STUDY: PIPER ALPHA CATASTROPHE

On the night of 6 July 1988 the oil production platform, Piper Alpha, operated by Occidental Oil in the UK sector of the North Sea, blew up and was completely destroyed. The disaster killed 167 men, 109 of them dying from smoke inhalation. No system existed to lead the men on the platform to safety. Only 61 survived.

A leak of gas condensate, which later exploded, was caused when a pump was activated while, unknown to the control room, it was under repair. A blank flange fitted to a valve was not leak-tight. The initial explosion caused extensive damage and spread fire through the platform. Gas pipelines leading to other platforms in the area ruptured and intensified the blaze.

Lord Cullen, who led and wrote the report on the disaster, concluded Occidental Oil had not provided adequate training to make its work permit system effective; monitoring of the system was inadequate; communication was poor. Action following a 1987 fatality involving a failure of the work permit system had no lasting effect on practice.

The report said Occidental management should have been more aware of the need for a high standard of incident prevention and fire-fighting. They were too easily satisfied that the work permit system was being operated correctly, relying on the absence of feedback of problems as indicating that all was well.

> The management adopted a superficial attitude to the assessment of the risk of major hazard. They failed to ensure emergency training was being provided as intended. The platform personnel and management were not prepared for a major emergency as they should have been. The safety policies and procedures were in place; the practice was deficient.

Occidental Oil's UK assets were subsequently acquired by another oil company and it has vanished as an entity in the UK North Sea.

CASE STUDY: PADDINGTON RAIL DISASTER

Two commuter trains crashed into each other at high speed at 8.11 am on 5 October 1999, killing 30 people and injuring 160. Today, if you went out on to the street and asked people to name the two train companies involved, chances are most people would not remember. Would you?

But ask people to name the company that was vilified by the press after the accident and everyone would say 'Railtrack'. So why did Railtrack get it in the neck when most people can't even remember the names of the train companies – Thames Trains and Great Western Trains?

The answer, we suggest, is that when the accident happened Railtrack had no credit left in its 'reputation bank'. In fact, its account was in the red. There were a number of reasons for this:

- a widely held perception that Railtrack put 'profits before safety' – that the only stakeholders it cared about were its shareholders;

- recommendations after the Clapham and Southall crashes had not been implemented;
- the perception that rail services had deteriorated since privatization;
- Railtrack bosses were 'fat cats' and paid too much.

Because Railtrack had no reputational credit among its stakeholders, other than shareholders, when the accident occurred, it instantly became the villain of the piece. It possessed no reputational credit upon which it could draw, in this worst of all possible circumstances, to help it through.

Needless to say, as soon as the two train companies involved saw that Railtrack was getting all the blame from the media, they both introduced a 'no interview' policy and vanished without trace (not a bad policy in the circumstances).

Immediately after the accident, Railtrack responded well. Its CEO, Gerald Corbett, was on the scene within the hour giving media interviews, but after a few days he got tired of media questioning and handed the role over to other executives in the company. His refusal to appear on *Newsnight* because 'he was too tired' became a headline story in the print media.

In our experience, it is always a mistake to change the spokesperson role in a major crisis because viewers and listeners begin to identify with, and often sympathize with, the spokesperson. Of course it is a tiring, and sometimes irritating, role, but you absolutely cannot give up on it until media appetites are satisfied. As we often say to our clients: 'This is like wrestling a gorilla; you take a break when the gorilla takes a break'.

One of the substitute spokesmen then went on the BBC Radio 4 *Today* programme. In response to a question from interviewer John Humphrys, he angrily stated, 'It's about time we stopped this national *hysteria* about the safety of rail travel'. He used the 'hysteria' word at a time when the front carriages of the two trains were still locked together, some of the bodies had still not been identified, and Paddington station was still closed – inconveniencing thousands of commuters.

What he said was strictly true – rail travel is the safest form of travel after air travel. But he failed to factor in what we call the 'emotional dynamics' of the situation and caused a national outrage through his remarks. Railtrack's share price spiralled even further and the company was forced to issue a public apology later that day.

The company went on to take another extraordinary action. In a major crisis, when the company becomes the focal point of attention from hundreds of reporters, the only sensible way to communicate with them is via news conferences (see page 211), supported by constant updates of a website if possible. Inexplicably, but probably on bad advice, Gerald Corbett chose to visit the offices of the main London-based newspapers to give individual interviews. He began with the *Daily Mirror* because it is the tabloid most widely read by the Railtrack workforce. The workforce by this time were in a highly demoralized state. Passengers were spitting at them and they were threatening to go on strike over safety issues.

However, during the course of the interview, Gerald Corbett got a question he found to be insulting. It went along the lines of, 'Mr Corbett, if the inquiry finds Railtrack to have been negligent, will you resign and do you expect to be prosecuted for corporate manslaughter?' These are perfectly legitimate questions and are perfectly answerable.

But Mr Corbett took umbrage and stormed out of the *Daily Mirror* offices – hotly pursued by *Daily Mirror* photographers. Next day he found himself on the front page under the headline, 'RATTLED! Railtrack boss walks out of interview over "deeply offensive" question'. This triggered a smear campaign by the *Daily Mirror* and the whole one-to-one interview strategy backfired.

Later, the Hatfield tragedy occurred and, under huge pressure from the Prime Minister and Deputy Prime Minister, Corbett had no option but to resign.

What have been the consequences for Railtrack? They began with the company being stripped of its safety role, which was handed over to the government's Health and Safety Executive; £280 million being wiped from the company's value in 10 days because of a collapse in the share price; and deepened loss of stakeholder confidence in the company.

Paddington always seemed to be an accident waiting to happen. As the *Wall Street Journal* wrote at the time of the accident, 'There is no conflict between safety and profit, unless you assume it's good business to kill your customers, smash up your capital stock and expose yourself to tort litigation'.

By May 2001, Railtrack had reported a much-worse-than-expected loss of £534 million for the year. This was the company's first loss since privatization and was largely due to a £733 million payment spent on a rail renewal programme and compensation claims in the wake of the Hatfield crash in October 2000, which claimed four lives. The disruption led to huge compensation payouts to train operating companies.

Finally, in October 2001, the company was declared bankrupt, de-listed from the London Stock Exchange, and today represents one of the UK's most embarrassing corporate failures.

Three brief examples of crises in the 'accident' category but some themes are identifiable: the confusion of image with reality; the belief that because it hasn't happened in the past, it won't happen in the future; the vain hope that because 'the procedures' have been written the accident can't happen and, in each case, a failure to communicate appropriately.

CEOs ARE NOT INFALLIBLE

In the examples of Brent Walker and Ratner, why, instead of shouting 'stop', have the combined forces of non-executive directors, auditors, public relations advisers, investment analysts and journalists been so often complicit in encouraging chief executives to believe in their own infallibility?

These are circumstances which particularly affected – but not exclusively – the kind of entrepreneurial, share-price-driven companies which came to fame in the 1980s. The crises which affected them have tended to be financial rather than operational.

In some famous cases, outright fraud has either temporarily weakened a company (Guinness and Mirror Group) or destroyed it altogether (Barings Bank and Enron); in others, excessive appetite for acquisitions, or exposure to property, has stretched the balance sheet to breaking point. In another 'business' category, clever, well-focused businesses such as GPA (in aircraft leasing) and Tiphook (in containers) were suddenly revealed to have misread the downturn in their own highly specialized markets.

The common thread here is that, in almost every case, there is one person in charge usually the founder of the business, a natural optimist, risk-taker and autocrat, perhaps with no more than two or three long-standing associates whom he really takes into his confidence.

CASE STUDY: MARKS & SPENCER

Marks & Spencer, under the stewardship of its autocratic former boss, Sir Richard Greenbury, completely failed to spot changes in consumer buying habits of clothing and consumer expectations of a more exciting shopping experience.

Because for a time, indeed for a long time, Marks & Spencer customers all wanted to look the same ('middle class, middle aged and middle England', as someone quipped) it didn't mean they were going to stay like that forever. The problem was compounded by a corporate culture that discouraged entrepreneurial flair and rewarded conformity and sycophancy.

Where was the risk radar screen in St Michael House? Certainly not switched on. Marks & Spencer was not boycotted. It was just abandoned.

To make matters even worse, the company had a policy of no communication with the press under Sir Richard. But if a journalist dared to write a story about the company and got a fact wrong, it has been alleged that Sir Richard would call the hapless journalist personally and blow him (verbally) to kingdom come. Needless to say, when Sir Richard retired and the company was on the skids, there was a legacy of embittered journalists only too happy to sharpen their knives and stick them into the company.

Veteran company doctors have been quoted as saying that if there is one reliable indicator of a company that will eventually run into trouble, it's having a charismatic, high-profile chairman. Tiphook's founder-chairman Robert Montague, suntanned, Ferrari-driving sponsor of the Conservative winter ball, has been cited as a classic example. But this may be an unduly pessimistic view; Richard Branson (Virgin) and Anita Roddick (The Body Shop) still buck this trend.

Nonetheless, a past president of the Society of Insolvency Practitioners has said the most common misjudgement made by companies in incipient financial difficulties is that they are not quick enough to change the person at the top.

The one sure way to buy the company time when it is on the edge of trouble is to appoint a new chief executive. So long as he (or she) can put up a reasonable business plan the banks will almost always give the new CEO six months.

PRODUCT-RELATED CRISES

The contamination scare which prompted the withdrawal of millions of bottles of Lucozade from shops throughout Britain (13 November 1991) is a nightmare of a kind which has come to haunt a growing number of consumer product companies over the past two decades.

In 1990 Perrier was forced to recall every bottle of its popular sparkling water worldwide after some were found to contain traces of benzene. More recently, in June 1998, Coca-Cola faced a contamination scare in Belgium, but appeared to have learnt none of the lessons from the Perrier experience. (See page 150.)

A few years prior to the Perrier incident, Tylenol, a headache pill made by Johnson & Johnson in the United States, was temporarily withdrawn after an extortionist laced capsules with cyanide, killing seven people.

The cost of dealing with such recalls can be huge. Industry experts have estimated that the cost of recalling suspect products from shops is nine times as much as delivering them in the first place.

This pales into insignificance, however, when compared to the costs of lost production and rebuilding public confidence in products once they have been declared safe. Johnson & Johnson is estimated to have spent more than £50 million to recover from the Tylenol crisis, and Perrier twice as much. However, the manner in which each company managed its product crisis was entirely different – as were the consequences.

CASE STUDY: THE TYLENOL TALE

Never in corporate history has an organization in crisis gained as much public and editorial sympathy as Johnson & Johnson did in the United States for its conduct throughout the Tylenol-related poisonings and their aftermath. The day before cyanide-laced Tylenol tablets caused deaths in the Chicago area in September 1982, Tylenol commanded 35 per cent of the US adult over-the-counter analgesic market, accounted for some $450 million of annual sales and contributed over 15 per cent of Johnson & Johnson's overall profits.

At first, just three deaths from cyanide poisoning were associated with the capsules. As the news spread, as many as 250 deaths and illnesses in various parts of the United States were suspected of being part of a widespread pattern. Eventually enquiries from the media alone were logged at over 2,500.

After testing 8,000,000 tablets, Johnson & Johnson found no more than 75 contaminated tablets, all from one batch. The final death toll was seven, all in the Chicago area, but the alarm had been spread nationwide. Surveys showed later that 94 per cent of consumers were aware Tylenol was associated with the poisonings.

Key to the success of the way in which the Tylenol case was handled lay in the assumption of the 'worst possible scenario'. Ironically, the closest thing the company had to a crisis plan was its credo that its first concern must be for the public and its customers – a credo which ultimately saved its reputation.

To its credit, Johnson & Johnson lost little time in recalling millions of bottles of its extra-strength Tylenol capsules. The company reportedly spent half a million dollars warning doctors, hospitals and distributors of the possible dangers. At the same time, the *Wall Street Journal* wrote: 'the company chose to take a large loss rather than expose anyone to further risk. The "anti-corporation" movement may have trouble squaring that with the devil theories it purveys'.

The company also resisted the temptation to relaunch the product as soon as it was known to be safe and the lunatic who contaminated the capsules had been arrested. At the time the US government and local authorities in Chicago and elsewhere were pushing for new drug safety laws. Johnson & Johnson saw a marketing opportunity and took it by edging out its competitors in the $1.2 billion analgesic market. It was the first in the industry, after the recall, to respond to the 'national mandate' for tamper-resistant packaging and new regulations imposed by the US Food and Drug Administration.

Johnson & Johnson later went on to relaunch the product and win the Silver Anvil Award of the Public Relations Society of America for its handling of the crisis. Within five months of the disaster, the company had recovered 70 per cent of its one-third share of this huge market. The company had clearly positioned itself as the champion of the consumer, given meaning to the concept of corporate social responsibility, and demonstrated communication expertise hard to equal since.

The plaudits which Johnson & Johnson received leading to, most importantly, market share recovery, stemmed from its decision to anticipate the worst. The company could have restricted the recall to the Chicago area and saved itself millions of dollars. Had it done so, however, its Tylenol sales would almost certainly have suffered more dramatic losses because of poison-tampering hysteria. Their losses would have been far more difficult to recover because of continued uncertainty and loss of public trust. What was happening to Tylenol users in Chicago was receiving coast-to-coast television coverage in America. (If you had been sitting in your New York apartment, had seen the news about Tylenol, and then developed a headache would you have rushed out to the corner drugstore to purchase a bottle of Tylenol? Most unlikely.)

CASE STUDY: WHAT TOOK THE FIZZ OUT OF PERRIER

In complete contrast to Johnson & Johnson, when Perrier found traces of benzene in its water, it dismissed the problem as 'a little affair which, in a few days, will all be forgotten'. Less than 24 hours later Perrier shares were falling like ten green bottles off the wall as more contaminated samples were discovered around the world.

In the United States the company decided voluntarily to clear millions of bottles from supermarket shelves. The company in France put this down to American wimpishness rather than a real health scare. To some extent the difference in outlook by the two countries was reflected by their marketing techniques. In the United States Perrier advertisements proclaimed 'Perrier is Perfect' while in France advertisements claimed *'Perrier C'est Fou'*, ie it is crazy, bubbly and enlivens the spirit.

The company's spokesman in France went on to imply consumers in France were less neurotic than in other countries; they didn't worry about such things. Maybe not, but his remarks were reported in other key markets and the company's apparent lack of concern for its customers caused outrage. Company executives in different countries made conflicting statements and clearly no worldwide strategic recall plan was in place.

Under increasing pressure, four days after the initial discovery of the benzene traces in the United States, Perrier decided to withdraw the product worldwide amid proclamations that 'with this action we have saved the image of Perrier all over the world'. By then, however, the damage to the product's reputation had been done. The company had been seen to procrastinate and be inconsistent in its messages about the seriousness of the problem. It was ridiculed by the media (in this country particularly by the now defunct *Today* newspaper).

People drink bottled water partly because they think it is chic and partly because they believe it to be purer than tap water. It is certainly marketed on a 'platform of purity'. Implementing a worldwide recall of a key product is a huge decision to take because of the financial consequences, especially when the reality of the size of the problem is tiny. However, the company which is not seen to take seriously the genuine concerns of its customers, does so at its peril.

Research undertaken across Europe by MORI for design company Henrion, Ludlow & Schmidt in 1995 found Perrier's corporate identity to have been the second most damaged as a result of corporate error. The most damaged was believed to be Shell's after the Brent Spar debacle. Interestingly, the survey was conducted in the same year as the Brent Spar issue but *five years after* the Perrier recall (see Figure 7.2).

Even after Perrier's chaotic recall the situation might have been recoverable. A brilliant advertising campaign signalled the end of the problem and that Perrier was back. But it was back, inexplicably, in 750 ml bottles instead of the original 1 litre bottles – yet it cost at least the same amount as the original bigger bottle! The inference seemed to be that customers should pay the cost of the company's own negligence. The company never recovered market share and, with its own share price weakened, became easy prey for a predator. Nestlé soon came along and swallowed it up.

Which specific corporate error or blunder of recent years had most effect on a company's identity?

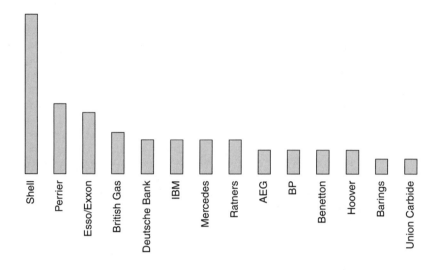

Source: 'Silver Lining', MORI, 1995

Figure 7.2 *The effects of crises on different organizations' standing*

CASE STUDY: COCA-COLA

Lessons it might have learnt from history

On 8 and 9 June 1999, more than 230 schoolchildren in Belgium claimed illness after drinking Coca-Cola products. More customer complaints came in during the following days. A further 80 complained of similar symptoms in France. The general symptoms included vomiting, dizziness and headaches. Ultimately, in March 2000, results of an independent investigation by Belgium's High Hygiene Council at the government's request revealed that the vast majority of those people with the symptoms had suffered mass sociogenic illness (MSI), or 'mass hysteria'. What emerged from Belgium was an organization unable to handle public perceptions in a crisis. While Coca-Cola searched for the facts – hard to establish when dealing with MSI – it failed to address the relationship between stakeholders and its own reputation.

On the morning of 8 June, children in Bornem, near Antwerp, who had drunk 200 ml bottles of Coke and Coke Light complained of the symptoms. The headmaster immediately called Coca-Cola Belgium and the company launched a high-priority investigation into the possible link between the illness and its products. It identified an 'off-spec' batch of the product manufactured in Antwerp most probably caused by defective carbon dioxide. In the afternoon of the same day Coca-Cola issued a product recall for that batch number, and by the end of the following day all the bottles had been removed from shelves. The head of sales for Coca-Cola even visited those in hospital to check after their welfare. So far so good for the world's biggest brand.

However, on the day of the incident Flemish commercial TV station VTM had run the news story during a prime-time bulletin that 37 schoolchildren had fallen ill after drinking *cans* of Coke. The company called the station to ask for a correction to bottles in any subsequent bulletins.

The next day other schoolchildren, and indeed adults, across Flanders said they were suffering as well. These cases, however, referred to cans (produced in Dunkirk), not the batch of bottles from the Antwerp plant. In fact, it later emerged that 49 per cent hadn't actually touched a Coca-Cola product at all and the symptoms were the consequence of MSI. Understandably, Coca-Cola could not find a fault causing these new reported cases.

From 10 June, and mistakenly, the company took an increasingly centralized approach to its communications response – with heavy involvement from its Atlanta headquarters. For four days, Coca-Cola's message remained that it was merely a bad odour that was causing the nausea and other side effects, but there was no risk to public health. As a precaution, the batch of defective product was recalled, but with no evidence of a fault related to the cans, there was no reason for a wider/total recall. However, as a consequence of the company's failure to provide a clear explanation, the Belgian Minister of Public Health simply ordered Coca-Cola to withdraw all products for which his ministry had received complaints. On Monday 14 June – the day after general elections in which the government suffered defeat for its alleged mishandling of the discovery of the carcinogen dioxin in a range of meats, eggs and various dairy products – he ordered a total recall of all Coca-Cola products.

Cold, scientific news releases were posted on the company's website, which failed to take account of the emotional dynamics of the situation. For those suffering and the wider public, this felt like a dismissive uncaring corporate response, triggering widespread anger and public concern, evidenced by the deluge of calls to Belgian poison centres – 900 calls in one day.

Independently a Belgian professor, and acknowledged authority on these matters, hypothesized in a television interview that it was MSI without having checked the patients first. There was understandable outrage from parents – and the credibility of this hypothesis was immediately undermined. As the facts got out of control, Coca-Cola stopped communicating while desperately looking for an explanation to offer the health minister.

It was only after the Belgian and French governments insisted that the products were withdrawn that the company finally mobilized the chairman and CEO, Douglas Ivestor, for a visit to Europe to help manage the crisis and bring it to a close. Coca-Cola took the right steps by withdrawing the contaminated batch initially, but then lost the high ground when it began arguing against a total product recall.

Its biggest mistake, however, was in failing to empower local Belgian and French managements to take care of their own communications response. Back

151

in Atlanta, the corporate communications people had little idea that the Belgian government – at election time – was in a crisis of its own over criticism for the way it had handled the simultaneous dioxin food health scare. The government was anxious to prove to the electorate that it did take food safety issues seriously, and jumped at the chance of forcing Coca-Cola to withdraw all its products.

In France, the government was equally anxious to show its concern over food safety issues and quickly followed the Belgian lead. The governments looked like the good guys and Coca-Cola was definitely the bad guy.

Not communicating is not an option – if you haven't anything to say, then explain that and the reasons for it, and add when you do expect to have information. While Coca-Cola was frantically trying to identify the causes for the apparent anomalies in the consumption patterns, the Belgian Minister for Health was anxious to hear what went wrong directly from the company, not the media. In that context, Coca-Cola was not open about the fact that it didn't know.

It seems almost inconceivable that the biggest brand in the world, valued at $50 billion, did not act more promptly and with more regard for the protection of its most precious asset – its brand. The root causes of the wholly inappropriate response lay in what we call the 'head office knows best' syndrome, and an overly internalized perspective on the crisis at hand. Global organizations are like octopi; all the operations are at the end of the 'tentacles', and this is where there is the most potential for things to go wrong. The centre of the octopus must train and empower management at the end of the tentacles to take the right decisions and make the right responses, because they know the local scene best.

The cost of Coca-Cola's mistakes was enormous:

- At the end of 1999 the company announced a 31 per cent drop in profits.
- By losing free media opportunities to reassure the public as the crisis unfolded, Coca-Cola had to launch costly, post-crisis advertising and promotional campaigns.
- Competitors seized the opportunities to fill Coca-Cola's empty shelf space and challenged the company's 49 per cent share of the market.
- The total cost to the company was $103 million (£66 million) – nearly double the original estimate.
- The majority of media coverage on Coca-Cola following the crisis referred to a company 'struggling to rebuild its reputation'.

These mistakes might easily have been avoided if Coca-Cola had taken a quick look at the Perrier case study.

After the Belgian contamination issue, the new CEO of Coca-Cola reorganized the company away from its centralized structure, and introduced an appropriate balance between local autonomy and global coordination. Coca-Cola now has systems in place to ensure that all offices are equipped to handle crises in their own localities, and can disseminate information internally to enable other markets to manage any consequences in their countries. Moreover, the other key principle now is to manage crises as they are perceived from the outside – perception is reality.

And then this happened.

COCA-COLA'S DASANI
Lessons it learnt from its own history

The withdrawal of its bottled water, Dasani, in the UK after just five weeks on the shelves is often referred to as another Coca-Cola disaster. However, if anything, it is a good example of effective crisis management; with clear and focused objectives to successfully protect the company's reputation. Often in crisis management it is important to identify what is the acceptable cost or what needs to be sacrificed 'for the greater good'. This was exactly the stance taken by Coca-Cola with Dasani in the UK.

The Dasani brand was first introduced to consumers in the United States in 1999 as a bottled, purified water, and had become a huge success there. The United States was a growth engine for purified water (from mains supply) as opposed to source water (for example, from an alpine glacier or natural spring). Dasani quickly grew to become the number two bottled water brand, behind Pepsi's purified water, Aquafina, with sales growing by 50 per cent each year to reach 1.3 billion litres.

Dasani's purification process involves taking a mains water supply through four stages of production before it is bottled. Passing it through three separate filters is followed by a 'reverse osmosis' filtration perfected by NASA to purify fluids on spacecraft. The pure, filtered water then has minerals added to enhance the 'pure taste' before ozone is injected to keep the water sterile. Following the clear success of the brand in the United States, Coca-Cola planned to replicate it around the globe.

The plan in Europe was to roll out the Dasani brand across the UK, Germany and France. Extensive market research in 2003 identified that taste was the most important factor for British consumers in choosing a bottled water, not its source. After countless 'taste test' focus groups, the right mix of added minerals was identified to appeal to the British palate. The purified water was to be produced at Coca-Cola's plant in Sidcup, Kent, and in the autumn of 2003 the new product was successfully sold into the retail trade with a full explanation of the process. The British Dasani met with the tastes of the public, and the shops were right behind the product: everything was geared up for the consumer launch on 10 February 2004.

February 2004 was when the problems started for Coca-Cola

While Coca-Cola was forthcoming to the trade on the purification process of Dasani, it appeared it was less prepared to be so open in its marketing to consumers. The front of the distinctive blue packaging carried the label 'pure' and the back 'purified'. Neither was technically incorrect, but nowhere in its packaging or marketing did it overtly explain the source of the water (the mains) when extolling the virtues of its purification process. This left a potential window of opportunity for knockers to claim that Coca-Cola was covering up. The company seriously underestimated the response of its bottled water competitors as it aimed to come marching in on their market share.

The Natural Mineral Water Association (NMWA) got active. Its first act after the Dasani launch was to lodge an 'official complaint' about the 'pure' claim with the UK Food Standards Agency (FSA), the industry regulator. It then put the wheels in motion for a media reaction to the product.

BBC Radio 4's *You and Yours* programme delivered a balanced feature on 'why Coke was targeting water', and *The Grocer*, the food industry's highly influential trade magazine, ran a piece on the 'actual' source of Dasani. The journalist of the article didn't think anyone else would pick up on it, but *The Grocer* is almost required reading for the consumer affairs writers of national newspapers seeking to scoop the next scare story. It was actually the Press Association that picked up on the story first, and after it appeared on the newswire the story went ballistic.

The following day the story was splashed across the daily papers. Headlines like 'The real sting', a play on Coke's 'The real thing' slogan, and the more obvious 'Coke sells tap water for 95p' could hardly have been any worse for Coca-Cola and its new baby. The tabloids drew on the uncanny parallel with an episode in the BBC sitcom *Only Fools and Horses*, in which Del Boy and Rodney take ordinary tap water from their Peckham allotment and bottle it up to sell as Peckham Spring. 'Are they taking us for plonkers!' yelled the *Daily Star*.

The company responded by re-emphasizing that Dasani was purer than tap water thanks to its sophisticated processes. The media went to the mains water suppliers' association, Water UK, for comment. It expressed concerns that Dasani was implying that tap water was impure. Far from it, Water UK rallied, consumers did not need to buy Dasani to get excellent quality, healthy water; 'Tap water is pure'.

At this stage the Dasani brand was taking a series of heavy body blows from the widespread media scrutiny. The product itself was a perfectly valid, and potentially highly desirable and successful, entrant into the market. However, Coca-Cola had not effectively tuned in the risk radar to the potential issues and the behaviour of key stakeholder groups. It completely underestimated the reaction of its competitors, and in not appreciating the public sensitivity around certain potential issues, left the door open for NMWA attack. Water has a peculiar place in our collective psyche. It is one thing we almost expect for free (like air). We grumble about our water rates/metering, and it took years for mineral waters to grab a foothold in the UK. The fact that Coca-Cola was not seen to be open about the 'tap water' source for Dasani led to the automatic assumption that Coke was trying to hoodwink consumers into buying something that wasn't what they thought it was. Nobody likes to be taken for a fool, and the media loves a 'rip off Britain' story.

For a newly launched brand with an image problem, the last thing it needed was a health scare. It got one. On Sunday 14 March, Coca-Cola Division Technical was informed that one sample of Dasani water was found to contain a level of bromate exceeding the specified maximum allowed. Coca-Cola ran a textbook product test and recall procedure. Following confirmation of the bromate levels and the cause from subsequent testing, Coca-Cola informed the FSA and agreed a course of action with it. The levels of bromate exceeded the UK standards (although they were lower than European standards), and while the FSA confirmed that there was no immediate health or safety risk, on 19 March the product was withdrawn by Coca-Cola as a precautionary measure.

Product recalls come and go all the time, and if handled sensibly and in a straightforward manner can have little impact on the good standing of a brand. However, Dasani was a brand on its knees following the media onslaught. Coca-Cola was facing a crisis with potentially widespread international consequences. Wise decisions were required on how to manage the product recall in order to minimize the damage.

The Coca-Cola Incident Management Crisis Resolution Team (IMCR), comprising UK-based representatives from both the company and the bottler, worked day and night to manage towards the most successful outcome. Coca-Cola's director of communication for Europe and the Middle East, Jonathon Chandler, led the international communications aspects. His objectives were clear: to protect the global reputation of Coca-Cola, to protect the reputation of Dasani in its 20 markets outside Europe, and to be seen to act responsibly in the UK.

Coca-Cola had to act quickly and decisively to control the communications agenda and avoid media speculation escalating the issue globally. It had to be open – seen to do the right thing and heard to say the right words – to deny oxygen to speculation and leave the story with nowhere to go.

The company broke the announcement over the newswires, and the communications team then handled over 100 media interviews during the course of the day. 'We volunteered to withdraw the product, and were able to make clear we understood the problem, its significance and that we knew how to fix it,' said Chandler. The media announcement was crucial to the whole process. Explains Chandler:

> A story like this is going to go around the world, whether we like it or not. What counts at this moment is whether the story is clear, accurate, and people can decide for themselves whether it is relevant to them. We satisfy billions of consumers in 200 countries with more than 300 different brands; we had a situation unique to one brand in one country. We spoke to the newswires first as I believe they share the same objectives of accuracy and objectivity. That ensured the rest of the world got the story accurately and from a reliable source, rather than through the sensationalist lens of the British tabloid press. It takes time to get round to everybody in the media at times like that. But during the news cycle, nobody was left unanswered.

The immediate withdrawal of Dasani from the UK market, after the product recall, was the acceptable price to pay in meeting the company's objectives. In announcing the product recall the company nailed the issue tightly to the British product and was seen to act responsibly. The issue was restricted to the specific mineral composition of the UK Dasani. All other Dasani markets were equipped with the facts and able to validate the safety of their own products, proactively communicating their test results.

Coca-Cola had learnt some very valuable lessons following the Belgian incident in 1999. The Incident Management and Crisis Resolution Team concept was created after that situation to work in tandem with Coca-Cola's many global bottling partners. It moved swiftly into action and enabled speed of action through local ownership of the issue as opposed to the centralized approach that had existed before. As Chandler says, local ownership was critical. The company was able to work promptly with the local regulator, act immediately and address all the relevant stakeholders while simultaneously equipping other Coca-Cola markets with the information and tools to manage the issue in their countries.

In light of the image problems for Dasani in the UK, the decision to withdraw completely was seen as the company acting responsibly, and removed any fuel for the story to escalate. Analysts welcomed the approach, and the Coca-Cola share price was not affected. The company was able to protect its Dasani interests elsewhere in the world, and it is not even beyond the realms of possibility that due to the thoroughness and responsibility of its approach Coca-Cola may well be able to reintroduce the brand back into the UK in the future.

However, well as the crisis response was managed, the fact remains that it only truly became a crisis because of the escalation of other issues that impacted the standing of the Dasani brand. A recall of a product of good standing is infrequently a crisis, but the baggage attached to Dasani made it one in this case. More honed processes for identifying potential issues at their emerging stage and addressing them before they escalate would have helped Coca-Cola in this instance. Ironically, the company had recognized this and was in the process of introducing a new, more rigorous stakeholder review procedure at the time of the Dasani situation. This new approach to its marketing planning process is now widely used across Coca-Cola.

WHO WILL HAVE A CRISIS?

Next week there can't be any crisis. My schedule is already full.
Dr Henry Kissinger while US Secretary of State

Companies could cite a variety of reasons which prevent them from addressing crisis issues before they occur. Some believe their size, location or the type of business they are in will protect them. Others believe issues and crisis management to be a luxury, or believe crisis is an inevitable cost of doing business. (Indeed, a survey conducted a few years ago among prominent US businessmen found they believed a crisis in business was as inevitable as paying taxes and death.)

In our experience, some executives have difficulty admitting to themselves that their companies could face a crisis because in doing so they would have to question the excellence of their company and, in some cases, even their own professionalism.

Others subscribe to the fallacy that well-managed companies simply do not have crises. This trait can affect even the most public relations conscious companies. Indeed, it can affect them more than others. When Nestlé was attacked for selling infant formula in developing countries, where it was often mixed with contaminated water, the company's belief in its own caring, nurturing image made it difficult for senior executives to accept the criticism. There was a prevailing belief that anyone who attacked Nestlé must be a loony or a communist or both.

According to business academic Ian Mitroff, in his book co-authored with Thierry Pauchant, *We're So Big, Nothing Bad Can Happen to Us* (1990), 'how people react to crises provides one of the most powerful windows, if not *the* most powerful window, into the souls of people and their institutions'.

He divides 'crisis-prone' corporations into two types: destructive companies, which believe it is their fundamental right, even their duty, to exploit all human, financial and natural resources for the profit of their shareholders; and tragic companies, which understand the need for change but do not have the emotional or cultural resources to make it happen.

Mitroff cites Exxon Corporation as a 'destructive' company (see Chapter 8) for which little can be done; 'but tragic companies can be helped by outside experts, analysts who can identify problems not apparent to those too close to them and inhibited by fear for their jobs'.

As recently as the early 1990s some companies (especially in the United States) even avoided crisis anticipation because of legal liabilities they might assume in doing so. The concern was that if companies identified potential risk areas and failed to guard against them, they might be more responsible legally than if they had not bothered to investigate in the first place.

There used to be an attitude of what you didn't know wouldn't hurt you. Nowadays, however, the courts say if you didn't know you should have known (see Chapter 10).

In this age of corporate accountability, and for all the reasons we have argued in previous chapters, the truth is that no organization is safe from a crisis and the potentially lasting damage it can cause. It is no longer a question of whether a major crisis will strike; it is only a matter of when, which type and how.

WHAT KIND OF CRISIS WILL HAPPEN?

In research conducted for us at the start of the 1990s by Business Planning & Research International among senior executives from the *Times Top 1,000* companies, the following crises were regarded as most likely to occur:

- environmental pollution;
- product defect;
- unwanted takeover bid;
- sabotage;
- death of senior management member;
- kidnap of senior management member;
- computer breakdown;
- industrial dispute;
- fraud.

More recent research among senior UK company executives, conducted by Infoplan in 1994, showed a shift in belief as to what kinds of crises might occur. The majority of respondents from 250 major British companies thought sabotage, extortion and product defects were the most likely forms of crises (see Figure 7.3). It is interesting to note the underlying current of optimism here that the most likely forms of crises were seen to be events 'done to the organization', ie, sabotage and extortion, rather than any fault caused by management error – a hope which is certainly at odds with slightly more recent findings from the United States.

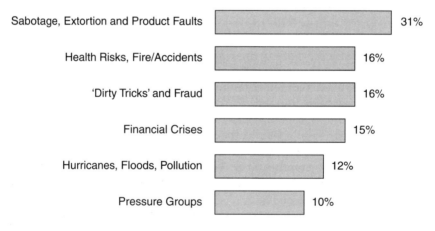

Source: Infoplan International, Japan, 1994

Figure 7.3 *The most likely causes of crises according to respondents*

Research conducted in 1995 by the Kentucky-based Institute for Crisis Management showed that company executives and consultants had been focusing on the wrong kinds of crises. Business crisis stereotypes such as fires and explosions accounted for only 17 per cent of 1995 crisis news stories. The real problems had revolved around white-collar crime, labour disputes and company mismanagement.

The fastest growing categories in the US were class action lawsuits, executive dismissals, hostile takeovers and sexual harassment – all of which had more than doubled since 1990. The news stories on these management crises were small in number compared to white-collar crime, labour disputes and mismanagement but they invariably attracted the media's attention because of the gut-wrenching personal and professional problems which they surfaced (see Figure 7.4).

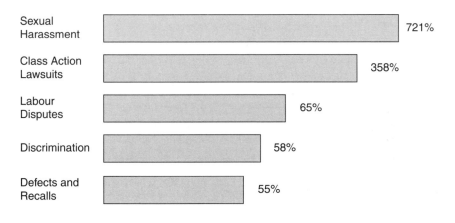

Source: Institute for Crisis Management, Kentucky, USA

Figure 7.4 *Fastest growing business crisis categories 1990–95*

This same research also revealed that executives not employees had been responsible for most crisis news coverage in the 1990s – management decisions were directly or indirectly involved in 78 per cent of 56,000 crisis news stories.

The most crisis-prone US industries in 1995, measured by the number of crisis news stories devoted to them, are shown in Figure 7.5.

For the purposes of the remainder of this book we are going to use our own definition of a crisis:

an event which causes the company to become the subject of widespread, potentially unfavourable, attention from the international and national media and other groups such as customers, shareholders, employees and their families, politicians, trade unionists and environmental pressure groups who, for one reason or another, have a vested interest in the activities of the organization.

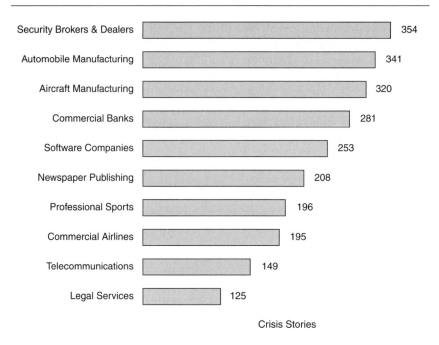

Source: Institute for Crisis Management, Kentucky, USA

Figure 7.5 *Most crisis-prone industries in 1995*

Foot-in-mouth disease: careless talk costs – reputation

Often an organization can find itself slap bang in the middle of a crisis when it has done nothing wrong by deed. Out of the blue, a company can find itself at the centre of outrage and with its reputation in tatters. It can occur without any emergence of an embryonic issue, without any stakeholder or NGO pressure and without any accident. Sometimes all it takes is a careless phrase, a throwaway line or an 'off the record comment'. It is always entirely self-induced, and can occasionally destroy an organization that has actually done nothing wrong. Usually it is the consequence of a company or individual having no empathy for its most important stakeholders – not holding them sacrosanct and being dismissive of them.

The following are just some examples of instances where careless 'gaffes' by executives have cost their organization:

● In 2003 Barclays Bank boss, Matthew Barrett, said the firm's credit card was too expensive for him. He told astonished MPs at the

Treasury Select Committee that he didn't borrow on credit cards as it was 'expensive' and no way to fund 'chronic borrowing'. One MP accused Barclays of 'bare-faced cynicism' for an offer to cardholders that allowed balance transfers from rival cards without incurring any interest – as long as the cardholder spent at least £50 a month on the card. He condemned cash-back offers as 'a bait and trap'.

- Stagecoach chief executive Keith Cochrane compared US bus passengers to riff-raff, in the US magazine *Forbes*, leading to a fall in share price. Stagecoach seems to have a habit of publicly bad-mouthing its customers: colourful chairman Brian Souter once described all northerners as 'beer-drinking, chip-eating, council house-dwelling, Old Labour-voting masses'.

- Retail entrepreneur, and darling of the City, Philip Green was forced to offer an unreserved apology in 2003 to the Irish in a bid to prevent a customer boycott. Attacking the *Guardian*'s financial editor, Paul Murphy, during an investigation into his accounts, Green said: 'He can't read English. Mind you, he is a f***ing Irishman.' Green referred to nationality several times while attempting to prevent the paper writing about his accounts. He was forced to apologize and said he had not meant to offend.

- Another entrepreneurial doyenne, Anita Roddick, spoke frankly when she described the Body Shop's anti-ageing cream as 'complete pap' and said that women who worried about their wrinkles would be better off 'spending the money on a good bottle of pinot noir'.

- In 2001 Top Man brand director David Shepherd said a typical customer at their stores was a young hooligan buying a suit for his first court appearance.

- Newcastle United Football Club's chiefs, Freddy Shepherd and Douglas Hall, branded Geordie women 'dogs' and said club shirts cost £5 to produce and sold for £50. Mass outrage ensued among probably the most loyal and dedicated fans in England, and the club risked disenfranchising one of its most powerful assets.

- Camelot's Dianne Thompson had to live with her suggestion in 2002 that punters would be extraordinarily lucky to win on the National Lottery. 'People have realized it probably won't be you. You would be lucky to win a tenner,' she confessed, and sales of tickets continued to plunge.

- Also in 2002, Sir Keith Whitson of HSBC said he would rather use cheap workers in India or China than his own British call-centre staff. He said the bank could get work done in Asia 'for a fifth of the price by smartly dressed employees who were keen to turn up to work'.

- And finally, the most famous gaffe in British corporate history – Gerald Ratner's description of his firm's products as 'total crap' in 1991. Ratner, whose company that year produced profits of £110 million as Britain's biggest high-street jeweller, made his remarks at the Institute of Directors (IoD). Ratner was reported by the *Financial Times* as saying, 'We do cut-glass sherry decanters complete with six glasses on a silver-plated tray that your butler can serve you drinks on, all for £4.95. People say "How can you sell this for such a low price?" I say, because it's total crap.' Ratner paid a terrible price for his comments: investors forced him to leave the board of his own company, and the profits soon turned into a loss of £122 million as consumers reacted with disgust. Eventually the Ratner name, which had unofficially become 'mud', was dropped in favour of Signet. The reason? Gerald Ratner made fools of the customers who had made him his fortune – they were so 'stupid' they would pay money for 'crap' products. He lost everything because he wanted to get a laugh from his peer group audience at the IoD.

SUMMARY

- Beware the obsequiousness of advisers.
- Don't confuse image with reality.
- Don't believe it can't happen because it hasn't before.
- Don't believe that writing the 'procedures' will prevent it from happening.
- Communicate at all times at all levels.
- Faced with disaster, consider the worst possible scenario.
- Be prepared to demonstrate human concern for what has happened.
- Never underestimate genuine concerns of customers.

8

Perception *is* the reality

Are you going to believe what you see or what I'm telling you?

Groucho Marx

Virtually every crisis contains within itself the seeds of success as well as the roots of failure. Finding, cultivating and harvesting the potential success is the essence of crisis management. The essence of crisis *mis*management is to make a bad situation worse. Many would argue, for example, that President Nixon's cover-up of the Watergate break-in created a bigger crisis than the original transgression would have produced.

Successful management of a crisis situation is about recognizing you have one, taking the appropriate actions to remedy the situation, being *seen* to take them and being *heard* to say the right things. Companies often misclassify a problem, focusing on the technical aspects and ignoring issues of perception – as we have seen with Intel's Pentium chip and Shell's response to Greenpeace over the disposal of the Brent Spar.

When Intel finally offered to replace the defective chip only an estimated 1 to 3 per cent of individual consumers (who constitute two-thirds of the purchasers of computers with Pentium chips) took up the offer. It wasn't that people wanted a new chip; it was just that they wanted to know they could get a new chip if they wanted one. As everyone knows, banks don't want borrowers to pay off their loans; they just want to know that borrowers *can* pay off their loans.

The problem in this stage of crisis management is that perception truly does become reality. In the case of Shell and Brent Spar, as the *Wall Street Journal* reported at the time: 'Shell made a strategic error. In a world of sound bites one image was left with many viewers: a huge multinational oil company was mustering all its might to bully what was portrayed as a brave but determined band'. Whatever the reality of the situation, Shell found itself floundering on the shoals of worldwide media perception.

Ordinary people couldn't get their heads round Shell's scientific and environmental arguments. The company's response focused almost entirely on the print media when television is by far more the most influential, and therefore important, medium. The television pictures showed water cannons being sprayed at the 'brave but determined band'.

Exxon Corporation's handling of the *Valdez* oil spill also taught students of crisis management important lessons in how poor communication can create a perception which does not reflect the reality – lessons we observed and did our best to remember when we were called in to help with the *Braer* disaster off the Shetland Islands in 1993 and the *Sea Empress* disaster in Milford Haven, Wales, in 1996.

A TALE OF THREE SORRY TANKERS

CASE STUDY: *EXXON VALDEZ*

How pouring oil on water created plenty of troubles

On 24 March 1989, at 2100 hours, the 987-foot *Exxon Valdez* oil tanker left the harbour of South Alaska's Valdez and entered Prince William Sound bound for California. The seas were calm and the weather was good. A local pilot, who had guided the super-tanker out of the port, was taken off shortly after 2330 hours. Twenty minutes later the *Exxon Valdez* ploughed into rocks and America's worst oil spill disaster had begun. Ten million gallons of oil spewed out of the vessel into Prince William Sound, a rich natural habitat. The disaster became instant world news.

Exxon, one of the five largest companies in the United States, had been under the leadership of Lawrence G Rawl since 1986. The son of a truck driver, an ex-marine, and with 37 years as an employee of Exxon before becoming chairman, Rawl was known for having a strong dislike of publicity and journalists. He perceived the media as a danger, to be avoided at all costs.

When the media asked for a comment at Exxon's headquarters in Houston several hours after the disaster it was told this was a matter for the Exxon

Shipping Company. They could not and did not want to make any further comment. When asked if the chairman would be interviewed on television, the response was that the chairman of the board had no time for that kind of thing.

Later, a spokesperson for Exxon Shipping coolly informed the press that emergency procedures and manuals existed for such events. Meanwhile the entire world was watching televised pictures of these emergency procedures failing as thousands of birds, otters and seals died in the oil slick.

Emergency procedures should apparently have been initiated by the Alyeska Pipeline Company, a consortium of seven oil companies that use the Alaskan pipeline. In the event of disaster, the consortium would be the first to act. But in this case even the most basic steps were not taken, and a ship specially designated for fighting oil pollution was left sitting in the dock for some time.

After more than a week Exxon was still pursuing a policy of 'no comment'. The publicity became so hostile that eventually Frank Iarossi, the director of Exxon Shipping, flew to Valdez to hold a press conference. This ended in a bitter battle with fishermen and journalists. Iarossi retaliated and the one small opportunity to cooperate and communicate with the press was lost. Iarossi's subsequent daily briefings were likened to the press conferences during the Vietnam War: generals who summed up small successes only to be immediately confronted by journalists who had seen completely different things on the battlefields.

Suddenly the chairman, Lawrence Rawl, decided to appear on television. He was interviewed 'live' and watched by millions of extremely angry Americans right across the United States. The first question put to him concerned the latest plan for the clean-up. He hadn't read it. He explained: 'it is not the role of the chairman of a large worldwide corporation to read every technical plan'. His arrogance was blatant.

When asked about the public relations disaster his company was facing – Esso products were being boycotted in the United States by this time – he replied: 'the reason we've got this public relations disaster [admitting he had one] is because of the media's reporting of the situation'. He proceeded to place the blame for his company's problems at the feet of the world's press. He showed no emotion over the enormous environmental disaster and offered no apologies to fishermen whose livelihood had been destroyed.

He didn't bother to go to Alaska to see for himself the damage which had been done until a fortnight after the event. When he did go the media was kept unaware of his visit. The damage to Exxon's reputation was complete.

The consequences for the company and the rest of the industry were dire. It is estimated the spill cost the company – in fines, clean-up expenses and lost market share – at least $16 billion.

New legislation was imposed on the oil tanker industry requiring all new ocean-going tankers to be built with double hulls. Experts in the shipping industry suggest double hulls are potentially more dangerous than single hulls because of the risk of a build-up of gas between the two hulls. Having seen the *Braer* and *Sea Empress* disasters first hand, it is easy to form the view that four hulls would not have prevented those oil spills. The new legislation appears to be a cosmetic, knee-jerk political reaction by governments that felt they had to

165

be seen to 'police' the wicked oil tanker and oil industries – a perception of wickedness created by Exxon's appalling communication in the aftermath of the *Valdez* spill.

Lessons from *Exxon Valdez*

When a tanker spills millions of gallons of oil into the sea, or an aeroplane falls out of the sky, or a ferry turns over in Zeebrugge harbour, people's first reaction is one of shock. It is difficult to accept that such disasters can still occur in this age of advancing technology and environmental consciousness. But, ultimately, no one expects there to be a zero-risk associated with any industry. Accidents do happen, whether in our private lives or in business.

This initial sense of shock, however, quickly turns to anger if the company at the centre of the crisis is not seen to take the appropriate action and to say the appropriate words. People need to be quickly reassured about certain things, essentially that:

- Everything (hopefully) was in place to try to prevent the accident from happening in the first place.
- Nonetheless, given the nature of the industry the company works in, it had the foresight to anticipate the possibility of such an event occurring and knew what to do to remedy the situation as far as possible, and as quickly as possible. In other words, to have the ability to paint a picture in words of a group of competent, caring people who swung into action really quickly to handle the situation.
- *The company really cares about what has happened.*

Exxon failed miserably on all three counts. In the aftermath of disaster, no action demonstrates more a company's concern for what has happened than the top man or woman being seen to go to the site, to be seen to take personal charge of the aftermath, and to communicate three simple messages:

- This is what has happened.
- This is what we are doing about it.
- This is how we feel about what has happened.

People will still feel aggrieved by what has happened but the anger will be dissipated if the company is seen to do its best in what is likely to be the most difficult of all circumstances. It is people's anger which causes the lasting damage to organizations. It leads to product boycotts, shares being sold and more demanding restrictions and penalties.

CASE STUDY: *BRAER*

Behind the headlines

During the course of 5 January 1993, we watched on the office television the events following the *Braer* oil tanker's grounding on rocks off the Shetland Islands earlier that day. At 5 pm we received a telephone call from New York. It was the chairman of Ultramar Inc. whose oil formed the cargo of the *Braer.* Could we help?

He told us he was catching the overnight flight to Heathrow and would then fly to Aberdeen where we were to rendezvous the following morning. Michael Regester takes up the story:

I booked myself on the last flight that evening from Heathrow to Aberdeen. The plane was packed with journalists and press photographers all headed for the same destination.

From Aberdeen I called the oil journalist Philip Algar, already on the Islands. Philip had travelled to the Shetland Islands not in his capacity as a journalist but in response to a request from the owners of the *Braer* to act as their media adviser. He brought me up to date with the facts.

The 89,000 dwt tanker, carrying 84,000 tonnes of crude oil from Norway to Quebec, lost engine power early in the morning of 5 January. The owners believe pipes probably damaged an air vent, resulting in sea-water entering the fuel tanks.

The vessel subsequently went aground at Garth's Ness on Shetland. Dreadful weather, with winds up to 100 mph, thwarted salvage attempts. By the end of the week the entire cargo was spilt, causing considerable loss of wildlife and inflicting immediate damage on a part of the local salmon fishing industry.

Ironically, the bad weather responsible for the accident played a major role in dispersing the oil rapidly. Within a few weeks the tourist authority stated: 'everything for the summer visitor season is now back to normal. Indeed, if you missed the news of the *Braer*, and now visited Shetland, there is nothing whatsoever to indicate that the islands came close to such a disaster'.

The trouble was, you would have to have been a Martian to have missed the news of the *Braer.* Within 48 hours of the accident there were over 500 journalists on the Islands, all based at the tiny Sumburgh airport at the southern end of Shetland. The scenes were amazing. Shetland is not renowned for its overcapacity of hotels or cars for hire. Journalists were knocking on people's doors, asking: 'How much for a room for a few nights and the use of your car?' The nearest hotel we could obtain rooms at was 60 miles away. The two showers at Sumburgh airport had been rented out as editing suites to the BBC and ITN.

I had booked a private room at Aberdeen airport to brief the Ultramar chairman on the latest situation and organized a charter plane to take us on to the Shetland Islands after his arrival. All commercial flights were booked up for days.

When we are called into crisis situations, often at a moment's notice, it is usually by companies for which we have never worked before. The situation is already highly pressurized by the time we get there and it is important to establish a quick and trusting rapport with the senior people we are dealing with. As I shook hands with the Ultramar chairman and was about to bring him up to date our flight was called. Our take-off slot had been brought forward.

Once on board it was impossible to have a conversation such was the noise from the tiny plane bouncing around in 100 mph winds. Knowing we were likely to be surrounded by the media on arrival at Sumburgh I gave him a copy of the statement I had hoped to discuss with him in Aberdeen. I waited with some anxiety as he read it for this was to be a critical moment in the establishment of our relationship.

One of our golden rules concerns the order in which statements are made in crisis situations. Whether written or spoken they must always cover the following topics in the following order:

- people;
- environment;
- property;
- money.

This is simply because this is the order in which most newspapers and broadcast media will cover the story. But sometimes our clients, not unusually on the advice of lawyers, don't agree and prefer to say something banal like: 'We will issue a statement when we have all the facts'. I need not have worried. The chairman agreed with the statement and proved to be an excellent communicator.

Press conferences were held twice a day for the next few days. When dealing with such large numbers of journalists and television crews this is the only practical way of keeping them up to date (see Chapter 12). Philip Algar and I were keen for our respective clients to be represented at the press conferences organized by the Shetland Islands, in order to present a united team dealing with the situation. This was agreed.

At the first press conference in which we participated, Ultramar's chairman had only about 5 per cent of press questions directed at him. The vast majority were aimed at the owners of the *Braer* and the Shetland Islands Council which was in charge of the clean-up. I therefore suggested we participate in no more press conferences but advised the chairman to remain on the Islands in case ownership of the crude oil became an issue. He should not be seen to be 'running away' from the situation but I didn't want him as a sitting target if there was no interest in the oil's ownership.

Instead, we focused on giving one-to-one interviews for the North American press who had arrived and in assessing for ourselves the amount of damage to the Islands. In crises of this kind it is important to obtain your own record of what has happened – particularly for dealing with future insurance claims and assisting with official investigations (see Chapter 10).

I hired a filmcrew from Aberdeen. They wanted to fly over but we asked them to take the ferry so they could bring a car with them. That solved our own transport problem as well as providing us with the footage we needed. Later, the footage had an additional use when it was turned into a film for Ultramar employees and investors back in the States.

In crisis situations a primary consideration must, of course, be audiences. Who needs to know what and how quickly? While messages to each audience must be consistent it is not always possible to transmit them all at the same time to each audience. In the case of the *Braer* the key immediate audience for Ultramar was its shareholders. After all, everyone in the financial community knew the *Valdez* spill had cost Exxon $16 billion. Ultramar was a tiny organization in comparison. If its shareholders thought they were going to be facing a bill of similar proportions, what was going to happen to the share price? So a first action taken by the company was to get its shares suspended on the New York Stock Exchange until it could assess the company's likely amount of financial liability, and check it had the insurance policies in place to meet the liability. Having done this the situation was explained to shareholders and their advisers and, later that day, trading in the shares was resumed. In the event, they dropped just 25 cents on the previous day's price.

The 'information void'

The vacuum caused by a failure to communicate is soon filled with rumour, misrepresentation, drivel and poison.

Business academic C Northcote Parkinson

Meanwhile the appalling weather conditions on the Islands were preventing workers from stemming the leaking oil and helicopters from spraying dispersant. In fact, nothing was happening. This absence of activity led to an 'information void' – typical in a crisis situation.

Instead of communicating positive messages about what would be done to minimize the environmental damage once the weather had subsided, virtually nothing was communicated by those responsible for the clean-up.

The void was instantly filled with media reports that the Islands were 'covered with oil', that 'oil was carcinogenic' – you could get leukaemia from breathing the fumes. As a consequence, 'school children were being evacuated', 'sheep were being evacuated' and 'all the salmon fish farms were contaminated'. And so the media pollution went on.

After oil, the two most important industries in the Shetland Islands are the export of salmon to Japan, and tourism. Following the media reports, the Japanese refused to import any more salmon and tourism fell right away. In that year alone, the Shetland Islands Council reported a £1.3 million loss in tourism revenues and forecast a cumulative loss of £18.2 million by 1998. The public perception of the situation had become the reality.

These lessons were uppermost in our minds when we were called in by the Wales Tourist Board on 15 February 1996, after the *Sea Empress* hit rocks on its approach to Texaco's refinery in Milford Haven.

CASE STUDY: *SEA EMPRESS* IN DISTRESS

The Wales Tourist Board had a huge challenge on its hands to prevent a similar impact on Welsh tourism. Tourism in Wales generates about £1.4 billion per year and is directly responsible for employment of one in nine of the workforce.

The protracted delay in the salvage operation only fuelled the daily saturation coverage of oiled beaches and birds. Media reports in Germany, Denmark and further afield implied the whole of Wales was affected. The task in hand was to correct these misconceptions and convert the massive exposure of Pembrokeshire in the world media into an advantage.

Our strategy, which won immediate approval from the Wales Tourist Board, had to be aimed at supporting the tourist trade, reassuring holiday-makers and persuading the media that every possible effort was being made to clean the affected beaches and restore them to their natural state prior to the tourist season.

Less than a week after the spill the Welsh Tourism Fights Back campaign was under way. Colleague Rosie Clifford devised the theme: 'The Treasure is Still Here – But No Longer a Secret'. This was a reference to the Pembrokeshire coastline being known as the 'secret treasure of Wales'. The theme struck a chord and the 'treasure' frequently appeared in newspaper headlines.

We wanted to minimize the medium- and long-term damage to the tourist industry by capitalizing on the rapid and comprehensive clean-up operation; and to emphasize that only a small area of Wales had suffered. The majority of Pembrokeshire's beaches were unaffected. This would hopefully counteract the predominantly negative and exaggerated image of the extent of environmental pollution propagated by media coverage.

The campaign included:

- a telephone hotline to respond to holiday-makers concerned about their bookings; and to monitor public concern;
- organizing over 20 television and radio interviews for the Wales Tourist Board's chief executive, John French – over a critical 48-hour period when the issue was still headline news – to convey agreed messages;
- transmitting positive messages to key UK and overseas markets via British tourism offices overseas;
- consulting with Texaco, owners of the crude oil cargo, tourist operators,

accommodation and attraction owners, local authorities and other agencies to ensure consistent messages to key audiences;
● briefing HRH Prince of Wales and the Secretary of State for Wales on the campaign to gain their support.

The words of Wales Tourist Board chief executive John French summed up the passion and rigour with which the potentially damaging information void was filled to best advantage: 'the images which brought us worldwide attention were negative but now more people than ever before know of the beauty that can be found here. We were determined not to let the media's images outlast the pollution itself'.

Positive media coverage immediately began to outweigh the negative. On one day alone – St David's Day – the Wales Tourist Board press office broadcast its reassurance campaign live through 25 local radio stations reaching in excess of an estimated 1,000,000 listeners throughout the UK.

A study jointly published in July 1996 by the Welsh Economy Research Unit, University of Wales, Cardiff Business School and the Welsh Institute of Rural Studies, entitled *The Economic Consequences of the* Sea Empress *Spillage* (1996), concluded:

> the weighted anticipated impact of the spillage on tourism spending in Pembrokeshire in 1996 was an average reduction of 12.9 per cent and slightly less for south west Wales overall. Applying this average impact, supported by actual turnover experience in the early parts of 1996, to the total estimated tourism spend in Pembrokeshire in 1995 of £160 million, gives a gross estimated impact on tourism spending in Pembrokeshire of £160m x –12.9% = £20.64 million.

From a potential total loss of revenue from tourism expenditure in Pembrokeshire, and severe reduction in expenditure in other parts of Wales, the damage had been limited to 12.9 per cent. For once, the perception had more or less matched the reality.

SUMMARY

- Recognize you have a crisis.
- Be seen to take the appropriate actions.
- Be heard to say the right things.
- Remember television is the most important medium.
- Don't blame the media for your problems; it can be your best friend.
- People's anger leads to product boycotts, fall in share price and more demanding restrictions and penalties.
- Talk about people first, then the environment and property and, finally, money.
- Don't be a sitting target at press conferences.
- Anticipate the 'information void' and be prepared to fill it.
- Remember 'media pollution' can outlast environmental pollution and be more damaging economically.

9

The media in crisis situations

Four hostile newspapers are more feared than a thousand bayonets.

Napoleon Bonaparte

The chairman of Exxon's fear and distrust of the media became a self-fulfilling prophecy for him. Ignoring the media when dealing with issues and crises will always prove to be a catastrophic error of judgement. This may seem obvious but it is a mistake often made by organizations facing a tricky, potentially disastrous, situation.

For example, in the immediate aftermath of the Lockerbie disaster, Pan Am made a conscious decision to minimize communication with the press. The airline believed a policy of non-communication would somehow distance Pan Am's name from the tragic consequences of the disaster.

This was a huge error of judgement. In a situation like this the media will descend on the site of the accident like a plague of locusts which needs to be fed. If it isn't fed by the organization which finds itself, however inadvertently, at the centre of the crisis, it will feed from the hands of others. And become deeply suspicous of the hand which obviously isn't feeding it.

When questioned about the warning of a possible terrorist attack, Pan

Am initially said it was unaware of any warning. It was later revealed that all carriers operating in Europe, including Pan Am, had been informed. A cardinal public relations principle had been breached. Concealing the truth is simply not an option. There are too many eager sources and too many eager reporters. In crisis situations, it is imperative *to tell your own story, to tell it all and to tell it fast.*

So did Pan Am's CEO, Thomas Plaskett, go to Lockerbie, apologize, attend memorial services, atone for responsibility? He did not. The media made mincemeat of the airline. It was already in financial difficulty and the transatlantic route was its only remaining profitable one. Passengers lost confidence in the airline – in its willingness and ability to transport us safely from one side of the Atlantic to the other – and chose other airlines in preference. The boycott proved to be the final nail in the airline's financial coffin. It went bankrupt.

HOW JAL AND BRITISH MIDLAND GOT IT RIGHT

In contrast, when JAL suffered its worst-ever crash on 12 August 1985 – 520 people died – the airline followed an elaborate protocol to atone. Personal apologies were made by the company's president, memorial services were held and financial reparations paid. For weeks, more than 400 airline employees helped bereaved relatives with everything from arranging funeral services to filling in insurance forms. All advertising was suspended voluntarily. Had JAL not made these acts of conciliation, it would have courted charges of inhumanity and irresponsibility.

At the memorial service JAL's president, Yasumoto Takagi, bowed low and long to relatives of the victims, and to a plaque bearing the victims' names. He asked forgiveness, accepted responsibility and offered to resign. The maintenance chief committed suicide.

Marion Kinsdorf, a US business academic, has pointed out in *Public Relations Review* (1990):

> the airline's reaction reveals not only the Japanese tendency towards 'group think' but the consciousness of equality of each member of the group. In Japan, what is regarded as 'just' or 'moral' is what everyone in a particular group, at a particular place and time, thinks is right. As a result, the spokesperson or the president of an airline responds and behaves according to how the majority defines 'just and proper'. Hence, news is received differently.
>
> JAL's president's visibility, his offer to resign, becomes more symbolic. He was responding to deep thoughts and feelings. In a country where nonverbal communication is far more crucial and effective than the spoken, such an act of resignation becomes a nonverbal expression of apology.

From the day of the accident, JAL had mobilized its staff, from the president down, to offer gestures of apology and regret. When family members had to travel to a small mountain village to identify bodies, airline staff accompanied them, paying all expenses, bringing them food and drink and clean clothes. It spent $1.5 million on two elaborate memorial services and dispatched executives to every victim's funeral (although some were asked to leave). It also established a scholarship fund for children whose parents died in the crash.

Importantly also, JAL were quick to notify victims' families. Overnight it issued lists of passenger names. One relative of a victim on Pan Am's flight 103 was not told officially of her husband's death until six weeks after the crash.

Although JAL did suffer from some media criticism, and for a while lost market share, it eventually made a full recovery. Much of its response was driven by Japanese culture. One would not, after all, expect the chief maintenance engineer of a Western airline to commit suicide. But its response was seen, crucially by the media, to be humane, caring and responsible.

A similar response came from British Midland Airways when one of its Boeing 737s crashed near Kegworth alongside the M1 motorway just a few weeks after the Lockerbie crash.

The airline's chairman, Sir Michael Bishop, immediately raced to the scene of the accident giving live radio interviews from his car phone. His voice was patched into a live interview with Michael Buerk on the BBC's *Nine O'Clock News*.

His response was remarkable. Many people in senior managerial positions, fearful of being misreported by the media – and of the consequences of being misreported – won't give media interviews until they have all of the facts at their fingertips and have worked out all the answers to the potentially most difficult questions. In a crisis situation this can be disastrous not least because it will usually take many hours before this is possible. Communication *has* to begin immediately.

Sir Michael Bishop gave interviews when he had no knowledge about the cause of the accident; how many people had died, been injured, or had survived. Lack of information at the outset of a crisis is typical. Very little information will be available for several hours. Some facts will be known – 'one of our planes has crashed' – but not much else.

Faced with this dilemma, Sir Michael Bishop focused on expressing how he felt about what had happened and what he was going to do about the situation. He immediately began to 'manage' the flow and content of news to the media.

In essence, he said he was going to do everything in his power to ensure the families of victims were looked after properly, the injured received the best possible treatment; and no stone would be left unturned in establishing the cause of the accident to try and prevent such an accident from happening again.

There was not much 'content' to what he said but he understood and implemented one of the golden rules of crisis communication – begin it at once, from the top of the organization. Even though it was eventually found to have been pilot error which caused the crash, no one lost confidence in British Midland or in Boeing 737s. Ironically, some people have argued the airline's reputation was actually enhanced by the chairman's response. It was seen to be caring and responsible.

GAINING MEDIA SUPPORT

This may come as a surprise, but in our experience of dealing with the media in crisis situations its attitude will be, to begin with, at worst neutral and at best sympathetic – particularly if people have died or been injured. It is usually when the media believe the organization at the centre of the crisis is unduly slow in providing information, reticent about providing 'talking heads' for interview or thought to be withholding information, that it becomes hostile. The key to successful communication in crisis situations is to establish the organization at the centre of the crisis as *the single authoritative source of information about what has happened and what is being done about it.*

International research has shown the media to be by far the most credible source of information throughout the Western world, well ahead of governments and, with the possible exception of Italy, the church. By virtue of its 'believability' the media acts as the most important conduit to shaping people's beliefs and behaviour.

Ultimately, newspapers, television and radio news programmes are 'products'. Those which best meet the demands of the prevailing market sell the most or are watched and listened to the most. Those that don't get it right either go out of business (the *Today* and *Sunday Correspondent* newspapers are examples) or suffer a drop in sales or audiences.

The *Sun*, for example, suffered a drop in sales when it attacked pop singer Elton John. It underestimated the singer's popularity with its readers and the libel cost it £1 million in compensation. Similarly, the newspaper's sales dropped after its reporting of the Hillsborough tragedy.

CASE STUDY: HILLSBOROUGH

How the media can have its own crises

Newspaper comment is free but facts are sacred.
C P Scott, newspaper editor in 1926

Few tragedies have been so comprehensively recorded as the disaster at the FA Cup semi-final between Nottingham Forest and Liverpool at Sheffield's Hillsborough stadium in April 1989. As Lord Justice Taylor's enquiry was later to state, the deaths of 95 Liverpool fans had been a wholly avoidable tragedy, but one which had been long in the making.

Peter Chippendale and Chris Horrie provide a remarkable insight into the *Sun*'s handling of the Hillsborough tragedy in their book *Stick It Up Your Punter – the rise and fall of the* Sun (1992). They point out how Taylor's acerbic report threw into sharp relief the way the football authorities had connived with papers like the *Sun* to hype the former working-class game into the realms of television-led fantasy. Multi-million pound transfer fees for players had soaked up the money desperately needed to update ancient grounds and squeezed smaller clubs to the extent that facilities had deteriorated into shabby squalor. Taylor summed it up as 'the all-pervading stench of fried onions' and the sight of 'men urinating against walls because of the inadequate and foul toilet facilities' (Lord Justice Taylor, 1990).

The Hillsborough tragedy, as Taylor bluntly concluded, was primarily the fault of the South Yorkshire police in charge of crowd control. To relieve the increasingly lethal pressure of 5,000 Liverpool fans struggling to get through the bottleneck of the turnstiles, the police had given the order for the gates to be thrown open. But instead of routing the surging fans on to empty terraces, they had allowed them to take the route through a tunnel into one of the pens which was already overcrowded. From here there was no escape because of the wire cages enclosing the front.

As the inevitable push forward began, Superintendent David Duckenfield, in charge of the police, 'froze' in his control box and made matters worse by treating the fans' desperate attempts to escape by scaling the cage as a 'pitch invasion'. Only when it was too late did he allow the emergency gates to be opened, relieving the pressure.

Every second of the drawn-out horror unravelled itself, live, in front of a television audience expecting an exciting afternoon's viewing. The mass of sports photographers took thousands of pictures, many of which showed such harrowing details of death and suffering it was almost impossible to decide which could be printed. Some people would bay for the blood of the papers printing the most horrific pictures while others would pile into the shops to buy the ones with the most shocking images.

Deciding what words could be written about the tragedy should have been easier. However, the then editor of the *Sun*, Kelvin MacKenzie, chose words which turned the Hillsborough tragedy into an unparalleled journalistic disaster, with huge financial consequences.

On the Monday after the accident the *Sun* cleared page after page for different pictures and stories, pulled together under the tacky headline: 'Gates of Hell'. On the Sunday immediately after the match, newspapers had sold an extra 500,000 copies between them. On the Monday, public desire for more detail still seemed insatiable.

The *Sun*, like other dailies, had more time to reflect on which pictures to use. But as the official death list had not been published there was still no way it could tell in most cases whether the individuals pictured being crushed or lying on the pitch were now alive or dead. Like most of its rivals, it printed them regardless of causing unbelievable anguish to families and friends of victims.

It was not the *Sun* but the *Daily Mirror* with its use of colour, so making the pictures even more ghoulish, which brought the wrath of Liverpool down on its head on Monday morning. The editor's justification was that showing the full horror of the event would help to ensure nothing like it could happen ever again. One wonders if he would have used the same pictures had they depicted one of his own children?

During the Monday a new and more sinister factor began to surface in the story. From the start there had been an understandable knee-jerk reaction of blaming hooligans for the disaster, and it was this preconditioning which had largely accounted for Superintendent Duckenfield's automatic assumption of a pitch invasion. Even when most of the deaths had already occurred, television commentators had fallen into the same trap by excitedly screaming that fans were tearing down the hoardings. They were – but only to use as makeshift stretchers.

On the Tuesday morning the *Sun* started to blame hooligans for the tragedy. It asked: 'Is it fair to make the police the scapegoat for the disaster? It happened because thousands of fans, many without tickets, tried to get into the ground just before kick-off – either by forcing their way in or by black-mailing the police into opening the gates.'

The next day it went the whole hog. Beneath a huge headline, 'THE TRUTH', it stated:

- Some fans picked pockets of victims.
- Some fans urinated on the brave cops.
- Some fans beat up a PC giving the kiss of life.

The story began: 'Drunken Liverpool fans viciously attacked rescue workers as they tried to revive victims of the Hillsborough soccer disaster, it was revealed last night'. A 'high-ranking' police officer was quoted as saying: 'The fans just acted like animals. My men faced a double hell – the disaster and the fury of the fans who attacked us.'

This was an outrageous libel of all the people involved but was legally safe because no names were used – as Liverpool City Council found out later when it debated suing the paper. The people of Liverpool did the only thing they could do. They turned their anger on the newspaper itself.

Some newsagents put it under the counter; some refused to sell it. Granada TV news showed people burning copies. All over the city copies of the paper were being ripped up, trampled and spat upon. People carrying it in the street found it snatched out of their hands and torn to shreds in front of them; the paper disappeared entirely from Ford's plant at Halewood and dozens of land-lords banned it from their premises. Sales of the newspaper in Liverpool collapsed.

Newsagents slashed their orders by as much as 80 per cent. The *Mirror*, which had raised £1 million for the disaster fund by increasing its cover price, was piling into Liverpool to seize the opportunity it had been given and rapidly gained ground despite its original ghoulish pictures.

The newspaper industry had learnt that, as in any other industry, people won't buy products which have been 'contaminated'. Sales of the paper on Merseyside have never recovered to former levels.

THE MEDIA AS AN ALLY

In most cases, the media will act responsibly if it is handled in an open and honest way. Public relations activity in crises must never attempt to hide the facts of what has happened; it has to act as a facilitator to explain what has happened and as a 'driver' to ensure appropriate action is seen to be taken to remedy, as far as possible, what has gone wrong. To deliberately hide the facts is complete folly. Sooner or later they will be discovered and the situation will become worse because of accusations of a 'cover-up'.

There will always be some who view crisis management as a 'black art' and will not believe anything said to them. In our experience they are in the minority. There are some television programmes where the company will always be on a hiding-to-nothing because of their anti-business bias: *Panorama* and *Watchdog* are examples.

For example, on one edition of *Watchdog* in 1996 the programme had, in its view, cunningly placed hidden cameras and some valuables in cars to see if they would be stolen by employees of car valeting companies. Probably to its surprise, at some valeting premises the valuables were not stolen but returned to their owner. The programme did not bother to mention the names of those companies but of course told us the names of those which had pocketed the goods. Companies need to think carefully about appearing on programmes which focus exclusively on bad news.

In general, however, the media should be viewed as a potential friend rather than potential foe. It is important to establish and track its agenda. In the Shetland Islands, during the *Braer* disaster, we regularly mixed with reporters to find out what was concerning them and what news they expected to hear next. This helped to shape what was said at press conferences and written in press releases.

On another occasion we were helping a major pet food manufacturer which had received an extortion threat. The letter said unless £50,000 was paid into an account at the Halifax Building Society by a certain date, strychnine would be injected into a leading brand of dog food. A phial containing strychnine accompanied the letter to prove the extortionist had the poison.

This was different to the Tylenol situation because the crime had not yet been committed and, dare we say it, the threat was against dogs and not human beings. If the product were recalled as a precautionary measure the extortionist could have made the same threat to another of the company's products – where would it have ended? (This kind of extortion is often known as 'sweetmail' after a blackmailer in Japan, dubbed 'the man with 21 faces', repeatedly extracted large sums of money from a Japanese confectionery company, the size of Cadbury's, until it eventually went bankrupt.)

If we told the media what was happening and the story was published, what would happen to sales of the product? Equally, if the news leaked out, the media would rip the company apart for putting profit above all else. We decided the media had to become an ally.

We agreed with officers from Scotland Yard to hold a joint press conference at which we would inform the media about the threat but ask them not to publish the story until the villain had been apprehended. Scotland Yard explained coverage of the threat would make it more difficult to apprehend the criminal, might encourage him to carry out the threat; and might encourage 'copycat' crime. In exchange, we would hold regular press briefings to keep reporters up to date with developments and they could, of course, publish the story once the extortionist had been caught.

There were no legal sanctions to prevent the media from publishing the story. There were no legal reasons to prevent them. But not one newspaper or broadcast medium used the story because, we believe, the reasons given to them were entirely plausible and reasonable.

In the event, the extortionist never carried out his threat to the pet food company but switched his target to Heinz Baby Foods. Dealing with a threat to babies is entirely different from dealing with a threat to dogs. The police mounted a huge surveillance campaign at every Halifax Building Society cash dispenser and eventually the criminal was apprehended. Only then did the story become national news.

CASE STUDY: THOMAS COOK COACH CRASH

As we advocate throughout this book, a policy of open and honest communication and the preparedness to be seen to be taking the right action when a crisis hits can encourage the media to become one of your greatest allies.

The foundation then exists for an organization to emerge from the worst of all possible circumstances with its reputation intact. Evidence for this view is demonstrated by the Thomas Cook Holidays' response to the crash of a coach carrying British holidaymakers in South Africa.

On 27 September 1999 – when the public was still in shock over the Paddington rail crash, which had happened only a month previously – a coach carrying 34 elderly Thomas Cook holidaymakers, two tour guides and the driver, lost control and careered off the Long Tom Pass in the Drakensberg mountains, South Africa.

Twenty-six elderly British tourists and their South African tour guide were killed. Another tourist died two weeks later as a result of her injuries. Seven

British tourists, a tour guide and the driver of the coach survived the crash, many with broken bones and head and chest injuries.

As soon as Thomas Cook Holidays received news of the accident, it initiated its crisis response plan. Simon Laxton, Thomas Cook Holidays' Managing Director, set up an Incident Control Team (see Chapter 11) to manage media- and relative-response teams and to deal with all other aspects of the accident.

The Incident Control Team focused first and foremost on the needs of the victims and survivors of the crash and their families. A team of trauma counsellors, mortuary technicians and legal and customer advisers was immediately sent to South Africa to counsel survivors, and to coordinate communication with the police and the media. A coach engineer accompanied the group in order to initiate an independent internal investigation into the crash. In addition, Thomas Cook Holidays consulted its insurance providers, Axa, whose employees also flew to the scene to assist with coordinating insurance and medical claims.

A relative-response hotline was quickly established to deal with the thousands of calls expected from concerned friends and relatives. The number was quickly communicated to the public via major UK television bulletins.

Despite the fact that full details of the incident weren't yet known, the Incident Control Team recognized that friends and relatives needed reassurance that Thomas Cook Holidays was doing everything possible, and that everyone involved was being treated with the utmost care.

Thomas Cook Holidays received over 2,000 calls in the first 24 hours after the crash. Simon Laxton worked with the team and answered a number of calls himself. Additional staff were drafted into the relative call centre to cope with the growing number of enquiries from concerned friends and relatives. The company made sure that *all* its staff (including those in over 700 high street branches and all bureaux de change) were contacted, briefed and updated regularly to deal with members of the public who called or visited outlets for information.

The company made immediate contact with South African Airways to make arrangements to fly relatives to Johannesburg. The terms of the insurance policies taken out by the holidaymakers varied widely. Most allowed for only one relative to fly to the scene, so Thomas Cook Holidays agreed with Axa to overwrite these, enabling distraught relatives to travel in pairs.

Contact was made with the Foreign Office, the South African government, the British High Commission in South Africa and the South African police to ensure that relatives were kept informed and that those who flew to South Africa were protected from a pack of tenacious journalists clamouring for reactions and new information.

All the necessary financial and practical arrangements were made to ensure that relatives were given all the support and information they needed while also being protected from the media glare.

Thomas Cook Holidays proactively contacted all customers booked on the same tour two weeks after the accident and offered them the opportunity to cancel their trips without charge. Only six chose to cancel, demonstrating that Thomas Cook Holidays had not lost the trust or confidence of its customers.

Media attention around the world was immediate and intense. Over 500 media inquiries were received by the media team (which was outsourced to public relations firm JGPR) in the first 24 hours after the crash. TV crews arrived at the company's headquarters in Peterborough within two hours of the crash and 'camped' for days in the car park outside the building.

The company managed an all-too-rare achievement in its response to the media. It issued its first news release via the Press Association and Reuters *before* receiving the first media call. This action ensured all the media knew which telephone number to call for information and put the company on the front foot in terms of influencing the way the story was covered.

In total, 19 statements were issued over five days. Only two of these were issued on a reactive basis, responding to specific media demands. All emphasized concern about the care and well-being of the victims' families, survivors and their relatives, as well as explaining Thomas Cook Holidays' commitment to finding out the cause of the accident as soon as possible.

Thomas Cook Holidays' lawyers, Field Fisher Waterhouse, were brought in at the outset of the incident. Their role was to ensure that all legal aspects of the coach crash were thought through, that there was immediate and professional advice available on complex issues around insurance and liability statements, and to provide immediate access to any team member with a legal query.

Simon Laxton acted as Head of the Incident Control Team as well as primary spokesman for Thomas Cook Holidays. An effective spokesperson, able to convey both grave concern and decisive action, is essential in any situation involving loss of life or injury. Despite the pressure he was under, Simon Laxton made time to give all major television stations one-to-one interview slots twice a day. He showed journalists all the response teams at work and, through his honesty and transparency, won their trust.

Initial media speculation about the cause of the crash and safety record of the coach tour operator was immediately quashed by the company. Simon Laxton took care to reiterate the company's strict health and safety assessment of contracted operators and its confidence in the coach company, Springbok Atlas.

Teams flown to the scene of the accident were briefed to handle media inquiries and to protect the privacy of survivors and their relatives. A Thomas Cook representative was later based at the Millpark Hospital, Johannesburg, in order to deal with inquiries that might have been too intrusive for survivors and their relatives.

The core Incident Control Team (including Simon Laxton) relocated to Johannesburg on Wednesday 29 September, three days after the crash. As the volume of calls from both relatives and the media had subsided, the team felt that it was important to address issues in South Africa directly and to be with the families who had flown out. It also wanted to give relatives direct and personal support, and to ensure victims' bodies had been correctly identified prior to their repatriation to the UK. Some members of the team remained in Peterborough to sustain the incident response in the UK.

Of critical importance was the continued day-to-day running of the business. Liz Makin, Simon Laxton's deputy, took control of the rest of the business to ensure the company's many other customers received the level of service they would normally expect – in other words, that their holidays were not disrupted in any way by the coach crash.

Even though doctors at the Millpark Hospital were confident that it was safe for survivors to return to Britain by commercial airline, Thomas Cook Holidays, in conjunction with insurers Axa, decided to use air ambulances to ensure maximum comfort for those returning home.

The company also recognized the vital role the people of Lydenburg played during the accident. Many had gone to the scene of the crash to provide assistance to emergency teams dealing with the crash. A memorial service was organized by the South African authorities and attended by Simon Laxton, who wanted to thank the townspeople 'for their overwhelming compassion and support'.

Because of Thomas Cook Holidays' open and honest communication with the media from the outset about every action it was taking, media coverage was largely neutral and quickly shifted away from the Thomas Cook Holidays brand to road safety issues in South Africa.

There was no immediate or lasting damage to the company's reputation. The company's response reinforced its reputation as a responsible company genuinely committed to its customers' safety.

There was no backlash from families and friends of the victims. From the outset, it was clear that care of the survivors and all the families involved was the absolute priority. As a consequence, there was no financial impact.

CASE STUDY: INGHAMS AUSTRIA COACH CRASH

The UK travel industry certainly appears to be well versed in handling such crises. In August 2004, a very similar incident occurred in Austria when a coach full of holidaymakers overturned, ultimately killing six people. Tour operator Inghams was responsible for the trip and immediately leapt into effective action. The first messages from the company not long after the accident were ones of care and concern. The Inghams spokesperson revealed that a management team had been sent to the scene and that 'our thoughts are with those who have been involved in the accident and their relatives'. The company announced that transport would be arranged for UK relatives to travel to Austria as needed, and it opened a response hotline immediately for concerned family and friends.

The tour operator liaised relentlessly with local emergency services and with the Foreign Office to be able to provide regular updates to the media on the developing situation. The next day it made arrangements for the repatriation of survivors, and revealed that it had flown more than 20 relatives of the passengers out to Salzburg already. As news of the fatalities emerged, Inghams was quick to show empathy with those involved. In a statement it expressed its 'deepest sympathies to those involved and to their families and relatives' and paid tribute to the service provided by the Austrian medical and emergency services. As the event played out on 24-hour news channels, the value of its rapid, effective and sensitive approach would have become clear to the company.

Reporters giving live updates from Inghams' head office in London were sympathetic towards the company and appreciative of the flow of information. But it was when the likes of Sky News and BBC News 24 arranged interviews with relatives of the survivors that its reputation held strong. Talking live to the studio from their homes, parents were highly complimentary of Inghams for providing information and updates about their children. They also expressed gratitude for the offers made to fly them out to the scene. As one said: 'The tour operator has been brilliant and they couldn't have done more for us.' Doing the right thing and being seen to do the right thing is invaluable.

MONITORING THE MEDIA

As discussed in Chapter 5, monitoring the media on a regular basis is one important way to spot evolving issues before they become full-blown crises – sometimes we call it 'crisis creep'.

But if it *has* hit the fan, monitoring what the media is saying about the situation is a crucial part of the response. If a serious factual error is broadcast or printed then no stone should be left unturned to have it corrected. Once a serious mistake appears in print or is stated on the broadcast media it becomes set in cement and repeated everywhere. In particular, it is important to remember the print media watch the broadcast media. Anything said on television or radio is likely to surface in newspaper stories. Financial journalists talk to fund managers and investment analysts. The lay media talk to the specialist media.

Retractions are difficult to obtain. The media doesn't like to admit it got it wrong. A published 'letter to the editor' does not carry anything like the same weight as the original article. The first thing to decide is whether the mistake is serious enough to make a fuss. If the error is only marginal a retraction or published letter to the editor may only serve to draw people's attention to the error again. If it is truly serious help should be sought from the Press Complaints Commission in the event of a newspaper error. If the error has been broadcast by one of the independent television companies it will be dealt with by the Independent Television Commission (ITC). If the ITC receives more than five complaints from the public about a programme or advertisement it has to investigate the complaint. If the BBC has perpetrated the error, the complaint should be lodged with its own internal watchdog. If none of these actions has the desired effect, threaten a lawsuit. If that doesn't work, go to court.

SUMMARY

- The media cannot ever be ignored in crisis situations.
- Begin the communications process immediately.
- Crucial to the crisis response is for the CEO to be seen to take personal charge of the aftermath and to be the principal communicator – if he or she is good at it.
- In the aftermath, focus messages on how the organization feels about what has happened and what actions it is taking to remedy the situation.
- Establish the organization as the single authoritative source of information about what has happened and what is being done about it.
- Newspapers can be boycotted in the same way as other products.
- Monitor the media constantly throughout the crisis; leave no stone unturned in obtaining retractions for seriously inaccurate reporting.

10

The legal perspective

When lawyers talk about the law normal human beings begin to think about something else.

Richard Ingrams, former *Private Eye* editor

People are often quite rude about lawyers in crisis situations and, sometimes, this includes us. When we met with the chairman of Ultramar in the Shetland Islands one of his first questions was, 'Do we need to have a lawyer with us?' Our response was, 'Only on the end of the telephone'.

The problem can sometimes be that the training lawyers receive prepares them to think about crisis situations in a completely different way. Whereas we will advocate *telling it all, telling it fast and telling it truthfully*, lawyers will often advocate *saying nothing, doing nothing and admitting nothing*. What they don't always appreciate is the long-term consequences for an organization's reputation – and the knock-on effect on its financial bottom line. These can be far more damaging than any legal consequences.

Part of the trick is to get to the CEO of the company that is in trouble before the lawyer does. If he or she has already been in the hands of lawyers for several hours it often makes it more difficult to persuade the CEO to take a more 'open' course of action. Sometimes it makes it impossible. The lawyers advising the company that owned the *Bowbelle* dredger, which tragically collided into the stern of the floating disco *Marchioness* on the Thames one summer's evening in 1989, drowning 51 young people, wouldn't even allow the *Bowbelle*'s skipper to apologize publicly. The belief was saying 'sorry' amounted to an admission of liability.

This was blatant nonsense. Admitting sorrow does not mean the company is liable. What needs to be said is: 'We deeply regret this has happened and will leave no stone unturned in establishing the cause' – as Sir Michael Bishop did after the Kegworth aeroplane crash.

The intransigence of the lawyers, and the client's 'rabbit in the head-lights' faith in all they said, caused us to walk away from the *Bowbelle–Marchioness* tragedy – one of the very few times we have done so in 20 years of advising companies in difficulty.

The other part of the trick is to marshal arguments in support of a particular course of action in the same way as lawyers do – by referring to precedents. Having a detailed knowledge of crisis case studies, of what worked well and what didn't, will provide evidence to support advice. In part, we hope this book helps in providing such evidence.

LEGAL PITFALLS WHEN COMMUNICATING IN CRISIS

From a legal standpoint there are two cardinal sins which must never be committed when communicating in a crisis. The first is *never to admit liability* for what has happened. There will always be an official investigation of some sort into what has happened and this will establish who is liable. The second is *never to speculate* about the cause of the crisis.

When something goes wrong, the first question from the media and others is: 'How on earth did this happen?' And this is the one question which will always be impossible to answer, not least because the answer will not be available. *What* has happened will be known but *how* it happened will not. As we have seen already, an essential part of the response is to describe what has happened.

Reporters will push hard for speculation about possible causes. Speculative theories make the story more interesting. They may try to flatter the spokesperson by suggesting he or she has been in the industry for a long time and, given the seniority of the position, must have some idea about the cause. The temptation is to think: 'Yes, I am a senior person with long experience and I won't look credible if I am clueless about possible causes'. This temptation must be resisted at all costs, for two reasons.

If the speculated cause proves to be incorrect it will be taken as a delib-erate attempt by the organization to hide the true facts of the matter – in other words, it will be seen as a 'cover-up'. More importantly, there will be a clause somewhere in the organization's insurance policies which states the cause of any incident must be agreed with the insurers before it is made public. If it is not but is nonetheless made public, the insurance companies have the legal right not to meet subsequent claims.

In the aftermath of the *Herald of Free Enterprise* ferry tragedy, a senior spokesman for Townsend Thoresen, the ferry operator, fell famously into the speculation trap. And when we were advising the manufacturers of Cuprinol, the wood-staining and preservative product, during a crisis situation, we faced a huge dilemma with the company's insurers.

CASE STUDY: *HERALD OF FREE ENTERPRISE*

On 6 March 1987 the *Herald of Free Enterprise*, a cross-channel ferry operated by Townsend Thoresen, left Zeebrugge harbour in Belgium on a routine return voyage to Dover. Before the vessel had passed through the harbour exit it suddenly filled with water and turned over on to its side. The tragedy claimed the lives of 193 passengers and crew.

Shortly afterwards a senior executive from the company gave a television interview in which he was asked how the accident had happened. He speculated the ferry had 'hit the harbour wall' on its departure. 'Ferry hit the harbour wall' ran as the headline in newspapers for days. Thereafter the company battened down the hatches and gave few additional interviews, stating it had to deal with the operational aftermath of the tragedy.

This immediately made the media suspicious. The company's lack of communication prompted deeper investigation by reporters who soon established the ferry had not 'hit the harbour wall' but had sailed from Zeebrugge while closing its bow doors.

This caused huge quantities of water to enter the vessel and destabilize it. The media soon discovered Townsend Thoresen always operated their vessels in this way because it provided a quicker turn-round time at either end of the passage. Not only were accusations of a cover-up instantaneous but media reports claimed 193 people had died because of the company's 'corporate greed'. As with Pan Am after Lockerbie, the public lost confidence in the ferry operator and chose Sealink ferries instead.

The irony was that, just a few weeks before the tragedy, Townsend Thoresen had been acquired by the much bigger shipping line, P&O. The acquisition had been made largely because of the goodwill associated with the Townsend Thoresen name. After erosion of public confidence, however, P&O had no option but to paint out the name of Townsend Thoresen from vessel sides and replace it with its own. Townsend Thoresen, as an entity, vanished altogether.

Corporate manslaughter

As a case study, the *Herald of Free Enterprise* is important for another reason. It led to historic committal proceedings for manslaughter against

P&O European Ferries (Dover) Ltd, four of the company's directors and three of its employees. This was only the second time in the UK that a charge of corporate manslaughter had been brought. It was first brought against a Welsh construction company in 1965 following the collapse of a bridge.

The charge of corporate manslaughter seeks to establish a link of 'recklessness' from the board director ultimately responsible for a particular activity through to 'coalface' operatives directly responsible for the failure. If proven it can lead to huge fines for the company and prison sentences for the individuals concerned.

The charges against P&O European Ferries alleged there was an obvious and serious risk that, as a result of the failure of the defendants to do their duties properly, the ferry would sail with its doors open, capsize and cause death. The prosecution alleged the defendants either gave no thought to the risk, or recognizing it, nevertheless went on to take it.

As in the case of the Welsh construction company the case was thrown out by the judge for lack of evidence. He said there was no direct evidence available to the prosecution that a reasonably prudent person in the defendants' position would have perceived the risk as obvious or serious.

The case had been widely seen as a test of whether or not a company could be prosecuted for manslaughter and the judge's decision had far-reaching implications for similar prosecutions in the future.

Since then there have only been three successful prosecutions of corporate manslaughter. The first was against the leisure activity company that organized the fatal Lyme Bay canoe trip in 1993 resulting in the death of four sixth-form students, and the second was brought against the managing director of Jackson Transport in 1996, following the death of an employee who inhaled chemicals. The third, and to date final, successful corporate prosecution was brought in 1999, against the directors of haulage firm Roy Bowles Transport, who were found guilty of ignoring the excessive working hours of a driver who fell asleep at the wheel, killing two motorists.

The law was never intended to target small companies, and there have been serious doubts as to whether there will ever be a successful action against a large organization. Under current law, complex management structures mean that the bigger the company involved, the harder it is to apportion blame to corporations or individuals working within them. With negligent companies too often escaping charges, it has long been widely recognized that additional measures are needed to bring those responsible to account, a point underlined repeatedly following high-profile disasters such as Zeebrugge, Piper Alpha and the Paddington rail crash.

In 2000 the Home Office looked as though it was going to make good on government promises to end uncertainty over corporate manslaughter. It published proposals to create a new offence of 'corporate killing', and three new offences to cover individuals who cause death by recklessness or gross carelessness. The intention was to make it easier to bring successful prosecutions against organizations or individuals whose activities lead to fatalities. However, little progress was made following the consultation, despite a renewed pledge by the government to introduce legislation following the 2001 Hatfield train crash, in which four people died. In 2003 the then Home Secretary David Blunkett announced that a draft bill would be released 'shortly'. At the time of going to press it has been deferred again until after the 2005 general election.

Reforming the law has proved contentious and legally complex. One of the key issues is that of accountability: which organizations the offence should apply to, and who should be held responsible within them. Crown Immunity protects government bodies from current law, while private companies are not afforded the same luxury.

Business groups including the CBI are unhappy about this, yet the government argues that the measure is a necessity to prevent it from becoming embroiled in an expensive cycle of self-prosecution. Moreover, senior mandarins have warned that a loss of immunity would make it all too easy to prosecute civil servants, or worse, would result in ministers being found personally liable for policy decisions that result in fatality. Although how this will be resolved is a matter for speculation, at the time of writing the indications are that the government is likely to get its own way.

The difficulty in determining who is ultimately responsible was brought into sharp relief by the failed charges against Railtrack following the Hatfield crash. The difficulty with the existing corporate manslaughter offence is that prosecutors are required to prove the existence of an individual within the organization who has a culpable 'controlling mind' before it can be found guilty. Corporate manslaughter charges were brought against Charles Pollard, a Railtrack executive responsible for the track at Hatfield at the time of the crash, yet the judge rejected the charges.

One suggested solution for determining personal liability within the corporate killing bill has been to create a nominated individual within the company who would be named as having ultimate responsibility, and who could be prosecuted and even jailed, if found guilty. Although those lobbying on behalf of corporate killing victims supported this solution, indications are that the government has buckled under industry pressure, and the bill will not seek to make directors personally liable. Opponents argued that rather than improving health and safety, it would be impossible to choose between directors in allocating personal responsibility, engendering a 'scapegoat' culture where directors seek to protect themselves rather than workers or the public.

The most likely solution was mooted by the Department for Work and Pensions Select Committee, which has recommended higher fines and punitive penalties as a means to encourage a more stringent approach to health and safety among companies. In this case it would be companies, rather than individuals, that would be held responsible – the stigma of which would itself be intended as a deterrent. The option retains an element of personal liability which, although not punishable by a prison term, may involve, for example, community service.

The details of the final bill are currently unknown. Nevertheless, speculation that ministers would need a high-profile corporate manslaughter failure to move the corporate killing up the political agenda seems to have been well founded. At the time of going to print, a draft bill has been promised before the close of the 2004 Parliamentary session, with legislation expected immediately after the 2005 general election.

If the law is enacted (and there is no reason to suppose it won't be; since the early 1990s, every attempt to impose greater responsibility on the corporate world – from social responsibility, working conditions and safety to financial and environmental reporting – has been successful), there will be a number of serious ramifications for organizations.

The potential culpability of the company at board level for failures further down the internal chain will put a premium on reviewing internal health and safety communication procedures. As Bill Gates of Microsoft said, 'Gimme the bad news. It only makes us better!'

Boards will need to consider the reporting chain for safety incidents and board-level receptiveness to 'coalface' concerns. They will also need to consider bringing health and safety and human resource functions into the boardroom to ensure small safety problems are dealt with at an early stage, and that the full importance of reporting them is understood on the ground.

Of main concern to us, however, is the risk that fears of prosecution will dominate the company's response to an accident. The lawyers will move in with their 'do nothing, say nothing' approach and communications paralysis will set in – contrary to all the arguments and evidence demonstrated in this book for protecting reputation in difficult circumstances.

We talked to officials at the Home Office about these concerns in September 2004 and their response was reassuring. There is nothing in the new law that would prevent companies from pursuing a policy of open and honest communication in the aftermath of an accident.

In fact, open communication will be even more important. Such criminal prosecutions would be heard before a jury. Perceptions by jurors of how the organization was seen to behave and heard to respond immediately after a crisis will, in effect, be its character reference in court and form the basis upon which its reputation can be rebuilt.

The proposed legislation argues strongly for organizations to pay even more attention to their training and rehearsal programmes to prepare them to communicate effectively during a crisis. This approach needs to be discussed and agreed with company lawyers before any real-life scenario.

Should more evidence be required to demonstrate the inadequacies of an entirely lawyer-driven response, organizations need only to look at TotalFina's response to the *Erika* oil-spill disaster in December 1999 off the Brittany coast.

CASE STUDY: TOTALFINA AND THE *ERIKA* OIL-SPILL DISASTER

The *Erika*, a tanker carrying approximately 30,000 tonnes of heavy fuel oil, broke into two sections 45 miles south of Brittany's Finistère peninsula. Around 14,000 tonnes of heavy fuel oil leaked into the Atlantic, and 14,600 tonnes of oil remained trapped in the sunken sections of the hold. TotalFina owned the oil; Panship Management and Services owned the vessel.

The legal view at TotalFina was that the company was not responsible; it was the responsibility of the vessel owner, of whom no one had ever heard. The fact that the TotalFina brand was a household name around the world and that its reputation was its most important asset mattered not a jot, said the lawyers. The only response of any importance, according to the legal view, was to be seen as not liable. In other words, to do absolutely nothing.

Big, huge mistake. Within two weeks, the company's share price had fallen 5 per cent, the French government had intervened and demanded TotalFina's intervention and the company's boss, Thierry Desmarest, had been savaged by the newspaper *Le Figaro* in a way that no French businessman has been before or since.

Even so, the company did not issue a press statement until three weeks after the spill, which still asserted it was not responsible. Thierry Desmarest responded to calls for compensation on national radio by offering one day's pay to an environmental organization. Nice one, Thierry!

Within days of the spill, environmental groups were taking action against the company. Greenpeace began delivering barrels (for the collection of shoreline oil) marked with the logo 'TOTALly irresponsible – FINAlly guilty'. Green parties in Germany, France and Italy announced a boycott and a day of action against TotalFina on 30 December. Members of the French Green Party urged TotalFina shareholders to sell their shares in protest.

A worldwide internet campaign against the company was launched shortly after the spill. This enabled environmentalists in Brazil, France, Portugal, Spain, Germany, Israel and Italy to unite and speak with one voice. Letters were e-mailed from around the world directly to Thierry Desmarest and other members of TotalFina's international management team, calling for full restoration of all areas affected by the crisis, admission of responsibility for the incident and a pledge that TotalFina would stop using single-hulled ships over 15 years old.

Direct action against TotalFina followed as public anger grew at its slow and arrogant response. Demonstrations were organized in affected regions, at the company's headquarters and at Thierry Desmarest's home, where oil and sand were dumped. A parcel bomb was sent to a TotalFina service station and gas containers set alight by a radical protest group.

Eventually, the company did become involved with the clean-up, but the public perception was that it had been forced to. Fall in share price, a boycott in three countries, direct action, reams of negative publicity, likely regulatory back-lash – that's the result of a legally driven response with no thought given to the reputational consequences.

SO WHAT IS THE LAWYER'S ROLE IN A CRISIS?

It is about protection. Specifically, to protect:

- the company from criminal prosecution;
- the company from future liability;
- officers and employees;
- the company's position with insurers and regulators;
- documents.

In a crisis it is essential to preserve records of everything. There is a legal duty to preserve and eventually disclose in litigation relevant documents which are in the company's possession even if they are compromising or damaging. The legal process of 'discovery' demands all relevant documents to be handed over to officials investigating what has gone wrong, with the exception of 'legally privileged documents'. Legally privileged documents and communication are immune from discovery even, in some cases, from regulatory authorities.

There are two types of privilege, 'legal advice privilege' and 'litigation privilege'. Legal advice privilege is confidential communication between the client and the lawyer, whether the lawyer is from an independent firm or is the in-house counsel. Litigation privilege extends to confidential communication between the client or lawyer and third parties such as expert consultants, provided litigation has started or is in reasonable prospect.

Lawyers will advise companies to photograph or photocopy everything, particularly anything that may have to be removed by the company, the emergency services or regulators. It is also vital that any internal enquiry into an incident is led by a lawyer for it to have any legal standing. The lawyer will take detailed statements from employees, contractors and others involved in the incident as soon as possible and collect and secure any supporting documents or other form of evidence.

Counsel may want to see press releases before they are issued. This is fine if the lawyer understands the public relations requirements of a crisis. We have, however, seen clear, constructive, communicative, not legally damaging press releases turned into meaningless gobbledegook at the hands of a lawyer. The writing of press releases is the preserve of the public relations professional. Advice may be needed from the lawyer on the approach but not on the words used. One final point: press releases may be produced in court after a crisis because they provide a useful – sometimes damaging – 'snapshot' of the company's position at the time of issue – so they *do* need to be accurate.

COMPENSATION

Compensation for injured parties soon appears as an issue in newspaper stories covering a crisis. How much will be paid, by whom and how quickly?

A company that states publicly it will pay compensation to victims and their families is admitting liability for event. So this must be avoided unless liability has been proven. On the other hand, any suggestion of callousness or complacency on the matter of compensation is out of the question. An appropriate response runs as follows:

> Right now we are doing everything we possibly can to help the families of the deceased and to ensure those injured are receiving the best possible treatment. The question of compensation will be determined by the outcome of the official investigation.

EX-GRATIA PAYMENTS

Affected families may face immediate financial hardship in the aftermath of an accident. It is wise for companies to have in place a policy – as well as a readily accessible budget – to make sums of money available to such families, for example to meet funeral expenses. These are called 'ex-gratia payments'.

Ex-gratia payments do not constitute admission of liability. They represent an act of helpfulness – and are seen as such. If, ultimately, the company that has made such payments is found not to be at fault it can reclaim its costs from the insurance companies of whoever is found to have been at fault. Never, however, reveal the amounts involved. They are a private matter between the company and families involved. This can be stated publicly in response to media questions on the subject.

SUMMARY

- The long-term consequences for an organization's reputation, and subsequent knock-on impact on its bottom line, can be more damaging than any legal consequences.
- Expressing regret for what has happened does not constitute an admission of liability.
- Refer to precedents when arguing the communications case against the legal case.
- Never, ever admit liability unless it has been proven.
- Never, ever speculate about the cause.
- If accused, use authoritative third parties to demonstrate your innocence; your own protestations will rarely be sufficient.
- Don't dodge the compensation question.
- Be prepared to make ex-gratia payments; they don't constitute liability.
- Don't have blind faith in the advice of lawyers and insurance companies; they can get it wrong too.

11

Planning for the unexpected

Today my stockbroker tried to get me to buy some 10-year bonds. I told him: 'Young man, at this point I don't even buy green bananas'.

US congressman when getting on in years

Executives, preoccupied with the market pressures of the present quarter, are not inclined to pay much attention to planning for future crises. However, it is instructive here to recall that Noah started building the ark *before* it began to rain.

Crises are often turning points in organizational life. They represent opportunities to establish a reputation for competence, to shape the organization and to tackle important issues. In most crises, because time is at a premium and resource allocation critical, company executives need strategic guidelines on what kinds of action are needed.

CALM AND POSITIVE THINKING

Taking action in a crisis can be fraught with risk. A strategy is needed for deciding when to define a situation as a crisis, when to take action and to work with others in solving the crisis. Such a strategic sense is in itself a great advantage when tension develops. The ability to keep cool when everything is collapsing is a quality valued in leaders, especially since apparent confidence by the leader is so reassuring to subordinates. Advance planning makes it more possible to concentrate on the actual problem when it peaks, and provides a framework for action.

Crisis management is about seizing the initiative – taking control of what has happened before it engulfs the organization. Planning to manage crises and issues is the key to corporate survival.

Those who are alert to the possibility that any event, even a crisis, is an opportunity to gain friends, to enlist support and, possibly, to attract new customers or shareholders, are well prepared to seize the initiative. Failure to have in place well-tried and tested contingency plans for every kind of emergency means, when the unexpected does occur, the company can only assume a combative posture; it is, of necessity, put into a defensive frame of mind.

Assuming a primarily defensive position establishes a negative attitude. It focuses thinking on reacting to conditions instead of the company acting on its own initiative. When a whole company is put into a negative frame of mind it is virtually certain to be seen as arrogant and unsympathetic to others – evidenced by Exxon Corporation's response to the *Valdez* oil spill. Instead, when positioned to deal not only with the crisis but also the inherent opportunities, a proactive posture can be established which leads to a positive attitude rather than a siege mentality.

DEEDS VERSUS DECLARATIONS

A second principle, perhaps of even greater importance, is that deeds build a reputation far more effectively than words in advertisements or glossy brochures. In today's climate of corporate accountability, promises – words alone – are greeted with cynicism or disbelief. Such an approach actually creates a target for attack should the slightest lapse in performance occur. Nothing gladdens the public heart so much as a fall from grace by the excessively righteous. Self-aggrandizement campaigns lack credibility because everyone knows the sponsor accentuates the beauty spots and hides the warts.

A record of responsible deeds is a vital ingredient for a positive image. The essence of a good reputation rests not in trying to conjure up a good story to hide substandard performance, but in sensitizing management to the need to adjust performance so the deeds speak for themselves. The guiding principles of crisis management are to:

● Develop a positive attitude towards crisis management.

- Bring performance throughout the organization into line with public expectation. Build credibility through a succession of responsible deeds.
- Seek and act on the opportunities during a crisis.

It boils down to deeds versus declarations. A record of responsible deeds is the organization's insurance policy when and if something goes wrong.

PLANNING TO MANAGE THE CRISIS

Anything which can go wrong, will go wrong.

Murphy's Law

The principles applying to crisis management planning are broadly the same for virtually all types of corporate crises. Methods for implementing the plan will not vary greatly for different types of crisis. It is usually impossible to anticipate every crisis which can arise but there are steps every company can take to prepare for one.

A coherent approach begins with the identification of potential crises. These may include:

- existing situations which have the potential to become crises;
- crises which have beset the company in the past – or other companies in the same industry – and might recur;
- planned activity which may meet with opposition from stakeholder groups.

The need is to catalogue the areas of risk: to assess the risk parameters. From this starting point it becomes easier to think through the logical series of steps which need to be taken in the crisis management planning process.

The audit process needs to be undertaken against our definition of a crisis in Chapter 6. The list then needs to be prioritized. A list which is too long will lose credibility with senior management. Since 'buy-in' from senior management is crucial to the whole process of crisis management planning, the list should be prioritized according to likely impact on the organization's financial bottom line. This will attract and sustain senior management attention.

Having identified likely areas of risk, the next questions to ask are:

1. Does the company have policies and procedures in place to prevent a risk from turning into a crisis?
2. Do plans exist for dealing with every aspect of the crisis should it occur?
3. Have the plans been tested to ensure that they work satisfactorily?

Various supplementary, but equally important, questions may be added. For example:

4. Which are the audiences most likely to be affected by the identified potential crisis?
5. Do plans include procedures for communicating effectively to these about what has happened and what is being done about it?
6. Have the communications aspects of the plan been tested, as well as the company's operational response?

In short, planning for crisis management may be summarized as:

● *cataloguing potential crisis situations;*
● *devising policies for their prevention;*
● *formulating strategies and tactics for dealing with each potential crisis;*
● *identifying who will be affected by them;*
● *devising effective communications channels to those affected so as to mini-mize damage to the organization's reputation;*
● *testing everything.*

How to manage the process is shown in Figure 11.1.

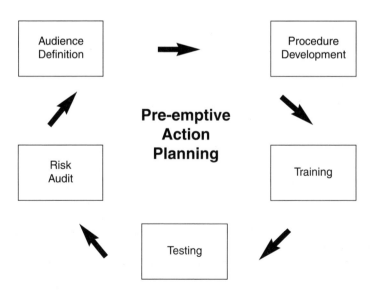

Figure 11.1 *Managing the process*

APPOINTING THE TEAMS

To manage and contain the crisis, three separate teams will be required; the Core Committee, the Crisis Control Team and the Communication Team (the role of the Communication Team is discussed in the next chapter).

The Core Committee

This will comprise main board directors whose role is to take the 'high ground' of the crisis, considering such aspects as:

- business continuity; product sourcing and supply;
- contingency budget approvals;
- high-level communication with, for example, the overseas head office, government ministers and members of parliament;
- content of messages for institutional investors, the media, customers, employees and other affected groups;
- the insurance position; liaison with legal advisers; ex-gratia payments;
- tracking what is happening to people; preparing to make hospital/ family visits;
- *above all*, ensuring the chairman or CEO is briefed and on the way to the site, accompanied by a public relations professional, as quickly as possible, to begin the media communication process.

Members of the team need to be grouped together in a 'war room' adequately equipped with telephones, fax machines, internet access, photocopiers, a television and radio (to monitor news reports) and boards around the room on which new information and decisions are recorded. The role of the log-keeper cannot be underestimated. He or she must be a long-standing company employee, intimately familiar with the business and its technical jargon but capable of writing clearly and succinctly in lay language.

It helps to have the boards inscribed with permanent headings so information can be clearly organized, for example:

People
Incident status
Environment
Weather
Product supply

Each team member must be assigned specific, individual responsibility for these key functions. They must be aware of their responsibilities and have rehearsed them. Each member of the Core Committee should have an 'alternative' in case someone is away. The team leader *must* chair regular information update meetings for all the team members, as often as every 15 minutes in a fast-moving situation.

The Crisis Control Team

The second team to come into play is the Crisis Control Team, responsible for the immediate 'hands on' operational response. The distinction between this team and the Core Committee is crucial. Neither should interfere with the other but the Crisis Control Team – which will be located at the site of the crisis – must keep the Core Committee constantly updated with developments. *It should have a member dedicated solely to this task.* Equally, the Core Committee – probably located at the head office – must provide the Crisis Control Team with strategic advice and rapid budget approvals for urgent areas of expenditure (see Figure 11.2, page 202).

The Crisis Control Team will also need a dedicated 'war room' for its members. Plans should include identification of an off-site 'war room' in case the site has had to be evacuated.

In addition to the materials and equipment already described, the 'war rooms' of each team should be equipped with plans depicting:

- locations of hazardous materials;
- sources of safety equipment;
- fire-water system and alternative source of water;
- stocks of other types of fire extinguishers;
- plant entrances and road systems, updated to include any road which is impassable;
- assembly points and casualty centres;
- location of plant in relation to the surrounding community;
- areas affected or endangered;
- deployment of emergency vehicles and personnel;
- areas where further problems may arise, eg fractured pipelines;
- area evacuated;
- other relevant information.

COMMUNICATION HARDWARE

Since the unexpected tends to happen at Sunday lunchtime or on Christmas Eve, a comprehensive, foolproof cascade call-out procedure is

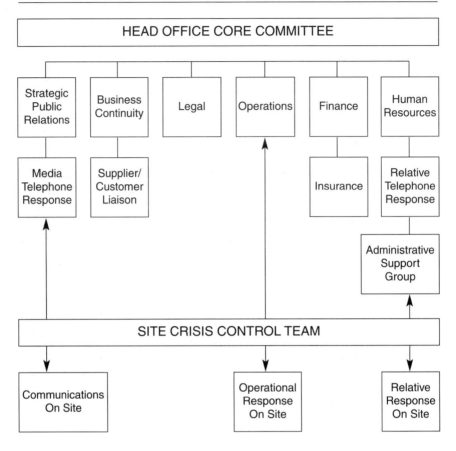

Source: Regester and Larkin training package

Figure 11.2 *Responsibilities and interactions of crisis teams*

required with back-up alternates to stand in for key individuals who are not contactable. The cascade principle involves each member of the teams having the responsibility to call out at least two other team members once he or she has been called.

Facilities and hardware for communication need to be checked. Are key individuals equipped with mobile telephones or pagers? How would the switchboard cope with floods of additional telephone calls? (Occidental Oil took 4,500 additional calls from the media and relatives in the first 24 hours after the Piper Alpha tragedy; Perrier took 3,000, over the same period, in the UK alone – see Chapter 12 for advice on handling telephone calls.)

CRISIS PREVENTION

While it will be the responsibility of the Core Committee, Crisis Control and Communication Teams to manage and contain the crisis, yet another group of people is required to ensure the crisis doesn't happen in the first place – we call this the Crisis Prevention Team. Ideally, it should be made up from members of the other three teams. It doesn't come into play when the crisis occurs but should have been instrumental in minimizing the size of the crisis if it does occur – and in preparing and rehearsing the other teams to respond effectively when it does.

Crisis prevention team

This team formulates and sets company-wide policies appropriate to the hazards or risks of the business. It needs to ensure managers of each part of the business have the funds and other resources required to enable them to comply with policies – *as well as responsibility for implementing them.*

Such policies need to go beyond ensuring the organization merely complies with existing regulations. They must endeavour to anticipate 'worst case' scenarios. This approach is likely to prove more costly but the cost involved of not setting such far-reaching policies can prove catastrophic in terms of human lives and the company's entire future. Developing policies against agreed company criteria will help to give them shape and depth. Such criteria can be developed by answering the following questions:

- Would this situation really affect our bottom line?
- How realistic is the identified potential crisis situation?
- Could corporate action halt or moderate the crisis?
- Does the policy stand up to public scrutiny?
- Are the resources to act available?
- Is the *will* to act present?
- What would be the effect of inaction?

A positive approach to crisis management demands the implementation of preventive policies which have been developed and checked on a regular basis. Part of the Crisis Prevention Team's remit must be to conduct audits to check policy implementation.

Take, for example, a manufacturing company being audited for implementation of policies to prevent a physical crisis. Each year the audit group might select an audit programme which examines different topics – safety and loss prevention, air and water quality, solid waste disposal, occupational health and product quality.

Sites selected for audit can be based on their risk potential, their recent performance and the length of time since last audited. To lend weight to the audit process, the Crisis Prevention Team needs to report twice yearly to the main board on the status of the risk audit programme and measures required to minimize new areas of risk.

This audit process works well because it takes an objective view of each situation and ensures appropriate standards are applied across all divisions. The continuing interest displayed by the board gives authority to the Crisis Prevention Team and ensures divisional and local management corrects deficiencies.

Auditing for potential financial crises

The same audit process can be applied to potential financial risks. For example, the Crisis Prevention Team adopts the protagonist role of an unwanted bidder and looks for tell-tale signs of weakness in the company's performance which could make it an easy prey. The danger signals are likely to include:

- static or falling earnings;
- poor return on capital;
- unhealthy dividend policy;
- bad cash management;
- too high gearing;
- poor investment policy;
- too many, difficult to justify, rights issues;
- unimaginative asset management (including well-stocked pension fund or cash mountain);
- neglected or poor communication with investors and their advisers;
- major shareholder suddenly disposing of shares;
- forthcoming tax or protectionist legislation;
- business synergy with the predator (improved earnings prospects of the combined companies);
- marketing synergy;
- knocking you out as direct competition;
- acquiring your management team;
- acquiring your production capacity.

External advisers – bankers, brokers and specialist public relations consultants – should be brought in to assist with the financial risk audit. Such advisers need to be reviewed regularly to ensure they are not also the advisers to potential predators.

The most important point to keep in mind is the worst case scenario approach. Organizations will rarely be criticized for considering every aspect of the situation and acting accordingly.

Appointment of the Crisis Prevention Team will demonstrate the orga-nization's commitment to responsible management of its business. If it does its job effectively, the team will minimize the risk of a crisis occur-ring in the first place, will help to contain it if it should occur, will reduce the potential damage to the organization's reputation, and will change the organization's culture from responsive to positive. In summary, the role of the Crisis Prevention Team is to:

- anticipate, clearly and comprehensively, all forms of crisis situations;
- develop strategies and procedures for dealing with them;
- check policies and procedures are implemented;
- ensure they are rehearsed and updated on a regular basis.

SELECTING TEAM MEMBERS

Various leadership styles emerge in crisis situations. While the 'human' participative manager is generally the most effective leader, he or she can sometimes inhibit the rapid decision taking required in an emergency. On the other hand, the authoritarian leader may act decisively at the expense of demotivating the team members and inhibiting creativity. It is vital for team leaders to recognize team members' different attributes and values and integrate them to maximum advantage during the crisis.

Members of all teams involved should be chosen for their personal qualities and talents – breadth of vision, ability to stay cool, knowledge of the company and its business, and the ability to make swift, clearly expressed decisions.

Some of the styles we have seen emerge include:

- *The 'ideas' person* – a creative member who is constantly injecting new ideas and suggestions. Some of these may be far-fetched but some may have real merit. It is vital for the leader to filter out the viable ideas and discard the remainder without discouraging the flow.
- *The communicator* – the individual who helps the flow of information both within and outside the team (not necessarily the team leader, although the team leader should possess strong communication skills also).
- *The doom merchant* – the devil's advocate who brings out the negative aspects of each proposed idea or solution.
- *The book-keeper* – the neat and orderly member who wants the records and logs maintained to perfection. This individual is more comfort-able in such a role than as a decision maker. Nonetheless, it is a vital role.

- *The humanist* – the people-oriented member whose solutions always focus on the human aspects of the problem – an important visionary in the heat of the moment.

PUTTING THE PLAN IN WRITING

The importance of putting the plan in writing cannot be overestimated. In our experience, too often the communication plans do not exist at all – or exist in the heads of a few individuals. Companies must overcome the 'Joe will know what to do if it happens' syndrome; Joe may be on holiday – or dead. Even if he is available, he will be too busy to explain plans which should be readily available for all concerned.

Absence of a written plan will cause hours of additional work for an already fraught management. People will fail to take basic actions; for example, failure to notify employees in an emergency will lead to a flood of unnecessary phone calls about the effect of the incident on work schedules. Valuable time will be lost and tempers grow short because names and telephone numbers are not available when needed.

Checklists of things to do and people to contact are invaluable in enabling the organization to 'hit the ground running' when the crisis occurs. In a chaotic situation it's a huge relief to be able to hand to subordinates lists of things to do, giving assurance that all the essential steps will be taken.

The plan must not be too long or rigid. It must provide the flexibility and framework which acknowledges the unpredictable aspects of any crisis situation; and give management the leeway to use common sense. It needs a structure, but a loose one.

Put the plan in writing and assign a 'champion' to ensure it is kept up to date with changes to the business and movement of personnel.

TESTING EVERYTHING

Remaining familiar with the plan's content is always a problem. The best way is through crisis exercise simulations to test effectiveness of procedures and training. But first those with key roles should receive training. There is no situation more demoralizing than running an exercise in which everyone comprehensively screws up. Worse, it puts management off doing it again. No one likes to make a fool of themselves.

A crucial ingredient to successful exercise simulations is getting the scenario right. Particularly if they have not previously participated in an exercise, management members will take part only reluctantly, believing they have 'more important things to do' and the whole business is a waste of time. If the scenario is in any way unrealistic they will refuse to continue and retire triumphant in the knowledge it *was* a waste of time.

When running the simulation, a good mechanism for making the mock incident evolve over real or imagined time is to feed in printed details of each new phase of the scenario and predetermined times.

For example, the person in charge of the response will receive a message stating:

> You have just learnt from the general manager of the company's manufacturing plant in Manchester that an explosion has taken place in or near the main chemicals storage depot. Several employees are unaccounted for, feared dead or injured in the wreckage. Reporters are arriving at the factory gate and many are phoning the company. The local MP is on the phone and wishes to speak to you urgently. Take appropriate action.

He or she will receive a series of such messages, sometimes at intervals of only a few minutes, and will then activate the Core Committee and Communications Teams. Role-playing journalists, relatives, MPs, investors, investment analysts and environmental lobbyists start putting pressure on the company. Television camera crews arrive at the head office, as well as at the Manchester plant, demanding interviews. Every aspect of the company's response procedures is put to the test.

The simulation should last for four or five hours. It should conclude with a 'live', filmed press conference and be followed up with an immediate debrief on the response – a 'hot washup'. Later, a more considered written report should be produced clearly identifying agreed areas for improvement and whose responsibility it is for their implementation.

In our experience, those who have participated in the simulation generally rate their performance unrealistically highly. This is to be expected because of the sense of reality and unusual nature of the experience. A second evaluation needs to be provided, by qualified outside experts, which, while constructive, is more realistic. Simulations should be run once or twice a year to ensure recommendations from the previous one have been implemented and to take account of changes in the business and movement of personnel.

SUMMARY

- Develop a positive attitude towards crisis management.
- Bring the organization's performance into line with public expectation.
- Build credibility through a succession of responsible deeds.
- Be prepared to act on the opportunities during a crisis.
- Appoint appropriate teams to prevent, manage and control crisis situations.
- Catalogue potential crisis situations.
- Devise policies for their prevention.
- Put the plan in writing.
- Test, test and test again.

12

Crisis communications management

Let our advance worrying become advance thinking and planning.
                                                    Winston Churchill

The best-laid plans are worthless if they cannot be communicated.

Speed is of the essence. A crisis simply will not wait. Tell it all, tell it fast, tell it truthfully – and don't stop until the plague of locusts has had enough or found a richer source of food elsewhere. It's like wrestling a gorilla: you rest when the gorilla rests.

STENA CHALLENGER GROUNDING

What was so impressive about Stena Lines' handling of the media during the grounding of the *Stena Challenger* outside Calais in September 1995 was its speed of response to the media and the way in which the company organized the flow of information.

Although none of the passengers or crew was injured, media attention was acute because of previous ferry disasters. Unlike Townsend Thoresen, Stena did not clam up. Within two hours of the *Stena Challenger* hitting the sandbank the company was communicating with the media about how much food and drink was on board; that plenty of telephone lines were available for the 172 passengers and 73 crew to contact anxious families; what it was doing to refloat the vessel.

In other words, the company concentrated on providing news about people first and, as we have seen, 'people' news must always take prominence over other information. It must be followed by news on the environment and property, if they have been affected, and lastly about money – what it is all going to cost.

The company's news handling deflected the media from focusing on questions about the navigation equipment and navigator; whether or not the skipper was drunk – as they did in the case of the *Exxon Valdez*. These are all questions it would have concentrated on in the absence of people-oriented news and, indeed, they were asked later. But by this time the story had died and only marginal coverage was given to such issues. Stena had survived the crisis and subsequently reported an increase in Stena Line passengers on the Dover–Calais route, with *Stena Challenger* carryings at normal levels.

A key to its successful response was its well-practised crisis management plan. A copy of the plan, with its practical information such as telephone numbers, contact points and clear procedures, is carried in the briefcases of the company's senior management in readiness for such an event.

The plan is activated by the master of any Stena Line ferry in distress: it is the master who puts into action an appeal for help. This produces a 'domino' effect at the company's headquarters in Ashford, Kent, with the ship and port management department which offers technical assistance necessary to manage the incident, and the four-strong public relations team who implement a media management plan. The public relations function ensures the ship management and technical teams are protected from media interference and can get on with rectifying the situation and ensuring passenger safety.

BACKGROUND INFORMATION TO SEIZE THE INITIATIVE

The first 24 hours are critical. The 'information void' will be guaranteed to loom because of lack of hard facts about the incident. The void, however, can be bridged by offering the media background information on the company or installation which has been affected. This produces two results: the first is the creation of valuable breathing space to gather and check information about the incident before its release to the media; and it demonstrates to the media that the organization is clearly going to cooperate and communicate with it. Reporters who gather or telephone to cover the story will usually know nothing about the company, its plant and operations. Offering background information enables them to begin framing the story they will later write or broadcast.

So it is essential to keep updated background information packs about the organization and each installation or part of the operation considered potentially at risk. They should include:

- colour and black and white photographs;
- diagrams;
- basic information about:
  - number of employees;
  - how long in business;
  - business description;
  - names of key executives;
  - safety record and practices.

Such packs located at the organization's headquarters as well as at each site at risk, where the media may descend in droves, will help the company to seize the initiative and prevent it from disappearing into the void.

SET UP A PRESS CENTRE

It may not be possible, or advisable, to hold press conferences on company premises. Reconnaissance work needs to be done near each site considered at risk and arrangements made, perhaps with a local hotel, town or village hall, which could be quickly established as a centre for the media during the emergency. The media should be informed of the times of press conferences – and these must be adhered to. It will talk to others between each conference but at least the company will have the opportunity to tell its own story once or twice a day, and to correct misinformation picked up by journalists. Around 10.30 and 15.30 are generally regarded as suitable times for holding press conferences because they meet the majority of deadlines.

MANAGING THE PRESS CONFERENCE

This can be a nightmare. Hundreds of potentially hostile journalists gathered at one location have been enough to make grown men cry. Training and preparation are the keys. The press conference site should contain:

- external telephone lines and handsets;
- a minimum of two fax machines;
- two entrances, one for use by management and the other by the media;
- a large diagram of the site or other visual aid material which will help to explain what has happened;
- background information press packs;
- refreshments (not alcohol);
- toilet facilities;
- adequate security measures to ensure control of persons, either on or off site, with particular regard to their safety.

Useful tips to assist with the successful management of press conferences include:

- Restrict the numbers of the management team to only those with specific knowledge of different aspects of the incident; *never* fall into the 'comfort in numbers' trap at the top table since this only provides the media with more targets to snipe at. Ensure it is chaired by a senior company executive *provided* he or she is a good communicator.
- Place a time parameter on the conference if members of management need to get back to dealing with the problem in hand; *never* less than 30 minutes. End the conference at the specified time.
- Try to issue a new press release at the *conclusion* of the conference. Have copies placed strategically at the exit door for the media so they are encouraged to use it, allowing the management to exit via their own door.

Press conferences rarely work well on television. It is best to arrange one-to-one television interviews after the conference. Never exclude television cameras from the press conference, however, as British Gas did famously when announcing the resignation of its much maligned chief executive, Cedric Brown, and the demerger of the company.

Although the company had arranged for one-to-one television interviews after the conference, broadcast journalists became infuriated when they and their cameras were excluded from the conference itself. Revenge was achieved by filming Cedric Brown leaving the conference, struggling to get through the throng of angry broadcast reporters, and being bonked on the head by a camera. A general picture of chaos – not helpful to the company's beleaguered reputation – was created which television companies delighted in showing the rest of the world on prime time news programmes.

Insist, however, that television cameras are situated at the back of the room and not allowed to gather round the table to get those nice close-up shots. This will only serve to further intimidate management and anger the print media who will not be able to see a thing.

There is another good reason for arranging television interviews after the press conference. If someone has made a mess of answering questions during the press conference the television interview provides an opportunity to rectify the error. When we were in the Shetland Islands during the *Braer* disaster, the vessel's owner was asked at one press conference: 'In the light of what has happened will you in future continue to route vessels through the narrow passage between the southern end of the islands and the north of Scotland?' He replied that thousands of vessels had plied this route for hundreds of years and he saw no reason for changing it.

This was a big mistake. The next day, the *Today* newspaper covered its front page with a huge photograph of a pathetic-looking oiled seal beneath the caption: 'I'd do it again – *Braer* vessel owner'. However, before giving a television interview for the BBC after the press conference he was suitably admonished by his public relations adviser and proceeded to provide the correct answer during the television interview: 'We will look carefully at the findings and recommendations of the official enquiry into the accident and, of course, we will adopt any recommendations which improve safety and minimize damage to the environment'. Millions more people watch television than read newspapers so, to some extent, the mistake had been rectified.

A final point to remember about giving television interviews after the press conference is that the company may be besieged with requests for such interviews and may not be able to cope because of other pressures. If this is *genuinely* the case, and can be seen as such, the 'pooling' arrangement can come into play. 'Pooling' simply means explaining to the broadcast media that there is insufficient time to meet all its demands for interviews but the company is prepared to give one interview which the broadcast media can share. The media will select from among its numbers who is to conduct the interview and which film crew will be used. They then share the resulting footage or radio tape.

DEALING WITH THE TELEVISION INTERVIEW

Training of television spokespeople is absolutely vital against crisis scenarios – partly to teach techniques and give confidence but also to discover who is good at it and who isn't.

Basic tips to remember are:

- Prepare three main points which, if appropriate, refer to people first, damage to the environment or property second and financial consequences third.
- If possible, rehearse the interview beforehand.

- Never speculate about the cause of the incident; instead say, 'The cause will be established once a full investigation has been completed'.
- Anticipate the worst possible questions and devise suitable answers.
- Praise the actions of third-party bodies, such as the police, fire brigade, etc.
- Never point the finger of blame at the company, employees or third parties.
- Eyeball the interviewer; never talk to the camera unless it is a down-the-line interview.
- Ensure the three main points are communicated irrespective of the questions asked.
- Jump on untruths, innuendo or misleading remarks immediately; interrupt if necessary.

COPING WITH HUNDREDS OF TELEPHONE CALLS

Few companies have more elaborate arrangements for dealing with incoming telephone calls from the media and relatives of employees than those in the oil industry. From our own experience of attempting and failing miserably to handle thousands of such telephone calls during one of the industry's worst disasters – at Bantry Bay in southwest Ireland, in January 1979, when an oil tanker, the *Betelgeuse*, blew up killing 50 people – we have helped the North Sea oil industry to pioneer a telephone response system which is today widely used by many of the utilities, airlines, chemical, pharmaceutical, engineering and food companies.

Since no company, whatever its industry, has a public relations or human resources department with sufficient people in it to cope with such pressure, the solution is to train employees from other disciplines within the organization in techniques for handling calls from these two vital audiences. Occidental Oil had a team of 40 trained responders in Aberdeen, and a back-up team of 20 in London, when the Piper Alpha production platform exploded late one evening in 1988. The teams helped the company to cope with some 4,500 telephone calls during the first 24 hours.

Responding to media calls

Incoming telephone calls from the media will far outweigh the numbers of reporters able to get to the site. Sometimes there is nothing to see, only people to talk to, as in the case of a company collapse or fraudulent activity. Aeroplanes, ships and oil rigs can disappear altogether. So the telephone becomes an incredibly important channel of communication.

We advise companies to designate a media telephone response room equipped with sufficient handsets and its own dedicated telephone number which can be quickly issued via the wire services in the event of an emergency. This prevents the main switchboard from becoming jammed up and allows the normal business of the day to continue. It can be a meeting room in which the handsets are stored in a cupboard ready to be plugged into jackpoints around the room at a moment's notice.

Other items to be kept in readiness for the media telephone response teams include:

- pads of numbered log sheets for each team member;
- a filing box for each individual;
- flip charts and pens;
- whiteboard and appropriate pens;
- map of the affected site;
- fax machine and photocopier;
- refreshments;
- 'fast facts' file about the company and affected installation.

'Fast facts' is a term we coined to describe the media telephone team's equivalent to the background information pack. Written in conversational language and carefully indexed, it contains the answers to every anticipated question reporters might ask in a crisis situation. It also contains a list of questions about every conceivable kind of crisis the company may face so the answers can be filled in at the outset of the emergency. These questions act as an *aide-mémoire* to obtaining crucial information which may be forgotten in the heat of the moment.

A common mistake made by companies in crisis is to issue information to the media only via press releases. But, as we will see, press releases can take a long time to prepare and distribute in crisis situations.

There must be a constant flow of information from the crisis management team's 'war room' to the media responders, so it is helpful to have the two teams located close to each other. Where this is not possible there needs to be an open telephone line between the 'war room' and the media responders so new information may be constantly accessed and passed on to media responders. New information, which is authorized for disclosure, is written on the whiteboards.

Whenever new information becomes available the supervisor in charge of the media response team – ideally a public relations professional although others can be trained in the role – gives the team a signal which means 'phones off the hook'. Responders finish their telephone conversations and the new information is gone through until every team member is confident about its meaning and comfortable with words to express the information.

Such briefing periods are also used to anticipate new questions which are bound to arise from the newly issued information. For example, the new information may state the site has been evacuated, but not where it has been evacuated to. The process of obtaining answers to these questions can begin immediately and, hopefully, be received before the question is even put.

RESPONDING TO CALLS FROM RELATIVES

This is often the most ignored area of crisis communication management yet it is one of the most important, for two reasons. Any inability to respond sympathetically with information about employees to callers will only add to their anguish. And it will frustrate and anger the caller who may resort to calling a local or national newspaper thereby compounding the public relations problem.

It is also one of the most complex aspects of the crisis communications response. Few organizations have efficient systems for tracking who was on the site when it happened, although these are improving. But if the company is unable to confirm quickly whether or not an employee was present and provide the caller with information about his or her status, initial anger will turn to fury.

Many companies ask employees to fill in forms stating which family member should be notified in the event of something happening to the employee – but don't keep these records up to date. People's situations change and information may be given unwittingly to the wrong person.

When the Piper Alpha tragedy occurred Occidental Oil flew relatives of everyone who had been on board the stricken platform to Aberdeen. It took over the Skean Dhu hotel at Aberdeen airport to accommodate everyone. Generous and correct though this action was, the company failed to keep track of who it was flying to Aberdeen. Some of the men working offshore were leading complicated lives and more than one wife claiming the same husband turned up at the hotel. The rest is best left to the imagination.

When the questions come they are nearly always the same:

- Was he there when it happened?
- If he was, is he all right?
- If he is uninjured, where is he now and when can I expect to see/speak to him?
- If he has been injured, how serious are his injuries and which hospital has he been taken to?
- Will you help me to get there?

If the worst has happened and the employee has died, this information must obviously never be given down the telephone. The police will want to inform the family but, if possible, they should be accompanied by a senior company representative.

British Airways EPIC Centre

The response system many companies employ to respond to relatives is modelled on British Airways' Emergency Public Information Centre (EPIC) near terminal four at Heathrow airport. It comprises a set of rooms only used when a plane has crashed or a crisis simulation test is being run. Because it is unique it is franchised out to other airlines.

Telephones are manned by flight attendants who have received additional training. A multiple language capability is important because of the different nationalities flying in aircraft. One bank of callers receive incoming calls, establish the name of the caller, who they are calling about, the nature of the relationship and where they can be reached. The caller is asked to wait by the phone until information can be given to them.

A second bank of responders establishes – in close cooperation with the British Transport Police located at Heathrow – the status of the passenger being enquired about and what information can be passed back to the relatives. Then follow all the logistical problems of flying relatives to hospitals and the scene of the accident.

In companies, the relative response team needs to be housed in a designated meeting room equipped in the same manner as the media responders. The two teams should not be located in the same room because of the different techniques employed. In essence, the media telephone response team is trying to give out as much accurate information as quickly as possible. The relative response team, initially at any rate, is trying to elicit information from callers.

Lack of resource may prevent using the double-banked system of British Airways, in which case one team will need to fulfil both functions. A separate administrative team should be set up, however, to deal with the logistics of getting family members to the hospital. The company will also need to ensure company representatives are at the hospital to assist family members.

THE NEWS RELEASE

The news release is a key communications tool in a crisis situation. It provides the company's official explanation of what is happening and may be used for expressing quotes from senior management on how it is 'feeling' about the situation. News releases should keep coming thick and fast throughout the crisis period.

A good idea is to number, time and date them, at the top of each release. This will enable journalists to keep tabs on the chronology of events more easily. It also enables media responders to ask which was the last news release seen by the journalist – and quickly ascertain the level of knowledge currently possessed.

In some situations, it is worth thinking about who else the media will contact for information about the emergency, for example, the police, fire brigade, local hospital and other third party agencies. These can be sent copies of the company's releases in advance of sending them to the media. Such third parties are often less well geared up to respond to the media and will be grateful for copies of the company's releases to help with their own response. It helps also, of course, in attaining a consistency of message from all those involved. (In Scotland, the police have the right to vet all press releases concerning death and injury from an industrial accident.)

One final point. It is sometimes possible to prepare 'pro-forma holding statements' in anticipation of a potential crisis, for example in the case of a physical accident; here is an example.

PRESS STATEMENT

<u>Date:</u>

<u>Time:</u>

<u>No:</u>

XYZ Company confirms an incident (state what if known) has occurred (state where and when) and coordination of emergency rescue services is being controlled by the site's emergency response team.

Firm details about the incident are not yet known, but every possible action is being taken to safeguard lives and the environment.
Background information about the site is attached and more information about the incident will be released as soon as it becomes available.

The following special telephone number has been issued by XYZ Company for media enquiries relating to the incident...

-end-

Press statements should always announce news in the following order:

1. nature of the incident;
2. location of the incident;
3. details of fatalities (numbers not names);
4. details of injured (numbers not names);

5. details of areas affected;
6. details of impact on the environment;
7. details of action to be taken for customers;
8. quote from senior manager expressing regret for incident and praise for those involved in all aspects of the emergency;
9. details about follow-up investigation into the cause of the incident;
10. reminder about site's safety record (if good) prior to the incident.

KEEPING EMPLOYEES INFORMED

Following a serious incident it is vital to keep employees informed of the situation and of developments. They should not learn new information via the media, as so often happens. Employees are the company's 'ambassadors' and need to be in a position to explain to customers, family and friends what is happening.

They should have access to company press statements prior to release. Where possible, briefings should be set up to provide an opportunity to ask questions; alternatively, they can be kept informed through e-mail, letters from senior management or printed newsletters. With employees it is important to obtain a sense of common ownership of the problem. Be honest and open about decisions being taken to solve the problem and share the entire remedial plan with them. Keep them updated regularly.

There should also be a policy in place which explains it is not the role of employees to talk to the media about the problem. It is impossible and would be wrong to try to 'gag' employees, but at least they will know what is expected of them if they are aware of the company's policy. This might run as follows:

> Should you be approached by a member of the press to comment about any aspect of the company's activities, please say you are not the best person to assist with their enquiry and the journalist should contact the press office.

USING YOUR WEBSITE

In the same way that the internet has been used by activists as a highly effective global mechanism for mobilizing opinion and action against organizations, company websites can provide a fast and effective means of communicating directly to stakeholders without the risk of 'interpretation' by the media.

Increasingly used by journalists as a source of company information, websites can play a crucial role in communicating to them and to other stakeholders. Use the website to post news releases and background information about a situation *in addition* to issuing news releases to papers, giving 'chat room' media interviews, responding to telephone media enquiries and holding news conferences.

Remember, though, that once information is on the website, it will be available globally. If you are dealing with a situation in which there is only local or national interest, it may be wiser to contain it to national boundaries rather than advertise it to the rest of the world.

Some companies employ the use of 'dark sites' on their website. The dark site is not normally accessible to people contacting the website; it is only activated by the company in an emergency situation. On to the dark site can be 'stored' prepared news releases which anticipate the most likely events that the organization might have to face, leaving gaps for the relevant details to be added when the need arises. Additionally, 'fast facts' about the sites, products or services likely to be impacted can be kept here too. The relevant information is then released from the dark site to the main website, saving huge amounts of preparation and approval time. Once the dark site has been activated it blanks out all other information on the website.

The website can also be used by the media and other visitors to download audio comments from company spokespeople about the situation – particularly useful for radio news broadcasts. Not long from now, the technology will exist for newsrooms to download live, broadcast quality, webcasts from company spokespeople for their television bulletins as well as online interviewing and news conferences.

THE ROLE OF THE EMERGENCY SERVICES

The police, in particular, can be of enormous assistance in crises of a physical nature. They can absorb some of the pressure through their own press and casualty bureaux working closely with the company involved in the emergency. They will also assume responsibility for ensuring bodies are identified by next of kin and for notifying families in the event of death caused by an industrial accident. Ideally, the police officer should be accompanied by a senior company representative so immediate condolences and assistance can be offered to the bereaved family. The police will not usually inform families of the injured unless the distances involved preclude the company from visiting the family. In most cases of injury, however, it is best to break the news by telephone so relatives can get to the hospital as quickly as possible.

The police will also be in attendance when survivors arrive at the hospital, or relatives and the media arrive at the site of the accident, to ensure control. They will organize traffic flows, establish meeting points, make secure the scene of the incident and organize appropriate resources.

It is important to remember that the police and representatives of the other emergency services involved in the situation, such as the fire brigade or HM Coastguard, will wish to communicate about what has happened; about the actions, bravery and equipment of their own men and women. The key is to ensure messages are coordinated and do not conflict with those being made by the company.

Company site managers should keep in regular contact with local police and fire brigades so relationships are maintained and roles defined. Informal agreements on lines of communication, wording of press releases and the release of new information can be drawn up. Sometimes it can be useful to invite a senior representative from the emergency services to attend company press conferences in order to present a 'united front'.

WHEN IT IS ALL OVER

Experience is the name everyone gives to their mistakes.

Oscar Wilde

In the aftermath of the crisis the temptation is to forget all about it as quickly as possible; to resume normal life. But surviving a crisis provides a huge opportunity for the organization to re-examine and reorganize itself to ensure it never again finds itself in a similar position. It can represent a turning point in organizational life, present opportunities to establish a reputation for caring and competence and rise from the ashes – chastened but in better shape to tackle the challenges of the age of corporate accountability. Never forget lightning *can* strike twice in the same place.

Attention needs to be given to employees and their families in the aftermath of crisis. Some may have been traumatized by the event. Some we know have left the organization because they could not face the possibility of a similar event happening again. Families who have been bereaved will often feel colossal anger towards the organization even though it may not have been at fault. The company can help by offering professional counselling. Sometimes it is possible to redirect anger felt for the loss of a loved one into a positive energy by channelling it into finding solutions to prevent the situation from ever occurring again; to make sense of what has happened by helping others in the future.

The continued inability of organizations – whatever their sphere of operations – to regulate their activities so the chance of crisis is minimized; a failure to check constantly that their deeds match their expectations and declarations; and lassitude over plans and preparations to deal with the worst, so that crisis can be quickly contained, must inevitably lead to greater constraints being placed upon organizations of all types.

The key to crisis management is crisis prevention, whether the vigilance and preparation is self-motivated or enforced by legislation. But if a fire does break out, comprehensive contingency planning can minimize the catastrophe; and a policy of open communication can minimize damage to corporate and individual reputations.

SUMMARY

- Ensure all key players keep a copy of the crisis management plan with them at all times.
- Have background information prepared.
- Set up a press centre.
- Ensure executives are trained to manage successfully press conferences, television, radio and print media interviews – against crisis scenarios.
- Establish trained telephone response teams to cope with media and relative calls.
- Keep news releases coming thick and fast; date, time and number them.
- Don't forget employees – they are the company's 'ambassadors'.
- Coordinate the response of the company and third parties.
- When it's all over, review the organization from top to bottom in the light of lessons learnt – lightning *can* strike twice.

References

Anderson, S and Cavanagh, J (2000) *Top 200: The rise of corporate global power*, Institute for Policy Studies.

Association of British Insurers (ABI) (2001) *Investing in Social Responsibility: Risks and opportunities*, ABI, London.

Brown, J K (1979) *This Business of Issues: Coping with company's environments*, Conference Board Report no 758.

Buchholz, R A (1988) 'Adjusting Corporations to the Realities of Public Interests and Policy', in *Strategic Issues Management: How organizations influence and respond to public interests and policies*, Jossey-Bass, San Francisco.

Chase, W Howard (1984) *Issue Management: Origins of the future*, Issue Action Publications Inc, Leesburg, Virginia, USA.

Chippendale, P and Horrie, C (1992) *Stick It Up Your Punter – the rise and fall of the* Sun, Mandarin Paperbacks, London.

Clifton, R and Maughan, E (eds) (1999) *Future of Brands: Twenty-five visions*, Macmillan, Basingstoke.

Corporate Public Issues and their Management, **26** (1) (January 2004), Issue Action Publications, Leesburg, Virginia, USA.

Crable, R E and Vibbert, S L (1985) 'Managing Issues and Influencing Public Policy', *Public Relations Review*, **11** (2).

Department of Health (DOH) (1997) *On the State of the Public Health: The Annual Report of the Chief Medical Officer of the Department of Health for the Year 1996*, DOH, London.

Elkington, J (2001) *The Chrysalis Economy: How citizen CEOs and corporations can fuse values and value creation*, Capstone, Oxford.

Environics International, Conference Board and Prince of Wales Business Leaders' Forum (1999) *The Millennium Poll on Corporate Social Responsibility*, Environics/GlobeScan, London [online] http://www.globescan.com/news_archives/MPExecBrief.pdf.

Grunig, J E and Hunt, T (1984) *Managing Public Relations*, Holt, Rinehart & Winston, New York.

Hainsworth, Brad E (1990) 'Issues Management: An Overview', *Public Relations Review*, **16** (1).

Hainsworth, Brad E and Meng, M (1988) 'How Corporations Define Issues Management', *Public Relations Review*, winter.

Heath, R L and Cousino, K R (1990) 'Issues Management: End of First Decade Progress Report', *Public Relations Review*, **16** (1).

Heath, R L and Nelson, R A (1986) *Issues Management: Corporate public policy making in an information society*, Sage, London.

Ito, Y (1993) *Beyond Agendas: New directions in communication research from a Japanese perspective*, Greenwood Press, London.

Jones, Barrie L and Chase, W Howard (1979) 'Managing Public Policy Issues', *Public Relations Review*, **5** (2).

Kinsdorf, Marion (1990) 'Crisis Management', *Public Relations Review*, **14** (4).

Larkin, Judy (2003) *Strategic Reputation Risk Management*, Palgrave Macmillan, Basingstoke.

Management Today, July 1994.

McCue, Peter (2001) 'Preventing the Crises you Can; Managing the Ones You Can't', speech at AAMC, Georgia, March 8.

Meng, M B (1992) 'Early Identification Aids Issues Management', *Public Relations Journal*, March.

Meng, M B (1987) 'Issues Management Today', Unpublished thesis, Bingham Young University.

Midwest Academy Manual for Activists (2000) *Organizing for Social Change*, Seven Locks Press, Maryland.

Mitroff, Ian and Pauchant, Thierry (1990) *We're So Big and Powerful, Nothing Bad Can Happen to Us, an investigation of America's crisis prone corporations*, Birch Lane Press, Secaucus, New Jersey, USA.

Hanna, Nagy (1985) 'Strategic Planning and Management: A Review of Recent Experiences', World Bank staff and working papers, no 751, Washington DC.

Post, J E and Kelley, P C (1988) 'Lessons from the Learning Curve: The Past, Present and Future of Issues Management', *Strategic Issues Management: How organisations influence and respond to public interests and policies*.

Sopow, Eli (1994) *The Critical Issues Audit*, Issue Action Publications Inc, Leesburg, Virginia, USA.

SustainAbility (2001) *Buried Treasure: Uncovering the business case for corporate sustainability*, SustainAbility, London.

Taylor, Lord Justice (1990) 'The Hillsborough Stadium Disaster', Cm 962, 29 January.

Tucker, Kerry and Broom, Glen (1993) 'Managing Issues Acts as a Bridge to Strategic Planning', *Public Relations Journal*, November.

Tucker, Kerry and Trumpfheller, B (1993) 'Building an Issues Management Tracking System', *Public Relations Journal*, **49** (11), pp 36–37.

US Public Affairs Council (1978) *The Fundamentals of Issue Management*.

Wartick, S L and Rude, R E (1986) 'Issues Management: Corporate Fad or Corporate Function?', *California Management Review*, **24** (1).

Welsh Economy Research Unit, University of Wales, Cardiff Business School and Welsh Institute of Rural Studies (1996) *The Economic Consequences of the* Sea Empress *Spillage*, July.

Winter, M and Steger, U (1998) *Managing Outside Pressure: Strategies for preventing corporate disaster*, Wiley, Chichester.

Zadek, S (2001) *The Civil Corporation: The new economy of corporate citizenship*, Earthscan, London.

Index

Page references in *italics* indicate figures